BOTTOM-LINE
PLANT
MANAGEMENT

BOTTOM-LINE
PLANT
MANAGEMENT

Martin R. Smith

PRENTICE HALL
Englewood Cliffs, New Jersey 07632

PRENTICE HALL
Englewood Cliffs, New Jersey 07632
Prentice-Hall International, Inc., London
Prentice-Hall of Australia, Pty. Ltd., Sydney
Prentice-Hall Canada, Inc., Toronto
Prentice-Hall of India Private Ltd., New Delhi
Prentice-Hall of Japan, Inc., Tokyo
Prentice-Hall of Southeast Asia Pte. Ltd., Singapore
Whitehall Books, Ltd., Wellington, New Zealand
Editora Prentice-Hall do Brasil Ltda., Rio de Janeiro

This publication is designed to provide accurate and authoritative information in regard to the suject matter covered. It is sold with the understanding that the publisher is not engaged in rendering legal, accounting, or other professional service. If legal advice or other expert assistance is required, the services of a competent professional person should be sought.

. . . From the Declaration of Principles jointly adapted by a Committee of the American Bar Association and a Committee of Publishers and Associations.

Library of Congress Cataloging-in-Publication Data

Smith, Martin R., 1934–
    Bottom-line plant management / Martin R. Smith.
       p.   cm.
    Updated ed. of: Managing the plant. c1983.
    Includes index.
    ISBN 0-13-087594-5
    1. Factory management. I. Smith, Martin R., 1934– Managing the
plant. II. Title.
TS155.S626   1991
658.5—dc20
                                                  91-21092
                                                    CIP

ISBN 0-13-087594-5

PRENTICE HALL
Business Information & Publishing Division
Englewood Cliffs, NJ 07632
Simon & Schuster, A Paramount Communications Company

Printed in the United States of America

About the Author

Martin R. Smith is president of Management Sciences International, Inc., a consulting firm that he founded in 1978 specializing in profit improvement. Smith has consulted with literally hundreds of companies, helping them improve their productivity and quality.

Before founding Management Sciences International, Inc., Smith was president, chief executive, and a member of the board of directors of SCMI, an Atlanta-based, foreign-owned importer and exporter of woodworking machinery and packaging machinery.

Smith is an operating executive, having served as vice-president and general manager for Dynapac, a foreign-owned manufacturer of construction equipment. Prior to holding that position, he worked in Ford Motor Company's automotive assembly division for several years in production, quality control, and industrial engineering.

Smith graduated from Clarkson College of Technology and later attended General Electric's management training program. He was registered as a professional engineer in California in 1978.

Smith served as a member of the board of QUALITY MAGAZINE and has presented seminars across the United States on such subjects as profit improvement, import-export, productivity, and quality. He has served on the board of directors and advisory panels of several companies.

Contents

What This Book Can Do for You and Your Plant's Bottom Line

This book provides literally *dozens* of usable techniques and ideas to improve profits and reduce costs, for fast-track, bottom-line payoff. These techniques and ideas can be applied to any manufacturing business, large or small, regardless of product line.

This book will help manufacturing managers everywhere become more successful in their jobs. Practical, proven ways to improve bottom-line results will accomplish this goal. Here are just a few examples of what this book can do for you.

- Shows how to *establish a manufacturing operating plan* and how to use that plan to achieve improved bottom-line results. Sample plans that can be adapted by any company are illustrated. See Chapter One.

- Explains how to *apply the most important financial yardsticks,* such as return-on-assets, expense budgets, and manufacturing variances to measure and control plant profitability. See Chapter Two.

- *Reveals proven organizations* for different types of manufacturing businesses and *explains productive organizational principles* not shown in most manufacturing handbooks. See Chapter Three.

- *Pinpoints 15 sure-fire control measurements* needed to measure, control, and correct manufacturing performance in all areas of the business to improve bottom-line performance. See Chapter Four.

- *Details a step-by-step organized, and dynamic cost-reduction program* that has been used by many companies to substantially reduce operating costs in labor, material, and overhead. See Chapter Five.

- *Shows how to establish a cost-effective, four-step quality program for manufacturing companies* and explains all the elements of the quality process. *Describes the QUALITISCORE™, a method used by literally hundreds of companies to make big improvements in their product quality.* A self-inspection checklist is also provided. See Chapter Six.

- *Reveals a powerful application of math-free statistical process control (SPC),* and then *shows how to use the SPC program to assure and maintain employee involvement.* See Chapter Seven.

- *Demonstrates a method assuring continued worker productivity and quality.* Provides a diagnostic checklist that shows you how to evaluate the attitude of your workers. Places in the hands of your workers powerful but easy-to-use techniques for improving their productivity. Shows how to build teams effectively and how to open channels of communication with workers. See Chapter Eight.

- *Describes a reliable method for forecasting production schedules and inventories* and takes you through the process step-by-step with examples. See Chapter Nine.

- *Reveals how to purchase materials and parts for the fewest dollars* by using productive buying techniques. Methods for controlling vendor performance (i.e., in terms of price, quality, delivery) are set forth. See Chapter Ten.

- *Shows how to use a material requirements planning system* to increase productivity and shrink inventory costs. The entire technique is demystified and explained in everyday terms. The essentials of the system are outlined as well as its control mechanisms. See Chapter Eleven.

- *Describes several practical techniques that a plant can use to schedule production and product delivery.* Shows how to use scheduling systems to achieve on-time delivery goals at the lowest possible costs. See Chapter Twelve.

- *Describes how to reduce lead times in manufacturing* through a powerful technique called "Priority Control." See Chapter Thirteen.

- *Spotlights nine tested ways to reduce inventory levels and costs.* Show how to use these universal techniques through different company case studies. See Chapter Fourteen.

- *Describes the various elements of a Just-in-Time program* and how it can help reduce inventory levels by up to 75%. The famous Japanese Kanban system is explained. See Chapter Fifteen.
- *Leads you step-by-step through the process of reducing your direct and indirect labor costs by 33%* through use of short-interval scheduling, one of the widest and most effective cost-reduction programs ever used by companies worldwide. See Chapter Sixteen.
- *Features a labor reporting system to control worker and machine performance* to improve productivity up to 50%. See Chapter Seventeen.
- *Provides a self-inspection checklist regarding the effectiveness of the manufacturing engineering effort.* Shows how to improve the effectiveness of that function. See Chapter Eighteen.
- Makes easy work of *measuring the effectivness of capital investments* to maximize ROI (return-on-investment). You'll learn how to audit the continuing effectiveness of investment dollars long after the expenditures have been made. See Chapter Nineteen.
- Shows how to *recapture one-third of wasted maintenance hours* lost in most manufacturing companies. See Chapter Twenty.
- *Gives you practical techniques to reduce new product costs 25%* and explains how to bring new products on-stream in manufacturing within planned budget and time constraints. See Chapter Twenty-one.
- *Explains in detail 12 ways to beat the union at the negotiating table.* Forecasts the union negotiating environment for the 1990s and shows you how to prepare to handle new union challenges. See Chapter Twenty-two.
- Lays out a method to show you how to objectively *evaluate and hire the best possible job candidates.* See Chapter Twenty-three.
- Tells *how to establish a dynamic 21-point safety program* aimed at reducing lost-time accidents and workers' compensation costs. See Chapter Twenty-four.

HOW THIS BOOK IS ORGANIZED

This program of bottom-line performance techniques is organized into 24 chapters, each aimed at a specific function of the manufacturing company. It presetns proven, practical, and profitable techniques for lowering costs and improving profits. Each chapter contains several methods that successful managers have used to make their functions more successful and more competitive.

This book features control measurements that not only *control* operations—they also *improve* them. It first describes the nature of controls and explains how controls should be established to assure simplicity and effectiveness in use. It then shows how to control and improve:

Direct labor performance	Inventory carrying costs
Downtime	Bill-of-material accuracy
Labor utilization	Quality costs
Productivity	Cost reduction efforts
Incentive coverage	Capital expenditures
Indirect labor performance	Grievances
Overhead costs	Discipline of the work force
Material burden	Maintenance costs
Inventory turnover	Absenteeism
Inventory accuracy	Accident frequency

These subjects are covered in sufficient depth to provide you with ideas, facts, and clear steps to apply the measures to your own operations. The section on cost reduction efforts, for example, lists twenty-nine areas for potential improvements and installation. In addition the following subjects are described:

- Just-in-Time and the Japanese Kanban system.
- Math-free statistical process control.
- Employee involvement and team building.
- How to evaluate your own quality system using a self-inspection checklist called the Qualitiscore™.
- Ready-to-use financial analysis for manufacturing operations and how to use the Dupont formula for determining return-on-assets.
- A diagnostic checklist to evaluate your employees' attitudes toward quality.
- Practical techniques to schedule the plant, including one dynamic method called Priority Control.
- One of the most effective ways to forecast inventory levels using a technique called Cycle Forecasting.
- A self-inspection checklist for manufacturing engineering.
- An objective method for evaluating job candidates called the JOBSCORE.

HOW YOU CAN USE THIS BOOK

This book can assist you in many ways. Here are a few suggestions:

- Use the book to establish controls for each segment of the manufacturing business. Methods and techniques for every segment are shown in detail.
- Train manufacturing supervisors by developing supervisory training courses aimed at increasing their knowledge of operations. The book is organized in such a way as to teach supervisors progressive lessons in management. Or, select individual chapters to correct supervisory deficiencies.
- Use the charts, forms, and tables for measurement, control, and improvement of manufacturing operations.
- Solve specific problems that need to be addressed by turning to the chapter that describes how to improve that segment of manufacturing operations. Point-by-point, compare *your* operations to the practices recommended in the book, then focus on correcting weaknesses.

Martin R. Smith

1

The Six-Step Formula For Increasing Manufacturing Profits

Effective manufacturing management does not occur spontaneously. It is neither a matter of luck nor simple perseverance. Effective manufacturing management is a direct function of solid and thorough planning, efficient and determined execution, and consistent and intelligent measurement and control. The effect of all three is synergistic; that is, the proper combination of all three factors produces results far beyond the individual ingredients. It is somewhat like the formula:

$$1 + 1 = 3$$

And it works.

Literally thousands of successful companies worldwide have unlocked the secret. These companies have learned how to plan, execute, and control. Their experience has shown them how to apply this basic theory to practical manufacturing management and how to achieve substantial bottom-line improvements.

This chapter provides a six-step formula for increasing manufacturing profits; these steps are briefly introduced in the following paragraphs.

Step 1: Establish an annual manufacturing operating plan derived from the company's annual profit plan. In your plan, describe in broad terms how manufacturing intends to achieve the company's profit goals.

Step 2: Develop a project control timetable that describes all major goals and shows their relationship to one another. In essence, your project control timetable should be a large project timetable where the annual manufacturing operating plan is segmented into individual projects for all of the operating departments of manufacturing.

1

Step 3: Develop specific manufacturing plans to achieve the project timetable. In your action plans, state what specific goals will be accomplished, who will be responsible for them, and when they will be completed.

Step 4: Describe manufacturing management concepts you want to achieve, such as quality improvement. These concepts should represent the collective wisdom of the organization and form a framework in which the action plans are made. A simple example would involve a company determined to have the best quality product in its industry. In such a case, action plans describing quality would recognize that certain steps must be achieved to introduce a new product within manufacturing. These steps represent the company's experience of the best way to proceed, and they would be stated in the action plan.

Step 5: Prepare supervisors and managers to execute the plan in the most effective way possible. This step is one of the most difficult to implement. Manufacturing people may have different interpretations of the plan or they may not understand it thoroughly. The job of the manufacturing manager is to assure that subordinates understand what must be done, and to win their full support of the plan. There are proven ways to do just that; they will be described shortly.

Step 6: Develop effective measurement and control. Measurement and control of the operating plan as a whole, and measurement and control of specific action plans, must be carefully developed *before action plans are released.* Quantitative measures

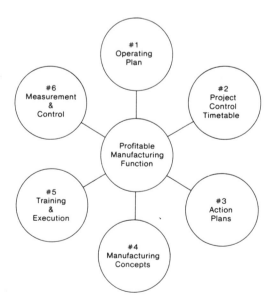

Figure 1-1   The Six-Step Formula for Increasing Manufacturing Profits

should be devised for each segment of the plan and periodic controls issued to assure that plans are being achieved.

Without measurement and control, it is very easy to fall behind schedule or to obtain mediocre or poor results.

The relationship of each of the six steps is shown in Figure 1-1. If each step is performed properly, a profitable manufacturing function will achieve its goals and contribute to company profitability.

HOW TO APPLY THE FORMULA

Many companies have evolved the six-step formula after years of trial and error. Some of these companies have refined the six-step formula to the extent that their planning and control functions are now almost a fine art. Typical companies in this category are such giants as Dresser Industries, Johnson and Johnson, and a host of smaller but very profitable companies such as Dynapac (a Swedish construction equipment manufacturer) and Tandem Computers (a West Coast computer company that grew from $100,000 in sales to $100 million in less than seven years).

Let's see how many companies develop and apply manufacturing operating plans.

STEP 1: LINK YOUR OPERATING PLAN TO YOUR PROFIT PLAN

Here's the procedure a plastics machinery manufacturer in New Jersey used to tackle Step 1 and develop an annual profit plan (See Figure 1-2):

1. *Calculate net sales* by subtracting *discounts* (price concessions to gain sales and generate prompt payment) from *gross sales*.
2. *Calculate cost of goods sold*, which represents the total cost of the manufacturing function, by deducting material, direct labor, and manufacturing expenses, as follows.

Determining materials costs

These costs are purchased materials and parts used in products to be sold. Material costs are generally recognized as (1) raw material—purchased materials waiting to be used in the product, (2) work-in-process—partially finished product, and (3) finished goods—product ready for shipment.

If the material is not used in the product, it is classified as an operating expense. Such items as tools, fixtures, jigs, and fuel (for heating) are examples of operating expenses.

Determining direct labor costs

Direct labor represents those labor costs used to form materials into products. Assemblers who put together product components, for example, would be classified as direct labor.

19X3
PLASTICS MACHINERY
COMPANY PROFIT PLAN
(MILLIONS $)

Gross sales		150
Less: Discounts		7
Net sales		143
Less: Material	55	
Direct Labor	15	
Manufacturing Expenses	20	
Cost-of-Goods Sold		90
Gross Margins		53
Less: Engineering	14	
Marketing	15	
Administrative	6	
Operating Expenses		35
Operating Profit		18
Interest Costs		4
Profit Before Taxes		14

Figure 1-2   Company Profit Plan

Determining manufacturing expenses

These costs are all those used in the manufacturing process other than direct labor and material. They can be countless, but include these prominent items:

- Salaries of manufacturing people
- Maintenance labor
- Inspection labor
- Warehouse and material handling labor
- Insurance and hospitalization
- Fuel and electricity
- Tools, jigs, fixtures
- Office and factory supplies
- Payroll taxes
- Depreciation
- Freight
- Rentals

3. *Calculate gross margins* by subtracting the *cost of goods sold* from *net sales*. The total of materials, direct labor, and manufacturing expenses constitute what is known as "cost-of-goods-sold" or, in other terms, the total cost of the manufacturing function. When these combined costs are subtracted from net sales the result is called "gross margins."

4. *Calculate operating profits* by subtracting *operating expenses* from *gross margins*. These expenses include the costs of running the product engineering, marketing, and general administrative functions such as top management, finance, personnel, data processing, and so on.

5. *Calculate profit before taxes* by subtracting interest costs from operating profits.

6. *Develop a manufacturing operating plan* based on this company profit plan. Figure 1-3 shows the manufacturing plan developed by this New Jersey company.

Production, expressed in number of units of machinery, shows the actual production for 19X2, the planned production for 19X3, and the variance between the two numbers. Notice that 19X3 production is planned to be 10 percent higher than 19X2 production.

19X3
PLASTICS MACHINERY
MANUFACTURING OPERATING PLAN

	Actual 19X2	Plan 19X3	Variance
PRODUCTION (NO. UNITS)			
Large machines	60	66	+10 %
Small machines	27	30	+10 %
Total:	87	96	+10 %
MATERIALS (MILLION $)			
Purchased materials	50	50	Flat
Purchased parts	3	5	+67 %
Total:	53	55	+ 3.6%
DIRECT LABOR (MILLION $)	14	15	+ 7.1%
MANUFACTURING EXPENSES (MILLION $)			
Machine shop	4	4	Flat
Fabrication	4	4	Flat
Assembly	4	5	+25 %
Materials handling	2	2	
Quality control	1	1	
Maintenance	1	2	+50 %
Manufacturing engineering	1	2	+50 %
	18	20	+11 %

Figure 1-3   Manufacturing Operating Plan

The remaining portions of the operating plan are in millions of dollars. Material costs are separated into two components: purchased materials and purchased parts. Purchased parts are those bought already fabricated such as nuts, bolts, screws, fittings, and bearings.

Material costs are projected to increase by 3.6 percent. When one considers that volume is increasing by 10 percent and that inflation is probably adding another 10 percent, the small increase in material costs is spectacular; it shows that purchasing agents are really doing a fine job.

Direct labor costs are also declining. They, like their material counterparts, are faced with both production and inflation increases of 10 percent; yet direct labor costs are up by only 7.1 percent.

Finally, manufacturing expenses are up by 11 percent, matching the increase in production. They too, are not as high as they might have been once inflation is taken into account.

Notice, also, that manufacturing expenses are segmented by departments rather than accounts. In practice, both breakdowns are used, so each department can plan and control individual accounts (fuel, salaries, etc.).

Match Your Manufacturing Capability to Your Company's Competitive Strategy

It is important that you match your manufacturing capability to your company's competitive strategy in the marketplace. For example, a U.S. company that manufactures electronic components had years ago relocated its manufacturing base to third-world countries, namely Taiwan and Singapore. As long as it manufactured the electronic components by the millions, this arrangement suited the company perfectly because labor costs in the United States were prohibitively high. The company, therefore, had relocated its plants overseas to cut its labor costs and to survive in a highly competitive marketplace. Engineering remained stateside at corporate headquarters.

In recent years, however, the company had acquired a medical electronics company in California and had farmed out most of this manufacturing capability to its plants in Taiwan and Singapore. This proved to be a big mistake. The new product line was substantially more complex than existing product lines, and product design changed frequently and rapidly in line with demands from customers in the United States. Since engineering headquarters were located in the United States, there were long delays in incorporating design changes and therefore many unhappy customers.

The company was forced eventually to brings its medical electronics division back to the United States for manufacturing. There proximity to engineering and to customers soon resolved the problem.

STEP 2: ESTABLISH A TIMETABLE

A construction equipment manufacturer in the Midwest developed the project timetable shown in Figure 1-4. The project timetable is the second step in the six-step formula, and it expresses those events that must take place within the calendar year to support the manufacturing operating plan. Notice that in the timetable, specific individuals have been assigned responsibility for project tasks. Normally, a project timetable is composed of three categories, as follows.

1. New Products

This includes the pilot plant (or prototype build) of new products along with early production when tooling, fixtures, methods, and standards are being implemented. This category also includes product line upgrades when existing products are improved or made less costly.

2. Facilities and Equipment

The second category lists plant expansions, new offices and buildings, and new equipment.

3. Manufacturing Systems

The final category shows all support systems needed to improve manufacturing's capability. This is, normally, the most extensive of the three categories. It details the work of industrial engineering, materials management, and quality control, to name a few. Typical projects would include the following:

MATERIALS MANAGEMENT SYSTEM

- Inventory control
- Production control
- Materials requirements planning
- Inventory accuracy
- Obsolescence and excess inventory reduction
- Bills-of-material accuracy
- Purchasing variance improvements

INDUSTRIAL ENGINEERING

- Cost reduction
- Incentive systems
- Methods and standards
- Labor reporting

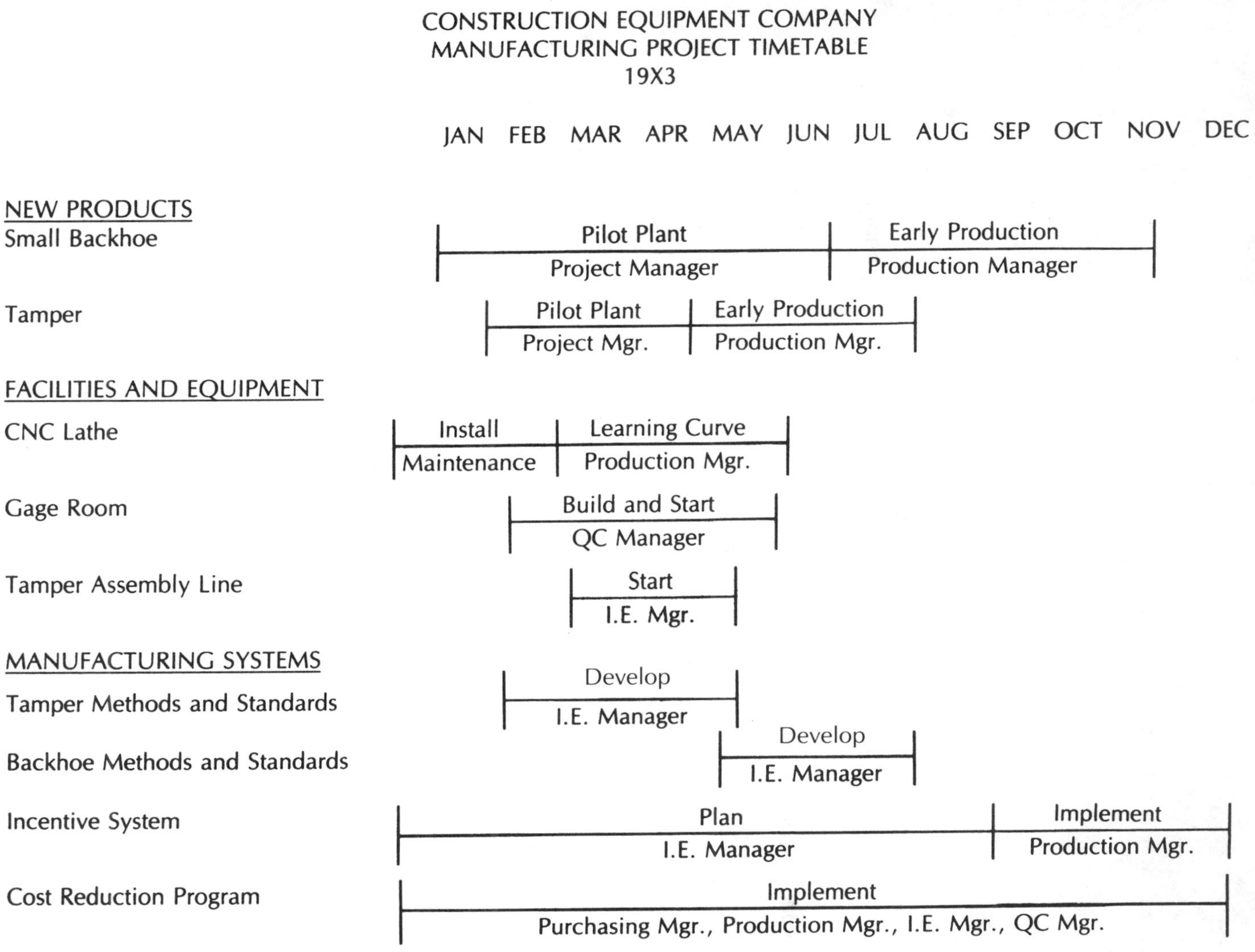

CONSTRUCTION EQUIPMENT COMPANY
MANUFACTURING PROJECT TIMETABLE
19X3

JAN FEB MAR APR MAY JUN JUL AUG SEP OCT NOV DEC

NEW PRODUCTS
Small Backhoe

Pilot Plant | Early Production
Project Manager | Production Manager

Tamper

Pilot Plant | Early Production
Project Mgr. | Production Mgr.

FACILITIES AND EQUIPMENT
CNC Lathe

Install | Learning Curve
Maintenance | Production Mgr.

Gage Room

Build and Start
QC Manager

Tamper Assembly Line

Start
I.E. Mgr.

MANUFACTURING SYSTEMS
Tamper Methods and Standards

Develop
I.E. Manager

Backhoe Methods and Standards

Develop
I.E. Manager

Incentive System

Plan | Implement
I.E. Manager | Production Mgr.

Cost Reduction Program

Implement
Purchasing Mgr., Production Mgr., I.E. Mgr., QC Mgr.

Figure 1-4 Project Timetable

8

QUALITY CONTROL

• Cost of quality reporting
• Scrap, rework, and warranty reductions
• Quality engineering systems

STEP 3: DEVELOP ACTION PLANS TO ACHIEVE YOUR OPERATING AND PROFIT GOALS

Action plans are the instruments that convert both operating plans and project timetables to reality through assignment of specific tasks designed to make things happen. Furthermore, they focus the resources of the manufacturing organization on significant tasks and help employees understand the goals.

A typical action plan, developed by the previously mentioned construction company, is shown in Figure 1-5. This particular plan shows specific ways to establish the cost reduction program outlined in the company's Project Timetable (see Figure 1-4). The firm took these steps to establish its action plan:

1. *Outline specific tasks* that must be accomplished to implement the new program. In this case, the construction company identified five separate actions needed to get its cost reduction program up and running.

2. *Assign each task* to both the department and individual responsible for carrying it out.

3. *Set deadlines* for accomplishing each task.

CONSTRUCTION EQUIPMENT COMPANY
MANUFACTURING ACTION PLANS
19X3

PROJECT TIMETABLE	ACTION PLANS	DEPARTMENT RESPONSIBLE	PERSON RESPONSIBLE	COMPLETION DATE
MANUFACTURING SYSTEMS				
Cost reduction program	(A) Develop program outline	I.E.	Barnson	1/1/X3
	(B) Set cost reduction goals	V.P. Mfg.	Jones	4/1/X3
	(C) Develop procedures	I.E.	Mattia	7/1/X3
	(D) Train supervisors in cost reduction techniques	Personnel	Green	9/1/X3
	(E) Begin program	I.E.	Barnson	10/1/X3

Figure 1-5   Manufacturing Action Plans

STEP 4: MAKE THE MOST OF COLLECTIVE MANUFACTURING WISDOM TO IMPLEMENT WHAT WORKS BEST FOR YOUR COMPANY

Every manufacturing organization develops its own set of guidelines of conduct over a period of time. These guidelines are really an expression of what has worked best for the organization based on its experience. Some of these lessons have been learned readily; some of them have been absorbed the hard way. But whatever method was used in its conception, these guidelines reflect the collective wisdom of the manufacturing enterprise. They form a framework within which manufacturing runs its business and executes its operating plans.

Dynapac, Inc., a Swedish-owned manufacturer of vibratory compactors (steamrollers) in New Jersey, has its own set of manufacturing "wisdoms." Some of these follow.

Six Ways to Make Your Employees a Vital Part of Your Team

1. Try to stabilize employment. Layoffs disrupt work-force morale. Loyalty is built through security.
2. Make sure all classifications of employees, salaried and hourly, are treated equally. This builds trust and confidence. It keeps unions from the door.
3. Provide job classifications for all employees and ensure that they are clear and understood by everybody. This prevents misunderstandings and dissatisfaction, and communicates to all the job to be done.
4. Rotate supervisors and support people periodically to broaden their understanding of the business and to generate fresh ideas.
5. Keep salaries and perquisites high enough to hold turnover down, but not so high as to price yourself out of the business.
6. Always negotiate with unions from a position of strength. More profit margins are lost through management vulnerability at contract time than most companies recognize.

Seven Ways to Improve Materials Management and Fatten Your Bottom Line

1. Keep work-in-process inventories high and finished goods inventories low. This permits the flexibility of changes dictated by sales requirements while keeping total inventory turnover high.
2. Have material sources for all major components as close to the factory as possible to provide for emergency shortages.
3. Maintain a secondary source for all major parts and materials. The competition will stimulate lower prices and improve delivery. In cases of a shutdown of one supplier, the other will be ready to keep your production lines moving.

4. Change vendors every five to seven years. A too-long relationship allows rigor mortis to set in. The new vendor will keep your purchase costs low and provide improved services.
5. When purchasing high cost or high volume parts or materials, always get a minimum of three bids.
6. When dealing with a vendor a long way from the factory, have the vendor maintain a sufficient safety stock at a warehouse near you should an emergency occur.
7. Keep all warehouses locked and have limited access to them to assure that unauthorized use of inventory does not occur.

Six Key Principles for Keeping Costs Low and Quality High

1. Always maintain an active and vigorous cost reduction program.
2. Train employees to understand that there is no such thing as an uncontrolled cost. Their understanding of this is essential to cost reduction efforts.
3. Control all operations and provide for quick feedback of results to operating management. The faster a problem is uncovered, the faster it is resolved.
4. Make designers, manufacturing employees, and servicepeople responsible for quality—*not* the inspectors. Top quality products and services will be the result.
5. Have sales- and servicepeople audit the product for quality conformance. Their viewpoints reflect the customers', and they will sometimes be different from what manufacturing people consider acceptable.
6. Keep support services lean; too many inspectors, mechanics, engineers, and clerks drain away profits.

Six Points to Keep in Mind When Planning Facilities and Buying Equipment

1. Plan capital budgets so replacement costs do not exceed depreciation charges for the period involved.
2. Do not buy secondhand tooling and machinery. The initial savings in capital will be more than offset by the loss in productivity caused by old machinery.
3. The simplest tooling is the best. It will get the job done at the lowest possible cost.
4. All tool, process, and industrial engineers should work for one year as production foremen. Understanding the problems of production will help them design better tooling and production processes.
5. Maintain work standards on all major production operations to evaluate and improve the efficiency of both machinery and operators.

6. Keep factories as small as possible; an upper limit of 200 people should be maintained. Anything above that causes loss of control and a separation between management and labor that has an unfavorable impact on profitability.

The Two Most Important Principles to Remember When Developing New Products

1. Freeze design of new products before production starts. A changing design during early production generates inefficiencies in production and causes high obsolete inventories.

2. Always pilot plant or run prototypes of new products using production tooling. What works in the laboratory may fail dismally in production if not tested first.

STEP 5: TRAIN SUPERVISORS FOR SUCCESS

The best operating plan has but scant chance of success if manufacturing supervisors do not understand its importance or if they don't properly understand their role in the plan. Probably the best way to obtain the commitment of supervisors to the operating plan is to have them participate in its development from the inception.

Here are the actions a surface mining equipment manufacturer in Ohio takes to involve its supervisory staff in developing the operating plan:

1. *Solicit supervisors input from the outset.* In this company, foremen, general foremen, and production superintendents prepare their portion of the operating plan by projecting capital requirements, direct labor needs, and operating expense budgets for the forthcoming fiscal year.

2. *Conduct a management review.* The operating plan is then passed on to the vice-president of manufacturing for review. This manager holds meetings with foremen, general foremen, and superintendents by department.

3. *Submit the plan to top management.* Once it is approved by consensus, the operating plan is given to the company president for review.

4. *Hold training sessions.* After its operating plan has been reviewed by top management, this Ohio company holds training sessions with production supervisors—the same employees who prepared the plan. These supervisors tell upper management how they intend to carry out the operating plan. Timetables and action plans are developed from these sessions.

Each level of supervision brings to the plan certain information which describes individual contribution. These are shown in Figure 1-6.

LEVEL OF CONTRIBUTION	PLANNED RESOURCES	
Foremen and general foremen	Section	Units of production
	Section	Direct labor hours
	Section	Overtime
	Section	Staffing levels
	Section	Indirect labor forecast
	Section	Forecasted downtime
	Section	Capital requirements
	Section	Operating expenses
	Section	Cost reduction projections
	Section	Quality levels
Superintendent	Dept.	Direct labor hours
	Dept.	Units of production
	Dept.	Overtime
	Dept.	Staffing levels
	Dept.	Indirect labor forecast
	Dept.	Forecasted overtime
	Dept.	Capital requirements
	Dept.	Operating expenses
	Dept.	Cost reduction projections
	Dept.	Quality levels
Vice-president manufacturing	Factory	All of the above
	Factory	Maintenance budget
	Factory	Quality control budget
	Factory	Purchasing budget
	Factory	Warehouse budget
	Factory	Delivery schedule
	Factory	Inventory schedule
	Factory	Inventory accuracy projection
	Factory	Salaried people requirements
	Factory	Industrial engineering budget

Figure 1-6   Contribution Level Table

STEP 6: DEVELOP EFFECTIVE MEASUREMENT AND CONTROL

Once action plans are developed, the mining equipment manufacturer prepares measurement reports to monitor results of the operating plan. Action plans are also followed closely to assure completion of stated objectives. Measurement and control techniques will be covered fully in Chapter Four, but suffice it to say for now that each major segment of the manufacturing business has measurements imposed upon it, and reports to measure progress are published regularly to correct deviations from the plan.

2

How to Use Financial Controls to Attack Problem Areas and Measure Profitability

The success or failure of any business is directly related to its ability to sustain profitable performance, quarter to quarter, year to year. That ability is dependent upon the company's success in the marketplace and its further success in holding down costs in the business, particularly in the manufacturing side where the preponderance of costs lie.

Financial controls enable the business to evaluate trends and detect problems on a timely basis. Without them, most businesses would falter, even perish.

WHY FINANCIAL CONTROLS ARE VITAL TO YOUR SUCCESS—AND YOUR COMPANY'S

Since financial performance dictates the success or failure of the business, it follows that financial controls constitute the most important and significant regulators of the business for the manufacturing manager. Your success or failure in directing the manufacturing function will depend largely on your ability to understand the financial aspects of your job and to react accordingly when unfavorable financial trends are detected.

Unfortunately, too many manufacturing managers do not understand the significance of financial controls. They focus on other technical aspects of their jobs where they feel most comfortable. Manufacturing managers who were former chief industrial engineers, for example, may focus on incentive standard problems and pay but scant attention to controlling costs. And while they are devoting inordinate time to incentives, financial problems may be developing; and those problems may cost the manufacturing managers their jobs.

It is a startling fact that a large percentage of manufacturing executives today do not really comprehend financial controls; nor do they perceive their use as a method of improving operations, establishing priorities for corrective actions, and measuring the results of people working for them.

ASPECTS OF FINANCIAL STATEMENTS MOST CRITICAL TO MANUFACTURING MANAGEMENT

To understand financial control, you must first grasp the basics of manufacturing financial statements. Although the statement of income and statement of financial position reflect the financial health of the entire business, certain portions of both statements pertain directly to the manufacturing manager and your area of direct control.

Figure 2-1 shows the statement of income for 1990 for a fictitious company, International Machinery, Inc., Parts Manufacturing Division (PMD). Gross sales are reduced by returns, allowances, and discounts, to yield net sales. Manufacturing's cost of goods sold is then subtracted to obtain gross margins.*

Cost of goods sold represents the cost of manufacturing the company's products, and consists of direct materials, direct labor, and manufacturing overhead, which are covered in the following section.

How Direct Materials Costs are Calculated

The cost of materials used directly in the company's products, in PMD's case, will be: (1) raw material—castings, forgings, and fabricated metals that will be machined by PMD to final configurations determined by drawings and specifications; and (2) purchased parts—final part configurations bought directly from vendors for assembly or part sales.

Computing Direct Labor Costs

Direct labor costs are those associated with manufacturing and assembling the product itself. Machine operators and assemblers who work directly on the product itself are classified as direct labor, as opposed to such people as inspectors, material handlers, and maintenance people (called indirect labor) who provide essential services in manufacturing but who do not work on or change the product configuration themselves.

---

*Only those portions of financial statements for manufacturing will be considered here. For a full discussion of financial statements as they relate to the entire business enterprise consult any number of financial textbooks.

INTERNATIONAL MACHINERY, INC.
PARTS MANUFACTURING DIVISION
STATEMENT OF INCOME
FOR YEAR ENDED DEC. 31, 1990

Gross Sales:		$45,750,525
Less: Returns and Allowances	$ 732,561	
Cash Discounts	683,228	
		1,415,789
Net Sales		$44,334,736
Cost of Goods Sold		25,110,706
Gross Margins		$19,224,134
Sales Administration	$ 700,335	
Sales Commissions	652,079	
General and Administrative	1,632,994	
Total		$ 2,985,408
Operating Profit		$16,238,726
Gain on Assets Sold	$ 950	
Rental and Interest Income	25,245	
Total		$ 26,195
Net Income Before Taxes		$16,264,921
Federal Income Tax		$ 7,807,162
Net Income		$ 8,457,759

Figure 2-1 Parts Manufacturing Division: Statement of Income for Year Ended Dec. 31, 1990.

Calculating Costs Included in Manufacturing Overhead

This final cost consists of all other manufacturing costs not considered direct materials or direct labor costs. Overhead includes such costs as indirect labor, taxes and insurance, heat, light, and power, depreciation, and indirect materials and supplies (tooling, janitorial supplies, lubricating oils, paperwork expenses).

Gross margins, then, reflect *manufacturing* profits before other company costs such as sales and administrative expenses are subtracted from gross margins. When they are subtracted, net income is the final result.

Figure 2-2 reveals PMD's balance sheet, also termed the statement of financial position. It lists assets, liabilities, and net worth of the business, in this case PMD. Those accounts concerning the manufacturing manager directly are inventories and plant and equipment.

The inventories account represents the different stages of product in manufacturing: (1) raw materials and purchased parts; (2) work-in-process which denotes the former raw materials and purchased parts somewhere in the process of being manufactured; and (3) finished goods inventory—the stock of completely manufactured products ready for sale. Inventories are a key determinant of a manufacturing manager's success, and will be discussed more fully later.

Plant and equipment includes buildings, machinery, and equipment. This subject will be discussed in more detail later. For the moment, just remember that plant and equipment represents an investment that must be made to yield attractive profits for the business. When a manufacturing manager seeks to add new plants and equipment, profitability must be carefully determined and actual results monitored to assure that the investments are paying off.

INTERNATIONAL MACHINERY, INC.
PARTS MANUFACTURING DIVISION
STATEMENT OF FINANCIAL POSITION
DEC. 31, 1990

Current Assets		
Cash		$ 658,007
Securities (at Cost)		525,362
Accounts Receivable	$ 7,894,210	
Minus Reserve for Bad Debts	24,000	
Net Accounts Receivable		$ 7,870,210
Inventories		
Houston	$12,003,865	
Pittsburgh	2,833,529	
Los Angeles	1,702,058	
Total Inventories		$16,539,452
Prepaid Expenses		9,406
Total Current Assets		$25,602,437
Plant and Equipment	$25,876,254	
Less Depreciation	12,325,976	
Total Plant and Equipment		$13,550,278
Total Assets		$39,152,715
Current Liabilities		
Accounts Payable		$ 1,823,151
Accrued Liabilities		1,602,252
Payroll Deductions		87,155
Total Current Liabilities		$ 3,512,558
Equity		
Corporate Clearing Account		$ 8,592,891
Divisional Control		17,335,627
Retained Earnings		9,711,639
Total Equity		$35,640,157
Total Liabilities and Equity		$39,152,715

Figure 2-2   Parts Manufacturing Division: Statement of financial position Dec. 31, 1990.

HOW TO CALCULATE RETURN ON ASSETS TO MEASURE YOUR PERFORMANCE

If you, as a person, invest money, your very first concern is "How much will I earn?" A business asks exactly the same question when it invests its money. When International Machinery bought PMD (once a flourishing, independent company) it did so because it anticipated a certain rate of return on its money.

Return on assets is the measurement of success ("How much did I earn in relation to my investment?)" that corporate management burdens its divisions with. Return on assets (ROA) is the ratio of net income to sales, multiplied by asset turnover, as seen here:

$$ROA = \frac{\text{Income before taxes}}{\text{Net sales}} \times \frac{\text{Net sales}}{\text{Total assets}}$$

By canceling out the net sales (in true arithmetical form), ROA then becomes:

$$ROA = \frac{\text{Income before taxes}}{\text{Total assets}}$$

ROA is the prime measurement of how well each division performs financially. It is the best way of answering the question, "How well did this division perform in relation to the assets it had at its disposal?"

As can be seen in Figure 2-3 at the right-hand side, PMD had a 41.46 percent return on assets before taxes. That number is truly phenomenal, and it is an indication of the truly exceptional job accomplished by PMD management.

Steps in Calculating Return on Assets

Here are the steps involved in making the calculation:

1. Add total assets. In Figure 2-3, total assets are classified in the upper left hand corner. These numbers are taken directly from the balance sheet (statement of financial position). They are added together to form the total assets shown to the immediate right of the left hand column.

2. Divide net sales by total assets to show asset turnover, that is, how many sales dollars were generated with the assets PMD had. Net sales is taken from the statement of income shown in Figure 2-1.

3. Determine net income before taxes by subtracting sales administration expenses, sales commissions, and general (administrative) expenses from gross margins. Then, add miscellaneous income to gross margins. These numbers are taken directly from the statement of net income shown in Figure 2-1. As seen in Figure 2-1, gross margins are the dollars left over after manufacturing costs have been subtracted from net sales.

4. Divide net income before taxes by net sales to derive return on sales (refer to

Figure 2-3 and the column to the immediate right of the lower left hand column). In PMD's case, this was a phenomenal 36.69 percent. This calculation shows how effectively division management held down costs in relation to sales.

5. Multiply asset turnover by return on sales to get ROA. In PMD's case, of course, ROA is 41.46 percent.

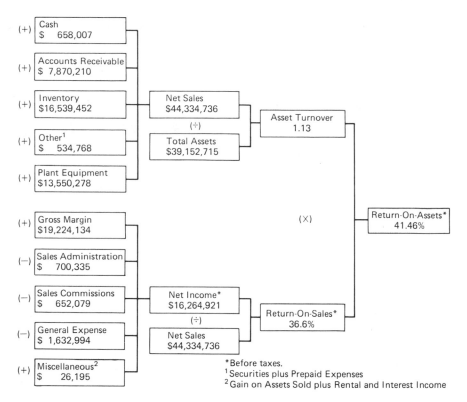

Figure 2-3   Parts Manufacturing Division: Return on Assets

While ROA is a picture of overall divisional performance, the chief contributor to results, either good or bad, is the manufacturing function. A glance at the numbers shown in the left-hand column of Figure 2-3 will tell you why. The manufacturing manager is responsible for inventories, plant and equipment, and gross margins. Those numbers are, by far, the most significant portion of all the numbers included in the ROA formula. The manufacturing manager's success is the prime ingredient of divisional performance, given a steady level of sales.

Control of ROA, therefore, is *the* paramount concern for the manufacturing manager. The balance of this book shows you just how to do it.

USING COST OF GOODS SOLD ANALYSIS TO MONITOR YOUR PROGRESS

ROA, while being the yardstick of divisional financial status, is only one of the several measures used by corporate management to control divisional performance. There are several additional measures which you should know to help you monitor progress to achievement of ROA goals. A description of the more popular of these follows.

Analyzing Gross Margins

Gross margins reflect that portion of money left over after manufacturing's cost of goods sold is subtracted from net sales. Gross margins, as a percentage of net sales, is a basic indicator of how good a job is being done to control manufacturing costs. PMD's gross margins for the past five years reveal an interesting trend:

	(Thousands Omitted)				
	1990	**1989**	**1988**	**1987**	**1986**
Net sales	$44,334	$42,105	$39,634	$30,912	$30,027
Cost of goods sold	25,110	25,263	28,536	22,878	23,727
Gross margins	$19,224	$16,842	$11,098	$ 8,034	$ 6,300
$\frac{\text{Gross margins}}{\text{Net sales}} \times 100 =$	43.4%	40.0%	28.0%	25.9%	20.9%

Note: Gross margins divided by net sales, as shown above, is multiplied by 100 to derive a percentage.

Gross margins for PMD have steadily improved from 1986, and are more than double that amount in 1990. That proves that manufacturing management has made steady improvements in reducing costs. The question now remains, "Where did the improvements occur?" Obviously, it had to be in materials, direct labor, or manufacturing overhead—the three ingredients of cost of goods sold. Let's analyze all three by breaking down cost of goods sold for the five-year period under study:

	(Thousands Omitted)				
	1990	**1989**	**1988**	**1987**	**1986**
Net sales	$44,334	$42,105	$39,634	$30,912	$30,027
Cost of goods sold					
Material	$10,322	$ 9,004	$ 8,225	$ 7,195	$ 7,248
Direct labor	4,379	4,980	5,163	5,632	5,465
Overhead	10,409	11,079	15,148	10,051	11,014
Total costs:	$25,110	$25,163	$28,536	$22,878	$23,727

Reductions have taken place in two of the cost categories relative to sales. Let's compare 1986 and 1990 to determine which costs were reduced and the extent of the changes over the five-year period. To do that we will take each of the cost categories (material, direct labor, overhead) individually and divide them by net sales for the year, and multiply the result by 100 to obtain the percentage of costs to sales:

	1990	1986
Material	23.3%	23.3%
Direct labor	9.9%	18.2%
Overhead	23.5%	35.6%

Example: Material costs for 1990 were $10,332 and sales were $44,334. Then, dividing material costs by sales, and multiplying the result by 100 provides the 23.3%

$$\frac{\$10,332}{\$44,334} \times 100 = 23.3\%$$

Material costs as a percentage of net sales have held steady over the last five years. At first, that might appear to be a flat trend. Yet if you consider the rate of inflation during that period of time, just holding material costs relative to sales is a major accomplishment (diminished only slightly by the fact that some price increases have taken place for the company's products during that time).

But where PMD really shines is in the substantial reductions made in both direct labor and overhead,. Here, obviously, is a company that has slashed costs to a minimum. Direct labor costs have actually been cut in half, from 18.2% in 1986 to 9.9% in 1990, and overhead has been reduced substantially during that same period, from 35.6% in 1986 to 23.5% in 1990.

What Inventory Turnover Tells You About Your Operating Efficiency

Inventory turnover is an indication of how efficiently a manufacturing organization is using materials which comprise the products. A low inventory turnover rate could indicate excessively high levels of usable inventory or high levels of obsolete inventory. If, for example, a certain part is selling at 10,000 pieces annually, and the usable inventory is 200,000 pieces, then an obvious condition of excess inventory exists.

Too high an inventory turnover rate, conversely, could indicate that not enough inventory is on hand to satisfy customer demands—a condition that results almost invariably in lost sales. This same condition can also be an indication of short machine run times with its consequent higher costs resulting from excessive machine setups and higher material handling costs.

How to Calculate Inventory Turnover. Inventory turnover is computed as follows:

$$\frac{\text{Manufacturing's cost of goods sold}}{\text{Average inventory levels during the year}} = \text{Inventory turnover}$$

PMD's inventory level for 1990 are shown in Figure 2-2. That number is $16,539,452.* Dividing that number into its cost of goods sold—$25,110,602—reveals an inventory turnover rate of 1.5 times.

How good or how bad is an inventory turnover rate of 1.5 times? To the uninitiated eye, it would appear very low. Many industry analysts would say that in a business like PMD's which manufactures to stock and produces high quantities of parts, turnover rates should be between 2.5 to 4.0 times.

Inventory turnover, however, is not a measure that stands alone. It must be analyzed in relation to company objectives. If you will recall the ROA formula shown in Figure 2-3, it is just as important to determine how much profit is being generated per turnover. In PMD's case, profitability was very high and the resultant ROA was exceptional.

The high levels of PMD inventory are the result of a deliberate management policy to provide quick deliveries of products to customers. PMD management recognizes that in its industry, delivery is a key ingredient of repeat sales, and it has consciously decided to hold finished goods inventory levels high to achieve that goal. Were it moving its inventories more rapidly, that advantage would be lost, and sales would probably be lower. That, in turn, would result in lower profit levels.

Using Manufacturing Overhead as a Yardstick of Performance

As explained earlier, manufacturing overhead is composed of all manufacturing costs other than direct material and direct labor. It is applied to overhead costs by means of an overhead rate that is calculated by dividing overhead costs by budgeted machine hours. PMD's manufacturing overhead costs for 1987 were budgeted at $10,655,000 for 1 million machine hours. The overhead rate, therefore, was *budgeted* at $10.65 per hour ($10,655,000 divided by 1 million).

In 1987, PMD's *actual* overhead was $10,051,000. A comparison of the budgeted versus actual overhead for that year follows:

	BUDGET	ACTUAL
Manufacturing overhead	$10,655,000	$10,051,000
Machine hours	1,000,000	800,000
Overhead rate	$10.65	$12.56

If PMD's manufacturing manager had compared manufacturing overhead dollars alone, he might have fooled himself into believing that PMD had been successful in controlling manufacturing overhead during 1987. Dividing machine hours into manufacturing overhead dollars to obtain an overhead rate, however, tells another story. The budgeted rate was exceeded substantially, and the results were nearly disastrous.

---

*We will use this inventory number for simplicity's sake. In actual use, the ending inventory figures for all four quarters would need to be averaged to determine average inventory.

Computing Fixed and Variable Costs

While direct material and direct labor dollars are relatively accessible for purposes of measurement and control (as you will see in later chapters), manufacturing overhead costs are not. Overhead is composed of a variety of costs, both fixed and variable, which need to be separated and measured to control overhead performance.

Let's first define fixed and variable costs before we move on to discuss how to control manufacturing overhead.

Fixed costs are those costs which do not change in response to a change in product volume. Typical fixed costs are depreciation, management salaries and benefits, taxes, rent, and heat, light and some power costs. (It must be remembered, however, that what you have just read is an *accounting* definition, for purposes of allocating and analyzing costs. From the viewpoint of the manufacturing manager, costs should *never* be considered fixed. That type of thinking will close your mind to possible reductions in fixed costs, such as selling unused plant space and equipment, combining supervisory positions, and eliminating salaried jobs, and so on.)

Variable costs are those costs that move, more or less, proportionately with product volume. Direct materials and direct labor are the prime examples. Others include indirect supplies, most power costs, and maintenance costs.

Now, let's examine manufacturing overhead costs for PMD's 1987 fiscal year. That was a relatively tough period for PMD; the division was experiencing all types of difficulties with bloated manufacturing overhead costs.

Figure 2-4 displays both budgeted and actual manufacturing overhead costs for PMD during 1987. The budgeted portion in the exhibit is divided into four parts, each expressing a different level of activity, as seen at the tops of the vertical columns opposite ("number of parts produced," "machine hours of operation"). This is called a flexible budget, and its purpose is to plan manufacturing overhead costs for different levels of production.

During 1987, PMD produced 3,500,000 parts and consumed 800,000 machine hours doing so. (That is shown under the far right-hand column titled "Actual Results"). For production of that many parts, only 700,000 machine hours should have been used. This can be verified by checking the budget for 3,500,000 parts produced. That is found in the fourth column from the left, and clearly states that 700,000 machine hours is the correct number for that number of actual parts produced.

How Manufacturing Overhead Is Measured and Controlled

So while we can see that PMD exceeded their overhead budget for that year, let's take a closer look at Figure 2-4 and discover just how bad things really were. It will first be necessary, however, to define the ways in which manufacturing overhead is measured and controlled.

Variances for manufacturing overhead are classically divided into three categories: spending, efficiency, and capacity.

Calculating Spending Variance. This is the difference between the actual cost and budgeted cost for actual machine hours expended.

Referring to Figure 2-4, the spending variance for PMD was:

Actual manufacturing overhead	$10,051,000
Budgeted manufacturing overhead (800,000 hrs.)	10,003,000
Unfavorable spending variance	$ 48,000

Calculating Efficiency Variance. This is found by comparing overhead costs of budgeted machine hours to overhead costs of actual machine hours. It is a measure of efficiency of machine hours used.

Again, referring to Figure 2-4, the efficiency variance for PMD can be calculated as follows:

Budget at 800,000 machine hours	$10,003,000
Budget at 700,000 machine hours*	9,676,000
Unfavorable efficiency variance	$ 327,000

*This is the amount of *required* machine hours when 3.5 million parts are produced—the actual case in 1987.

Calculating Capacity Variance. This measures the variance derived from performance attributable to operating the plants at below normal capacity. Normal capacity can be defined as *average* use of facilities over the past several years. In PMD's example, normal capacity has been set at 1 million machine hours based on prior years experience. A capacity variance will exist for PMD because in 1987 only 800,000 machine hours were used.

Once more, see Figure 2-4, for data needed to calculate the capacity variance for PMD, shown here:

Normal capacity	1,000,000 machine hours
Actual hours used	800,000 machine hours
Underabsorbed capacity	200,000 machine hours

Now that machine hours have been determined in the capacity variance calculation, costs must be applied. Since capacity variance measures the overabsorption or underabsorption of *fixed* overhead, variable costs are not considered (because they change with changes in product volume, while fixed costs do not). Using the fixed overhead rate shown in Figure 2-4—$7.39 per machine hour, the capacity variance is calculated:

Fixed Overhead Rate × Underabsorbed Machine Hours
        $7.39   × $200,000

                                                = Capacity Variance
                                                   $1,478,000

INTERNATIONAL MACHINERY, INC.
PARTS MANUFACTURING DIVISION
FLEXIBLE BUDGET*

	FLEXIBLE BUDGET				1989 ACTUAL RESULTS
Number of parts produced	5,000,000	4,500,000	4,000,000	3,500,000	3,500,000
Machine hours of operation	1,000,000	900,000	800,000	700,000	800,000
Variable overhead:					
Indirect materials and supplies	$ 1,116,000	$ 1,004,000	$ 893,000	$ 781,000	$ 946,000
Maintenance	810,000	729,000	648,000	567,000	648,000
Power	1,277,000	1,149,000	1,022,000	894,000	1,022,000
Other	60,000	54,000	48,000	42,000	50,000
Total variable costs	$ 3,263,000	$ 2,936,000	$ 2,611,000	$ 2,284,000	$ 2,666,000
Fixed overhead:					
Supervision	$ 3,003,000	$ 3,003,000	$ 3,003,000	$ 3,003,000	$ 3,003,000
Taxes and insurance	2,370,000	2,370,000	2,370,000	2,370,000	2,349,000
Heat and light	792,000	792,000	792,000	792,000	805,000
Depreciation	1,177,000	1,177,000	1,177,000	1,177,000	1,177,000
Other	50,000	50,000	50,000	50,000	51,000
Total fixed costs	$ 7,392,000	$ 7,392,000	$ 7,392,000	$ 7,392,000	$ 7,385,000
Total overhead	$10,655,000	$10,328,000	$10,003,000	$9,676,000	$10,051,000

Variable overhead rate per machine hr	$ 3.26
Fixed overhead rate per machine hr	$ 7.39
Total overhead rate per machine hr	$10.65

*Numbers rounded-off to nearest thousand.

Figure 2-4 Parts Manufacturing Division: Flexible budget

Combining Variances. Let's now put all three variances together and observe their cumulative impact on costs:

Actual overhead	$10,051,000		
		Spending	
Flexible budget for 800,000 hrs		variance	
Actually used	$10,003,000	$48,000	Controllable
			variance
		Efficiency	$475,000
		variance	
		$327,000	
Flexible budget for 700,000 hrs			
Required	$ 9,676,000		

The $475,000 represents that portion of the manufacturing overhead that could have been avoided had manufacturing management done a better job. It is an unfavorable variance that is strictly controllable.

Capacity variance, on the other hand, is related to product volume attributable to sales, and, as such, is beyond the control of the manufacturing manager. For PMD in 1987 it was an unfavorable variance. It does, however, signify a cost that must somehow be reduced so the division can remain profitable.

Both controllable and uncontrollable variances, when put together, look like this:

Unfavorable spending and efficiency variances	$ 475,000
Capacity variance	1,478,000
Total variances	$1,953,000

Manufacturing overhead costs are important to the manufacturing manager. Through use of a flexible budget and monthly reports of the variances indicated, you can keep the manufacturing overhead rate in line and hold costs to a minimum.

3

How to Organize Your Company for Maximum Profitability

The best manufacturing operating plan devised needs the proper vehicle to carry out its mission. The right manufacturing organization can make that happen. It will not guarantee results, but it will allow the mission the opportunity to be achieved successfully.

The wrong organization structure is a guarantee of failure. It focuses on weaknesses, does not capitalize on management strengths, and fails to zero in on the manufacturing strategy needed to achieve company profitability.

It would be deceptively easy to state that there is but one definitive organization structure perfectly suited to achieve manufacturing results. Unfortunately, that just isn't so.

There are many different and viable forms of manufacturing organization; and there are many factors that influence the proper selection: company age, technology involved, company size, product diversity, and management strategy, to name but a few.

FIVE FUNDAMENTAL ORGANIZATIONAL PRINCIPLES FOR SUCCESSFUL MANUFACTURING

Underlying every successful manufacturing organization are certain fundamental principles. These principles can be applied by any manufacturing organization.

1. *Make structure suit size.* As company size increases, manufacturing organizations will change commensurately. The small business utilizes an organization

28

substantially different from the medium-size business, and the medium-size business utilizes an organization different from the large company.

2. *Build organizations around product lines*. The most successful ones specialize, as illustrated by the Medical Electronics example in Chapter One.

3. *Separate management teams in decentralized organizations*. In all successful manufacturing organizations decentralization is a function of geography. As distances between the home office and factories increase, the necessity for separate management teams increases. For example, it is almost impossible to run a plant in California from a home office in New York.

4. *Hold line managers in production accountable for all results*: cost, production, productivity, quality safety, and hygiene. Support specialists can advise regarding decisions within their area of expertise, but production managers must always be responsible for results.

5. *Keep support staffs lean*. Too many specialists create a tendency to pay more allegiance to functional specialties rather than to manufacturing objectives.

ORGANIZING FOR PRODUCTIVITY

Let's examine some examples of the more productive forms of manufacturing organization. Bear in mind that there are infinite varieties of organization possible. Presented here are some of the more basic—but workable—structures. Embellishments can then be made according to the needs of the manufacturing organization.

How Company Size Changes as Sales Increase

In the fifties and sixties it was fashionable for smaller companies to copy the organizational structure of the successful General Motors Corporation. When Alfred Sloan's book, *My Years with General Motors*, appeared in 1964, that trend was reinforced. Subsequently, many companies learned the hard way that what suited General Motors did not necessarily suit them. Many executives discovered that their companies were just too different in many respects to mimic G.M. or any other organization.

A pharmaceutical company along the eastern seaboard grew from about $4 million in sales to about $100 million over 10 years. Figure 3-1 shows the manufac-

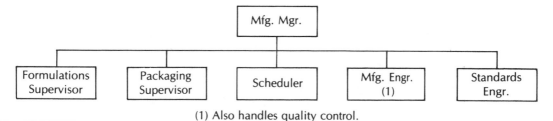

(1) Also handles quality control.

Figure 3-1   Pharmaceutical Manufacturing Organization of a Small Company

turing organization it used when it was still young, producing $4 to $10 million of goods annually. A manufacturing manager had five people reporting to him, as can be seen on the chart. Notice that the manufacturing engineer doubled as the quality control supervisor. In like fashion, most salaried employees wore two or more hats. The formulation supervisor, for example, also ran the receiving and shipping dock.

A few years later, when the same company had grown to about $30 million, the organization similarly grew to handle the expanded volume and product line. That organization can be seem in Figure 3-2. Notice that manufacturing line functions consolidated under an operations manager. The company, although still a one-plant operation, expanded sufficiently to justify the operations manager slot.

The same company eventually grew to the $100 million sales level, and the resultant decentralized manufacturing organization can be seen in Figure 3-3. Notably, two plant managers now report to a vice-president of manufacturing (the former manufacturing manager). Each plant has responsibilities akin to the operations manager of the former $30 million company. A headquarters staff has also been added using specialists in regulatory affairs, manufacturing engineering, and quality control. These specialists advise plant operators and help them to improve operations and reduce costs.

The regulatory manager's function is a good example of a special need demanding its own organizational prerogative. This advisory function interprets Food and Drug Administration (FDA) regulations and helps individual plants comply with those regulations. Obviously, this function would not be needed except in a company producing food, drug, or medical devices.

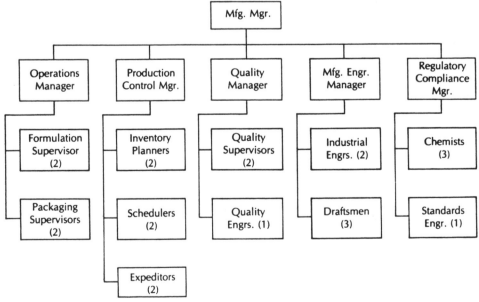

Figure 3-2   Pharmaceutical Manufacturing Organization of a Mid-Sized Company

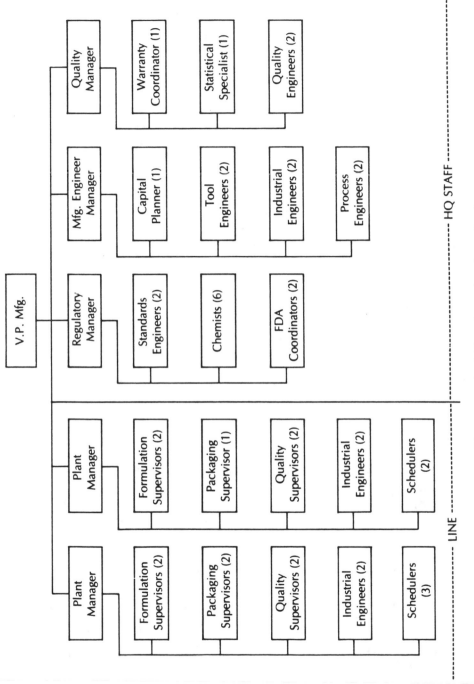

Figure 3-3 Pharmaceutical Manufacturing Organization Of a Large Company

How Unit Management Can Generate Greater Profits

Most manufacturing people are familiar with the classic line and staff organization which has been in profitable use for much of the last fifty years. Figure 3-3 is a typical example.

There has been a trend, however, in recent years to base the manufacturing structure on product lines rather than simple line and staff separations. The product line organization is referred to as Unit Management. It is a culmination of the desire to assign profit center responsibilities to product lines rather than plants. Proponents of the unit management concept of organization are convinced that greater profits will be the result.

A mining equipment manufacturer in the midwest produces three basic types of mining machinery: draglines, power shovels, and drills. For many years the manufacturer utilized line and staff manufacturing organization. But for many years drills took a backseat to draglines and power shovels, both larger products with higher sales volumes. A change in management brought with it a change in manufacturing organization to the unit management concept seen in Figure 3-4.

This company has three plants and, in the past, three different plant managers ran their respective plants and reported to the plant manager.

The revised organization assigned product line manufacturing responsibilities to unit managers. Each manager has a staff of people reporting to him, similar to what the plant manager formerly had, but now the unit manager is responsible for a specific product in all three plants.

Advantages of Unit Management. The unit management structure has the following strengths:

- It provides equal resources to all product lines. When using traditional line and staff organizations there is a tendency to shift resources to what is comfortable to work with while neglecting certain product lines that may be too difficult or too small in volume. The unit management concept assures recognition of all product lines.

- Product knowledge increases and, as a result, quality improves while both production and support people become more proficient in their product skills. This can (but will not necessarily) result in lower product line costs.

- Manufacturing unit managers work more closely with marketing managers who have the same product line focus. This almost inevitably generates lower inventories, as manufacturing people develop a "feel" for the marketplace demand of "their" product.

Drawbacks to Unit Management. There are, of course, disadvantages:

- Sometimes support costs climb as each unit manager adds staff people. For example, where industrial engineers were assigned to plants before, they are assigned to product lines now, and some overlapping of work to be done inevitably occurs.

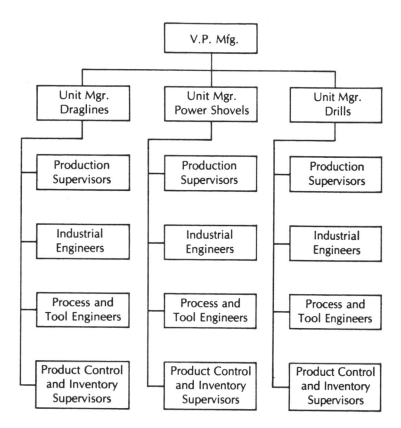

Figure 3-4   Product Line Manufacturing Organization

- Managers tend to become too specialized. Unfortunately, that reduces the flexibility of the organization.
- Confusion about "who is supposed to be doing what?" is a more dominant factor. When there is no plant manager it is often hard to determine responsibility and assign corrective action. Buck passing is more prevalent.

When to Use Unit Management. Unit management, as opposed to line and staff, can be used to advantage in the following situations:

- When some important product lines are being neglected.
- When a very close relationship between manufacturing and marketing managers is necessary to assure product line success.
- When a major new product is introduced into manufacturing.
- When there are diverse products being manufactured together.

The Advantages of the Matrix Organization

An organizational concept closely related to unit management is the matrix system. This type of unit functions best in an environment with diverse product lines, high levels of technology, and new product introduction.

In matrix management, each middle manager has two bosses. Figure 3-5 clearly depicts this relationship. While the plant manager reports only to the vice-president of operations, subordinates in materials, production engineering, and quality report both to the plant manager and to their counterparts at corporate headquarters, the directors of materials, production engineering, and quality.

The matrix organization combines functional and direct line reporting relationships. While the materials manager, for example, is responsible to the plant manager for day-to-day results, the materials manager is also responsible to the headquarters materials director for functional systems. The headquarters director is, in turn, responsible for uniform materials policies and procedures throughout the different plants and warehouses in the company. The advantage of this relationship is readily apparent when group purchasing replaces individual plant purchasing to take advantage of discounts associated with quantity buying.

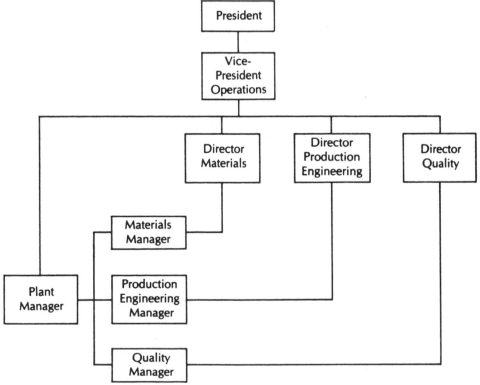

Figure 3-5   Matrix Organization for a Manufacturing Company

MRP or Traditional Planning and Control: Which Works Best for Your Company?

Although there are supposedly limitless variations of potential materials management organizations, they all are based on two fundamental organizational concepts: (1) the traditional production planning and control organization without materials requirements planning, and (2) the new materials management organization emphasizing the use of materials requirements planning.

Chapter Eleven describes a materials requirements planning system (MRP) in detail. MRP is a powerful computer planning tool developed about fifteen years ago to plan materials in the manufacturing process and minimize inventories simultaneously. It has revolutionized the production planning and control process by allowing managers to do a much better job controlling inventories, particularly in larger, more complex manufacturing operations where the manual control of inventories is inefficient.

Primary Planning and Control Functions. Figure 3-6 describes the typical production planning and control function still in overwhelming use in industry. It is composed of the five classical functions:

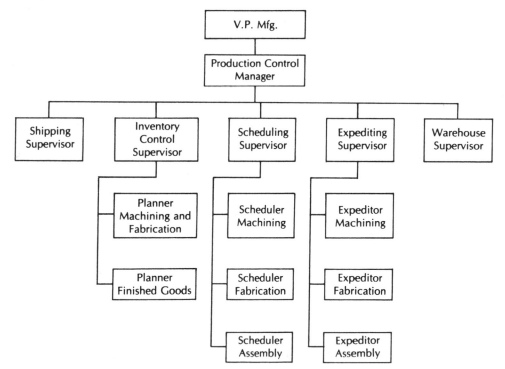

Figure 3-6 Production Planning and Control Organization (No Materials Requirements Planning)

- *Shipping*—Products, literature, and other related items sent by road, rail, and air.
- *Inventory Control*—The planning, monitoring, and control of raw materials, work-in-process, and finished goods inventories.
- *Scheduling*—Scheduling of raw material and parts receipts from vendors; scheduling of all manufacturing operations.
- *Expediting*—Control and follow-up of orders in manufacturing to assure schedules being attained.
- *Warehousing*—Storage of raw materials and parts awaiting usage in manufacturing or shipment to customers.

Primary MRP Functions. Figure 3-7 illustrates the newer materials management organization that uses material requirements planning. The primary functions of this organization are:

- *Shipping*—This function is the same as for the production planning and control organization.
- *Inventory Control*—This function is also the same.
- *Planning*—The job of planning in the materials management organization encompasses the functions of scheduling and expediting, shown in the production planning and control organization. Its job primarily is to use the computer's capability to derive parts requirements based on the MRP program and then to assure that the schedule is being achieved also through use of the computer. The basic difference between the planning function in Figure 3-7 and the scheduling function in Figure 3-6 is the MRP program.

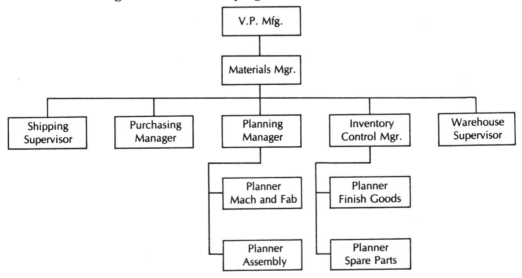

Figure 3-7 Materials Management Organization With Materials Requirements Planning

- *Warehousing*—This function, like the shipping and warehouse functions, is the same in both types of organizations.
- *Purchasing*—Under the materials management concept, purchasing is integrated with all other materials functions.

Comparing MRP and Production Planning and Control. The following matrix examines characteristics determining—in general—the use of each of the two basic materials management organizations:

Factor	Prod. Planning and Control	Materials Management
Plant Size	Small	Large
Number of Products	Limited	Extensive
Number of Parts in Product	Limited	Extensive
Product Complexity	Simple	Complex
Changes in Sales Forecasts	Few	Many
Product Options	Few	Many
Demand for Spare Parts	Light	Heavy
Cost of Inventory	Small	Large

MTP is a far more expensive system when compared with the manual methods used by production planning and control organizations. Therefore, as the matrix shows, the more complex the product line and the larger the manufacturing operations, the more applicable the use of MRP. Each case must be judged individually. The matrix serves only as a guide.

Two Proven Ways to Organize the Purchasing Function

There are two generally accepted and proven ways to organize the purchasing function, and each has its own merits.

Advantages of Commodity Purchasing. Figure 3-8 displays the purchasing organization for a lawn and garden manufacturer. Each of the buyers specializes in the purchase of specific commodities. This is referred to as "Commodity Purchasing." There are obvious advantages to this type of purchasing organization. Buyers get to know their own commodity fields quite well and can locate sources quickly; when one buyer purchases all of one commodity, larger quantity discounts can be procured.

When Product Line Purchasing Works Best. This same manufacturer of lawn and garden products at one time used the product line purchasing concept, as seen in Figure 3-9. This organization centralizes purchasing authority by product line. The buyer for lawnmower products, for example, would purchase *all* components for lawnmowers—sheet metal, commercial components, and plastics.

PURCHASING DEPARTMENT — LAWN AND GARDEN MFG.

```
                        ┌──────────────┐
                        │  V.P. Mfg.   │
                        └──────┬───────┘
                               │
                    ┌──────────┴───────┐
                    │ Purchasing Mgr.  │
                    └──────────┬───────┘
            ┌──────────────────┴────────────────┐
   ┌────────┴────────┐                  ┌────────┴────────┐
   │  Buyer—Sheet    │                  │    Expeditor    │
   │  Metal and Plate│                  └────────┬────────┘
   └────────┬────────┘                           │
            │         ┌────────────┐      ┌───────┴──────┐
            ├─────────│   Buyer    │      │  Inventory   │
            │         │  Plastics  │      │   Planner    │
            │         └────────────┘      └──────────────┘
            │         ┌────────────┐
            │         │   Buyer    │
            ├─────────│ Commercial │
            │         │ Components │
            │         └────────────┘
            │         ┌────────────┐
            │         │   Buyer    │
            └─────────│    MRO     │
                      └────────────┘
```

Figure 3-8   Commodity Purchasing Organization

The MRO buyer in both purchasing organizations does exactly the same job—purchases maintenance, repair and operating supplies (MRO). MRO constitutes hundreds, if not thousands, of supplies used predominantly by plant engineering organizations for building and machine repairs. Under the product line organization it is still preferable to have MRO items purchased by a separate buyer.

Product line buyers get to know their product lines quite well, and they can be held responsible for purchasing materials and parts for their product line. These are fundamental advantages of product line purchasing.

The disadvantages are pretty well what you'd expect them to be. Buyers don't specialize in commodity buying and, therefore, have only a sprinkling of knowledge of each commodity. In addition, quantity discount opportunities are smaller, since each buyer purchases a smaller quantity compared with the commodity buyer.

PURCHASING DEPARTMENT — LAWN AND GARDEN MFG.

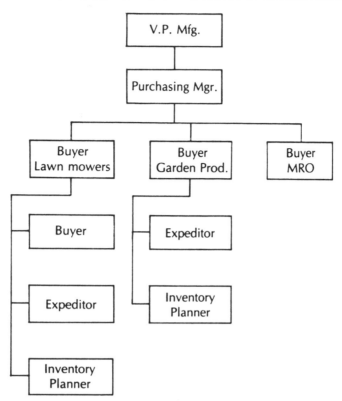

Figure 3-9   Product Line Purchasing Organization

Product line purchasing can be relatively advantageous when plants are widely separated and central purchasing administration is difficult. It can also be best for smaller firms with just a few major product lines.

Otherwise, the commodity purchasing organization offers a great deal. Most companies have found this organizational method to be preferable.

Two Leading Types of Manufacturing Engineering Organization

In manufacturing engineering organizations there are two dominant concepts in operation today. The two methods can be contrasted essentially through their degree of specialization.

How Nonspecialized Engineering Works. Figure 3-10 is an example of a non-specialized manufacturing engineering organization, normally seen in smaller

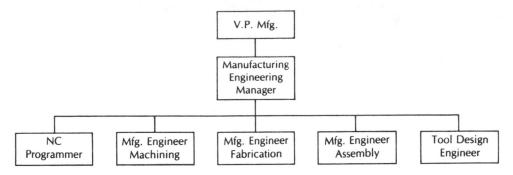

NOTE: All manufacturing engineers do their own time study,
methods work, cost estimating, and process engineering.

Figure 3-10   Manufacturing Engineering Organization for a Small Company Making Textile Machinery

companies. This organization is used by a small textile machinery company near Boston. In essence, a manufacturing engineer is assigned to each of the three major functional areas of the plant: machining, fabrication, and assembly. Each manufacturing engineer performs a variety of tasks: time study, methods, cost estimating, and process engineering.

The only specialization noted is for the Numerical Control (NC) programmer and the tool design engineer. Both of these jobs demand highly technical and specialized engineers, so it is not practical to have departmental manufacturing engineers assigned these duties.

How Specialized Engineering Works. The specialized manufacturing engineering organization for a large textile machinery company in Rhode Island is shown in Figure 3-11.

The process engineering, cost estimating, and industrial engineering functions (time study and methods) are separate functional entities. The NC programmer is assigned to the process engineering department; tool design, an expanded function for the larger textile machinery company, is also separated, as it was for the smaller company.

Drawbacks to each approach. The nonspecialized approach to manufacturing engineering develops well-rounded manufacturing engineers who specialize in functional operations, as opposed to functional specialties. As a company grows, however, it becomes increasingly difficult to rely on this type of organization.

The nonspecialized organization for a large company would inevitably result in the need for more engineers when compared with the specialized organization; thus, it would be more costly. The larger company also has so many machine tools and processes that the specialized manufacturing engineer would be unable to develop his knowledge of all the operations in his assigned area.

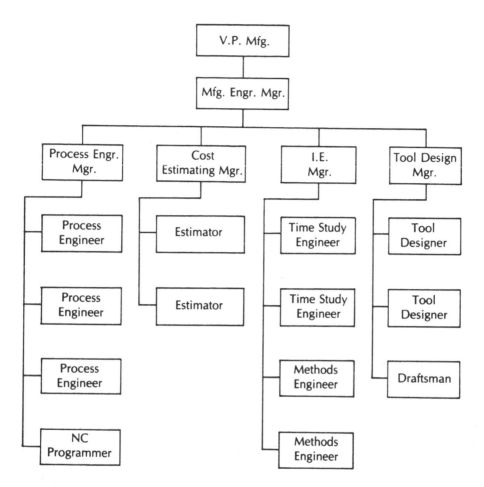

Figure 3-11 Manufacturing Engineering Organization for a Large Company Making Textile Machinery

How to Organize Quality Control to Improve Quality and Lower Costs

Regardless of the industry or technical complexity of the products or operations, or size of company, one type of quality control is superior to all others. That organization is seen in Figure 3-12.

The quality function is divided into two segments, line and growth. The line organization provides for the day-to-day activities of the quality control department, and the growth portion of that segment of the organization which accounts for improvements in quality methods, techniques, and processes. The growth portion is devoted to improvements. It focuses on improved quality levels and lowered quality costs, both of which go hand-in-hand. Chapter Six describes these functions in detail.

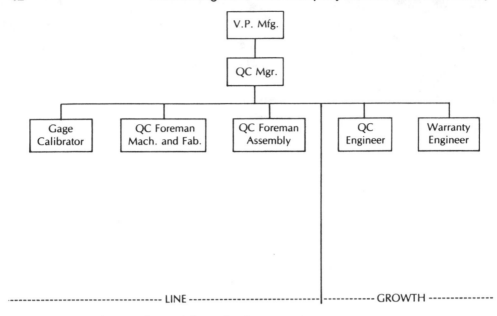

Figure 3-12   Quality Control Organization

HOW TO AVOID ORGANIZATIONAL MISTAKES

Too many companies in too many instances develop inappropriate organizations. When that happens, the wrong organization turns company strengths to weaknesses and perpetuates failure. Let's examine some of the most common errors.

Keep Small Companies Flexible and Responsive

Years ago, when General Motors was the largest and most successful organization in the world, it was common for many other companies to pattern their manufacturing organizations on that giant. One such company was a small toy manufacturer in New York State. A new top management loaded manufacturing with a top-heavy, specialized structure similar to the ones previously displayed in Figures 3-3 and 3-11. Although an attempt was made to keep staffing in each segment of the organization low, the sheer number of functions generated an excess number of employees. Overhead rates soared.

To make matters worse, the large, cumbersome structure caused unneeded delays of all sorts in manufacturing. It took about six months for the whole structure to collapse, and the company lost money for the year. A new management team soon was installed by an outraged board of directors. Learning from their predecessors' mistakes, the new management team implemented an organization similar to what is seen in Figure 3-1.

A small company needs a flexible and responsive organization. It just doesn't have the resources that a larger company has. An inflated organization might operate satisfactorily for a larger company, but it signals the death knell for a smaller operation. The sheer number of organizational levels combined with the vast number of functional specialties is simply too much. Organizational mire hinders the ability of the manufacturing organization to perform.

Know Your Optimum Size and Don't Try to Exceed It

By necessity, an automobile assembly plant deals with large numbers of employees. But even there, sheer size can generate inefficiencies. In the very large plants, managers tend to become administrators and lose their touch with day-to-day operations.

A large automobile assembly plant in New Jersey closed its doors in the 1980s. Hit by the recession of those years, the plant could not respond adequately with lower costs and top quality cars. The magnitude of operations was immense. Over its twenty years of operation it had been a steady source of cost and quality problems for the parent company, and it had seen a seemingly endless procession of managers during that time, all trying to improve operations. All failed.

In *all* cases, economic concentration of manufacturing facilities has its limits. There can be no doubt that smaller plants generally operate more efficiently than larger ones. Every plant has an optimum size. That limit is exceeded when top managers become removed from what is happening on the firing line. When they can no longer devote adequate time to plant activities, that is the time to call a halt to further growth and to start thinking of building a new plant.

Don't Overcrowd Your Reporting System

A mid-sized construction equipment manager on the east coast had the following manufacturing organization:

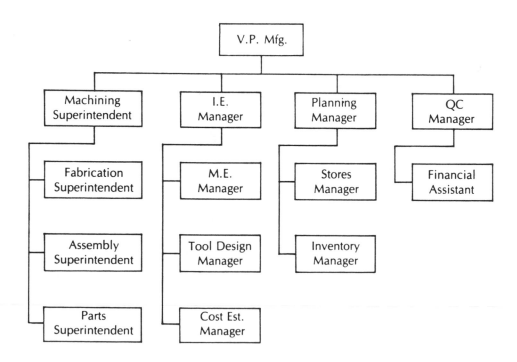

Thirteen managers in all reported to the vice-president of manufacturing. Rather than have the traditional four functional chiefs (production, materials, manufacturing engineering, quality) under his direct supervision, he elected to have all department heads report directly to him.

Needless to say, there is no way imaginable that the V.P. could properly supervise and direct all of these functions.

Not too long after the organization came into effect it began to crumble. A general lack of coordination among departments resulted in unachieved goals. Infighting became prevalent, and department heads began to set their own objectives, some of them running in counterdirection to their peers. A new manufacturing manager was soon hired.

Two More Tips for Profit-Minded Company Organization

1. Streamline management. Too many levels of organization slows the response of the organization to stated objectives. Compare the two following organizations, and decide for yourself which is more responsive to change.

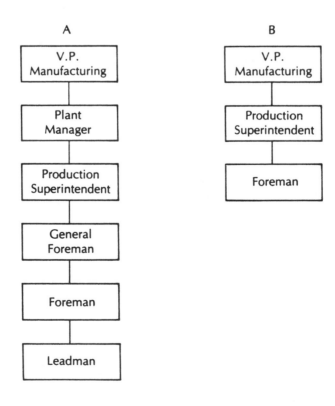

2. Reorganize only when absolutely necessary. Excessive reorganizations create feelings of insecurity; furthermore, they tend to focus the attention of the organization on "playing politics" rather than on accomplishment.

Put yourself in your employees' shoes. If you know there is going to be constant reshuffling, you will not only feel shaky about your position, but you will devote a good share of your time to assuring that you come out on top when the inevitable changes occur.

An organization should change, but only in response to new challenges—growth, shrinkage, new products, acquisitions, and similar definitive changes.

4

Fifteen Methods for Cutting Manufacturing Costs and Keeping Them Down

Once action plans have been established, and once the manufacturing organization is in place to achieve those action plans, some method of measurement and control is needed to assure the plans are being completed according to established timetables. Manufacturing controls are the proven method of accomplishing that goal.

HOW TO USE MANUFACTURING CONTROLS TO REDUCE COSTS

Effective manufacturing controls are superb tools for reducing costs and holding them down at lower levels. But they must first possess certain attributes to make them successful. They need these characteristics:

1. CONTROLS MUST BE SIMPLE. A control measurement must be both easily applied and understood. A good example is the measurement of direct labor efficiency that was changed in an aluminum fabrication plant in the south. Work standards were once expressed as "direct labor hours per 100 pounds produced." Nobody fully understood that type of standard. Foremen were confused. When direct labor standards were changed to "pounds per hour"

all of the mystery cleared; foremen were able to easily measure and understand the new standard and production was soon increased by 10 percent.

2. CONTROLS MUST BE EXPRESSED QUANTITATIVELY. An old management expression is "If you can't reduce it to numbers, it ain't worth a damn." Controls that are not measurable in numbers are too easily misinterpreted. Subjective judgments and opinions substitute for objective measurements. Progress, or lack of it, cannot be readily determined. Almost all manufacturing action plans are capable of being expressed quantitatively and should be, so that control over operations can be effective.

3. CONTROLS MUST BE TIMELY. What happened last quarter is of historical interest only. It is too late to do anything about it. If it is too late to take effective corrective action, then reporting is not timely. Measurements of operations need to be geared to the events being measured. Such important events as production and direct labor, for example, need to be measured *at least* daily, if not every few hours. The short interval of time between the event and its feedback to manufacturing management permits corrective action to bring the plan back into schedule before it is too late. In manufacturing operations almost all events need to be reported weekly or daily, seldom at longer intervals.

METHOD 1: CUT DIRECT LABOR COSTS

To show how direct labor costs can be reduced, let's examine a specific situation. The aluminum fabrication plant previously mentioned installed direct labor controls and was able to achieve an annual cost savings of approximately $1 million.

Use The Daily Labor Report to Track Efficiency and Downtime

The first control tool installed was the direct labor control report, shown in Figure 4-1. This report shows both the efficiency of the labor force by department, as well as its amount of downtime.

The left-hand column lists each of the aluminum plant's manufacturing departments. The next column to the right displays standard hours. These numbers reflect the total standard hours for the work performed in each department for the time period being measured, in this case one day.

Earned hours, the next column, shows actual performance measured in labor-hours. This example explains how earned hours are derived:

OPERATION	STANDARD HOURS
slit 6" coils	.5 per coil

In the aluminum plant, an operator would be required to slit sixteen 6" coils in an eight-hour shift to meet standard. Following are earned hours an operator will be awarded for different production levels of 6" coils:

ALUMINUM FABRICATION PLANT
DAILY LABOR REPORT
8/16/X2

DEPARTMENT	DIRECT LABOR MEASUREMENTS				
	STD HOURS	EARNED HOURS	PERCENT EFFICIENCY	TIME OFF-STD	PERCENT OFF-STD
Pre-Heat	260.0	260.0	100.0	20.0	7.1
Hot Roll	232.4	216.6	93.2	63.6	21.5
Pre-Heat	248.0	258.4	104.2	0	0
Cold Roll	231.5	217.6	94.0	48.5	17.3
Slitters	574.7	471.6	82.1	201.3	25.9
Anneal	148.0	148.0	100.0	0	0
Packing	470.0	456.4	97.1	50.0	9.6
Total	2164.6	2028.6	93.7	383.4	15.0

Figure 4-1   Direct Labor Control Report

NO. of 6" COILS SLIT	% EFFICIENCY	EARNED HOURS
4	25.0%	2.0
8	50.0%	4.0
12	75.0%	6.0
16	100.0%	8.0
20	125.0%	10.0
24	150.0%	12.0

Earned hours for the day are accumulated for all direct labor operations for each department and posted to the report shown.

"Percent Efficiency," the next column, is explained in Figure 4-1. For the day in question, the plant averaged 95.2 percent efficiency.

The final column of Figure 4-1, "Percent Off-Standard, displays the total time that direct labor employees are performing jobs not measured by standard hours. These hours can be caused either by time spent on direct labor jobs, which have not yet been measured, or by downtime. In the case above, the percent of time off-standard for the day amounted to 18.6 percent.

Create a Separate Daily Downtime Analysis

This report, also issued daily, expands information taken from the "Percent Off-Standard" section of the Direct Labor Control Report. It describes reasons for the occurrences of off-standard time. In essence, it is a downtime report.

ALUMINUM FABRICATION PLANT
DAILY DOWNTIME REPORT
8/16/X2

DEPARTMENT	PERCENT TIME OFF-STANDARD			DOWNTIME
	TODAY	YTD	19X1	REASONS
Pre-Heat	7.1	4.5	6.4	Thermostat Failure
Hot Roll	21.5	6.8	9.5	Roll Crack #3
Pre-Heat	0	3.1	2.9	—
Cold Roll	17.3	10.7	8.9	Elec. Failure
Slitters	25.9	8.5	10.3	Elec. Failure
Anneal	0	3.1	16.4	—
Packing	9.6	1.8	2.1	Interleave Quality Problem
Total	15.0	7.2	9.8	

Figure 4-2 Daily Downtime Analysis

The first column of Figure 4-2 lists the same production departments found in the Direct Labor Control Report. The second column shows the percentage of off-standard time also contained in the former report. The following column shows year-to-date results (YTD), and the next column displays last year's averages.

The final column, "Downtime Reasons," describes reasons for the current day's downtime.

Notice that downtime for the plant has been reduced from 9.8 percent in 19X1 to the current year's average of 7.2 percent through August 16.

The Daily Downtime Analysis is a useful tool for analysis of downtime, where it occurred, how extensive it is, and reasons for the downtime.

Create a Monthly Direct Labor Control Report

The final report used by the aluminum plant to reduce costs is historical in nature but useful, nevertheless, to compare direct labor performance over a period of time. This report is displayed in Figure 4-3.

The columns in this report are arranged the same as for the Daily Downtime Report, but the results for the current period are monthly, not the daily period of the Daily Downtime Report.

ALUMINUM FABRICATION PLANT
MONTHLY LABOR REPORT
AUGUST 19X2

DEPARTMENT	PERCENT EFFICIENCY			
	THIS MONTH	YTD	19X1	
Pre-Heat	95.2	93.8	85.4	—
Hot Roll	90.7	91.4	82.8	—
Pre-Heat	98.5	97.0	95.3	—
Cold Roll	97.3	98.1	104.1	—
Slitters	80.1	82.5	93.2	Electrical Problems
Anneal	102.1	100.8	70.1	—
Packing	93.2	90.6	93.4	—
Total	96.0	96.8	89.2	

Figure 4-3 Monthly Direct Labor Control Report

Notice that, while results for the current month and year exceed levels of the previous year, the slitter department's performance is depressed, and the reason given is electrical problems. A careful analysis of both daily performance and downtime reports by plant management should yield clues about reasons for the lackluster performance. Corrective action can then occur.

How to Calculate Savings by Monitoring Direct Labor Costs

A manufacturing plant that doesn't have direct labor control reports can generally realize a savings of 10 to 20 percent when the reports are published and used for corrective action. The savings are generated basically through reduced downtime, but some increases in direct labor performance can be anticipated. In the case of the aluminum plant that employed 320 direct labor people, the equivalent of 35 employees was eliminated over a period of eighteen months through implementation of direct labor controls. The breakdown was as follows:

DOWNTIME SAVINGS—ALUMINUM PLANT

DEPARTMENT	HOURS/YEARS SAVED	DOLLARS PER YEAR SAVED AT $10/HOUR[1]
Pre-Heat	4150	$ 41,500
Hot Roll	6670	66,700
Pre-Heat	6830	66,300
Cold Roll	4060	40,600
Slitters	14190	141,900
Anneal	5350	63,500
Packing	8170	61,700
Total:	49,420	$494,200

PERFORMANCE SAVINGS—ALUMINUM PLANT

DEPARTMENT	HOURS/YEARS SAVED	DOLLARS PER YEAR SAVED AT $10/HOUR
Pre-Heat	8990	$ 89,900
Hot Roll	6350	63,500
Pre-Heat	2280	22,800
Cold Roll	(1672)	(16,720)
Slitters	(3830)	(38,300)
Anneal	10150	101,500
Packing	Even	Even
Total:	22268	$222,680

TOTAL DIRECT LABOR SAVINGS—ALUMINUM PLANT

	DOLLARS	PERCENT
Downtime Savings	$494,200	68.9
Performance Savings	222,680	31.1
Total:	$716,880	100.0%

[1] The $10 per hour is based on an average hourly rate of $8 and a fringe level of $2 per hour (25 percent).

Notice that downtime savings are approximately double performance savings, and that performance savings are somewhat erratic with both the cold roll and slitter departments showing decreases in performance. Nevertheless, total direct labor savings amounted to over $700,000 for the entire plant.

Four Ways to Measure Direct Labor Control

Many other measurements of direct labor can be made to control and correct costs. Some of the more prevalent are as follows:

1. Calculate Labor Utilization

$$\text{Utilization} \quad = \quad \frac{\text{Time Off Standards}}{\text{Total Time Available}} \quad \times \quad 100\%$$

Example: A production department with twenty direct labor employees shows the following statistics for one eight-hour production:

$$\text{Total Time Available} = 20 \times 8 = 160 \text{ Labor-Hours}$$

$$\text{Time On Standards} = 120 \text{ Labor-Hours}$$

$$\text{Time Off Standards} = 40 \text{ Labor-Hours}$$

2. Calculate Direct Labor Productivity

$$\text{Productivity} = \text{Performance} \times \text{Utilization} \times 100\%$$

Example: In the same department cited in the example on utilization, performance (percent efficiency of direct labor) was 95 percent for that shift.

$$\text{Productivity} = 95.0\% \times 75.0\% \times 100\% = 71.3\%$$

Labor productivity is a more encompassing index than separate measures of performance and utilization. It provides a ready measurement of direct labor productivity in a single ratio.

3. Measure Units Per Employee

$$\text{Units Per Employee} \quad = \quad \frac{\text{No. of Units Produced (Output)}}{\text{No. of Direct Labor Employees}}$$

Example: Continuing with the same department example, if twenty workers had produced 1000 valves during their shift, then:

$$\text{Units Per Employee} \quad = \quad \frac{1000}{20} \quad = \quad 50$$

This ratio is used only when high production volumes of discrete units are produced. If the same twenty workers assembled two tractors during one shift, use of the "units per employee" ratio would be meaningless.

4. Calculate Direct Labor Costs Per Unit

$$\text{Direct Labor Cost Per Unit} \quad = \quad \frac{\text{Total D.L. Costs}}{\text{No. of Units Produced}}$$

Example: If the twenty direct labor employees each were paid $10 per hour, then:

$$\text{Direct Labor Cost Per Unit} \quad = \quad \frac{20 \times \$10 \times 8 \text{ Hrs.}}{1000} \quad = \quad \frac{\$1,600}{1,000} \quad = \quad \$1.60$$

METHOD 2: INSTALL INCENTIVE COVERAGE TO INCREASE PRODUCTION

Every manufacturing organization must decide on whether or not it wants to use incentive systems to stimulate production output. Generally, incentive coverage yields more results in proportion to the amount of manual work involved. One hundred percent manual work, such as hand assembly of small components, is a natural for incentive coverage; an NC machine tool, where the machine controls the cycle, is at the other end of the spectrum.

Also, short-cycle, highly repetitive work is amenable to incentive coverage, while long-cycle, highly technical, nonrepetitive work, such as missile assembly, is not.

How to Measure Incentive Coverage

The first control tool when measuring incentive operations is the degree of coverage. This measurement is made in two parts:

1. Percent Employees Covered
2. Percent Operations on Incentive

In the first case it is relatively simple to measure the number of direct labor employees on incentive. Let's look at the case of the surgical needle manufacturer. Here, 550 employees were classified as direct labor. Of these, 490 were on incentive. Therefore,

$$\text{Percent Employees Covered} \quad = \quad \frac{490}{550} \times 100\% \quad = \quad 89.1\%$$

For most operations it is not necessary to have all direct labor employees on incentive. There are always instances when to do so would not be practical. A good example is a small section of direct labor employees doing all nonrepetitive miscellaneous operations. Standards here would be difficult to establish.

The latter measurement, "Percent Operations on Incentive," is an index that is somewhat better than "Percent Employees Covered" simply because *all* employees could be on incentive but have only 25 percent of their work on incentive.

$$\text{Percent Operations on Incentive} \quad = \quad \frac{\text{Operations on Incentive}}{\text{Total Plant Operations}} \times 100\%$$

Total plant operations, of course, refers only to direct labor work. The surgical needle manufacturer had 312 operations (counting all variations as measured by production routings), and 249 of those were on incentive. Therefore,

$$\text{Percent Operations on Incentive} = \frac{249}{312} \times 100 = 79.8\%$$

Generally speaking, incentive coverage of 80 percent to 90 percent is considered acceptable, but each company must make its own determination, and that is usually done by measuring production increases generated by the incentive system.

How to Calculate Average Earnings

Average earnings is defined as those earnings derived from operations not on standard. In most union shops, average earnings is a negotiable issue, and payment resulting from average earnings is based on what each individual operator averaged on incentive for the past week. If a drill press operator, for example, ran several jobs not yet measured on incentive (usually new jobs) his *incentive* pay for those jobs would be the average incentive pay he earned during the previous week.

Average earnings is payment of something for nothing. Since unmeasured work is looked upon as a fault of management, unions are generally successful in their demands for average earnings. In that case, the measurement of average earnings becomes a significant ratio for management.

$$\text{Average Earnings} = \frac{\text{Average Earnings}}{\text{Total Incentive Earnings}} \times 100\%$$

The surgical needle manufacturer had the following average earnings for one calendar year:

$$\text{Average Earnings} = \frac{\$241,632}{\$1,550,750} \times 100 = 15.6\%$$

No matter how you look at it, either 15.6 percent or $241,632 is too much. Most average earnings are better held to maximums of 5 percent to 7 percent.

Measuring the Results of Incentive Coverage: Percent Performance to Standard

This ratio is the most significant one in measuring the results of incentive coverage. It shows increases in performance that can be directly related to increases in production.

The surgical needle manufacturer, before incentives, had the following annual performance:

$$\text{Performance} \ = \ \frac{\text{Earned Hours}}{\text{Standard Hours}} \ \times \ 100$$

$$\text{Performance} \ = \ \frac{398,140}{563,178} \ \times \ 100 \ = \ 70.7\%$$

After installation of the incentive system for one year, their performance had improved 25 percent (despite their large average earnings) as seen here:

$$\text{Performance} \ = \ \frac{506,442}{571,280} \ \times \ 100 \ = \ 88.7\%$$

In terms of actual improvement in performance,

$$\text{Percent Improvement} \ = \ \frac{88.7\% \ - \ 70.7\%}{70.7\%} \ \times \ 100 \ = \ 25.5\%$$

The 25.5 percent improvement in performance represented a real gain of equal amount in production output.

METHOD 3: PRUNE INDIRECT LABOR COSTS

Indirect labor costs constitute a significant portion of overhead, and overhead is that type of cost that must be constantly pruned to keep it from growing. A manufacturing team that ignores those costs will soon find its costs escalating beyond control.

Typical indirect labor costs are:
- Material Handlers
- Warehouse personnel
- Truckers
- Inspectors
- Pipefitters
- Machinists
- Electricians
- Millwrights
- Tool Grinders
- Tool Crib Attendants
- Sweepers
- Janitors
- Clerks
- Supervisors
- Managers

The list is seemingly endless, since any variation of clerk, for example, can be added to the list.

A large manufacturer of rebuilt bus transmissions and electric door openers for subway trains in New Jersey found itself with a burgeoning indirect labor force as the business grew quickly from a "Mom and Pop" operation to a mid-sized manufacturing company. It found that application of two basic measurements of indirect labor permitted the company to reduce and hold indirect labor costs by about 75 percent of its former level.

Comparing Indirect to Direct Labor

The first of these measurements is shown in Figure 4-4. Section "A" displays the total number of direct and indirect employees on the books for 19X0, 19X1 and the first four months of 19X2.

A ratio of direct labor divided by indirect labor is then developed. Notice that this ratio was 3.90 in 19X0 and 4.92 to 4.95 for the first four months of 19X2. This represents an improvement of 26.4 percent, as seen here:

$$\frac{4.93\% - 3.90\%}{3.90\%} \times 100 = 26.4\%$$

XYZ COMPANY
INDIRECT LABOR CONTROL
APRIL 19X2

A. DIRECT TO INDIRECT

	19X0	19X1	1/X2	2/X2	3/X2	4/X2
DIRECT	460	495	483	485	485	482
INDIRECT	118	118	98	98	98	98
DIRECT/INDIRECT	3.90	4.19	4.93	4.95	4.95	4.92

B. INDIRECT CLASSIFICATION

	19X0	19X1	1/X2	2/X2	3/X2	4/X2
INSPECTORS	29	29	22	22	22	22
TOOL CRIB ATTENDANTS	4	4	2	2	2	2
SWEEPERS	6	6	3	3	3	3
MAINTENANCE	28	28	24	24	24	24
WAREHOUSE	30	30	29	29	29	29
TRUCK DRIVERS	21	21	18	18	18	18
TOTAL:	118	118	98	98	98	98

Figure 4-4   Comparison of Indirect to Direct Labor

    Section "B" shows the actual number of indirect employees by classification, and reveals reductions made in each classification of indirect labor.

Measuring Indirect Labor as a Percentage of Cost of Sales

The second measurement used by the manufacturing rebuilder was the ratio of indirect labor costs to cost of sales. Use of that ratio permitted an unbiased and objective look at progress—or-lack of it—in controlling indirect labor costs. The ratio is:

$$\text{Indirect Labor Costs Ratio} = \frac{\text{Indirect Labor Costs}}{\text{Total Cost of Sales}}$$

    For the manufacturer being studied, his 19X0 and Jan.–April 19X2 ratios are seen here:

19X0

$$\text{Indirect Labor Costs} = \frac{\$1,963,520}{62,073,985} \times 100 = 3.16\%$$

Jan.-April 19X2

$$\text{Indirect Labor Costs} = \frac{\$\ 478,515}{21,173,228} \times 100 = 2.26\%$$

Change

$$\frac{3.16\% - 2.26\%}{3.16\%} \times 100 = 28.5\% \text{ Improvement}$$

    The 28.5 percent represents real dollar improvement adjusted for inflation, in terms of today's dollars.

METHOD 4: SLASH MANUFACTURING OVERHEAD

Overhead costs are composed of these types of accounts in manufacturing:

- Salaries
- Travel and Entertainment Expenses
- Overtime
- Due and Subscriptions
- Heat, Light, and Power
- Rent
- Insurance
- Supplies
- Training

- Rework and Scrap
- Depreciation
- Downtime
- Recruiting Expenses

Here's how a machine tool company in Ohio was able to lower manufacturing overhead. The company began by segregating overhead costs into spending and efficiency variances.

The spending variance is the difference between the actual overhead and budgeted overhead for actual standard hours of operation. The company had forecast a monthly rate of 70,000 standard hours at a total overhead cost of $280,000, as shown here:

Budgeted Overhead Costs: $280,000

Actual Overhead Costs: 255,000

Favorable Spending Variance: $ 25,000

Since actual costs were $25,000 less than anticipated, a favorable spending variance occurred. An annual rate of savings was then $300,000 ($25,000 per month × 12 months), as actually happened during the course of the year.

The company had been forecast to produce 1,200 machine tools during the year, and to consume 70,000 standard hours per month, or an annual rate of 840,000 standard hours (70,000 standard hours × 12 months). Instead, 760,000 standard hours were used to manufacture those same 1,200 machine tools. A favorable efficiency variance resulted:

Budget for 840,000 Std. Hrs: $3,360,000

Budget for 760,000 Std. Hrs: 3,040,000

Favorable Efficiency Variance: $ 320,000
                Total Savings:

Favorable Spending Variance: $ 300,000

Favorable Efficiency Variance: 320,000

Total Favorable Variances: $ 620,000

The very nature of budgeting overhead costs to manufacturing departments, then measuring and reporting them by area of responsibility, soon produces cost savings. Supervisors and managers, when aware of *where* costs are, and *how much* they are, are then in a position to apply their skills in cost reduction. The machine tool manufacturer was successful in reducing overhead because they intelligently applied those principles.

METHOD 5: REDUCE MATERIAL BURDEN

Materials, in this sense, means materials used in the sold product. It does not include supplies, tools, gauges, fixtures, or any other expense classified as manufacturing overhead.

There are two measurable variances connected with material burden: price and quantity. A drug company in Tennessee reduced material costs by 20 percent through control of those two variances. That amounted to a rather large savings since material costs are usually the largest single category of cost in a manufacturing company.

Price variances in material burden measure the difference between actual purchased prices and standard costs. If, for example, a purchasing department bought 1,000 bearings at $7.00 each, while standard costs had been forecast at $8.00

DRUG COMPANY
MATERIAL BURDEN ANALYSIS
JAN., 19X3

($)

	THIS MONTH		YEAR-TO-DATE	
PRICE VARIANCES	Standard	Actual	Standard	Actual
Soluble Materials	20,500	18,550	20,500	18,550
Dry materials	16,800	17,200	16,800	17,200
Liquids	2,500	2,400	2,500	2,400
Packaging	18,900	17,500	18,900	17,500
Total	58,700	55,650	58,700	55,650
///				
QUANTITY VARIANCES				
Weigh, Screen, Mix	12,500	10,660	12,500	10,660
Absorption and Mixing	13,100	12,770	13,100	12,770
Packaging	10,000	10,000	10,000	10,000
Boxing	3,000	3,200	3,000	3,200
Total	38,600	36,630	38,600	36,630

Figure 4-5   Analysis of Price and Quantity Material Variances

per bearing, a savings of $1,000 would have resulted (1,000 bearings × $1.00 savings/bearing).

Quantity variances in material burden reflect the difference between specified and actual usage. The drug company, for example, formulated batches of 5,000 gallons of a chemical mixture and bottled the resulting lotions. By measuring quantity variances, they were able to reduce waste (extractables) and then needed 4,500 gallons for individual batches as opposed to the original 5,000 gallons.

Both price and quantity variances were reported monthly in the report shown in Figure 4-5. The top section of the report shows price variances, the responsibility of the purchasing department, and quantity variances, the responsibility of production people. Both current month results and year-to-date results are reported.

METHOD 6: REDUCE INVENTORY

A toy manufacturer reduced inventory by $1 million through use of control measurements of its inventory turnover rate, as well as the size of its inventory during different stages of manufacture.

Measuring Inventory Turnover

Inventory turnover is the annual number of times that a plant ships products equivalent in value to the average monthly manufactured costs of its inventory.

The toy company, for example, reported this turnover for 1990.

$$\text{Turnover} = \frac{\text{Cost of Sales}}{\text{Average Monthly Inventory}}$$

$$\text{Turnover} = \frac{9,350,000}{3,230,000}$$

$$\text{Turnover} = 2.89 \text{ Times Per Year}$$

Figure 4-6 shows the toy company's turnover rates for the past ten years. Notice that when inventory turnover rates and other control measurements were instituted in 1985 improvements began.

A composite of these controls is seen in Figure 4-7, which represents the company's turnover plan for 1991. The importance of planning inventory plans cannot be underestimated. Careful planning here assures that material purchases, production plans, and inventory balances are thought out ahead of time. This type of foresight inevitably results in inventory reductions. Once managers and supervisors focus their attention on the subject, improvements are sure to come.

The inventory turnover plan shown in Figure 4-7 breaks inventory down into its three segments: Raw materials (purchases), W.I.P. (Work-in-process; this is inventory being processed in manufacturing), and finished product awaiting shipment. Notice that as Christmas approaches, total inventories increase in response to heavier demand.

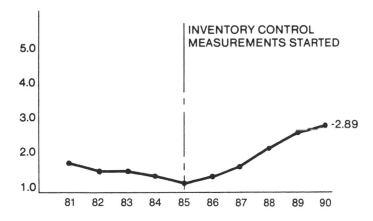

TOY COMPANY
INVENTORY TURNOVER RATE

Figure 4-6   Inventory Turnover Rates

TOY COMPANY
INVENTORY TURNOVER PLAN
1991

	COST-OF-SALES	INVENTORY			
		RAW MATERIAL	W.I.P.	FINISHED	TURNOVER
JANUARY	700,000	300,000	800,000	1,000,000	3.0
FEBRUARY	700,000	300,000	800,000	1,000,000	3.0
MARCH	700,000	300,000	800,000	1,000,000	3.0
APRIL	700,000	300,000	800,000	1,000,000	3.0
MAY	700,000	300,000	800,000	1,000,000	3.0
JUNE	700,000	300,000	800,000	1,000,000	3.0
JULY	700,000	300,000	800,000	1,000,000	3.0
AUGUST	1,000,000	700,000	1,000,000	1,500,000	3.2
SEPTEMBER	1,000,000	700,000	1,000,000	1,500,000	3.2
OCTOBER	1,500,000	700,000	1,000,000	1,500,000	3.2
NOVEMBER	2,000,000	2,200,000	1,800,000	3,000,000	3.5
DECEMBER	1,000,000	0	800,000	2,500,000	3.3
TOTAL:	10,700,000				

Figure 4-7   Inventory Turnover Plan

Actual inventory turnover results are published monthly by the toy company and compared to the plan.

Track Your Inventory Carrying Costs Carefully

In today's economy, inventory carrying costs of 30 percent of the value of the inventory are not uncommon. Therefore, the importance of keeping inventories to an absolute minimum to support delivery schedules is paramount.

This annual cost includes such major segments as:

SPACE COSTS

- Building and equipment depreciation
- Heat, light, and power
- Building and equipment maintenance
- Insurance
- Fire systems
- Plant protection

INVENTORY COSTS

- Interest on capital invested (about 20 percent)
- Transportation and handling
- Clerical costs
- Physical inventory costs
- Damage to inventory
- Obsolescence
- Theft

METHOD 7: MAINTAIN ACCURATE INVENTORY RECORDS

Accurate inventory records are of prime importance because if they are not maintained properly, variances in purchasing materials and usage of materials in production can be expected. If, for instance, an inventory record shows a balance of 100 bearings while an actual count reveals 75, a shrink of 25 bearings reduces inventory value by the cost of 25 bearings. Shrink is caused by many different things, among them:

- Clerical errors
- Failure to process paperwork quickly
- Unreported scrap and rework
- Misplaced inventory
- Theft

- Unauthorized material substitutions
- Inaccurate bills of material (see Method 8)

Monitoring Shrinkage Through Cycle Counting

A metal working company is the South countered this problem through cycle counting. Cycle counting is a system of perpetual physical inventory-taking, conducted on selected inventory parts every day, normally after business hours. It emphasizes the review of high value inventory parts. In cycle counting, employees physically count parts and check location accuracy as well. Mistakes are reconciled to perpetual inventory records.

Figure 4-8 shows a cycle count report used by the metal working company to reduce inventory shrink 60 percent. This report provides the following information:

- The actual number of different part numbers checked and the total number of parts counted.

CYCLE COUNT REPORT
WEEK OF SEPTEMBER 7, 19X1

NUMBER OF COUNTS

	PART NOS. CHECKED	NO. OF PIECES
Cycle Counter "A"	306	30,143
Cycle Counter "B"	294	32,650
TOTAL COUNTS:	600	62,793

NUMBER OF ERRORS FOUND

	NO. OF PIECES
Cycle Counter "A"	3.1%
Cycle Counter "B"	2.5%
TOTAL ERRORS:	2.6%

ERRORS IN DOLLARS

$$\frac{\text{No. of Pieces Wrong}}{\text{Total Inventory Counted}} = \frac{1633}{62,793} = 2.6\%$$

$$\frac{\text{Pieces Wrong}}{\text{Inventory Counted}} = \frac{\$21,528}{1,040,697} = \$2.1\%$$

Figure 4-8   Measuring Inventory Accuracy

- The number and percentage of errors found in actual pieces counted.
- A dollar amount on the errors found as well as a dollar and percentage figure based on the sample derived.

Use of this report (along with bills of material accuracy) enables managers to spot errors and take effective corrective action. It also gives a reliable picture of the estimated percentage of errors to be found in the inventory. In this case, shrink was reduced by 60 percent when management had the control tools in place to spot problem areas.

METHOD 8: CREATE COMPLETE AND ACCURATE BILLS OF MATERIAL

A key function of product engineering is the creation of bills of material that accurately reflect the type and number of parts to be used in the product. Inaccurate or incomplete B.O.M. (Bills of Material) directly affect the level of inventory accuracy. If a B.O.M. is wrong, unauthorized parts may need to be substituted, and this generates additional costs if the substituted parts are of higher value. It then also creates quantity variances in the parts being substituted because of unplanned issues.

Typical B.O.M. The bill of material seen in Figure 4-9 is typical of bills originating in engineering departments. Listed in the body of the bill are all of the components that make up the part described on the top of the bill, in this case a tension bracket,. The bill of material is used by all relevant departments—manufacturing, engineering, and accounting—to extract the information they need to do their jobs as shown below:

Engineering—Uses B.O.M. to list and specify all components, materials, and parts in the product.

Manufacturing—Structures the bill according to sequence of manufacture (called a production routing) and specifies work methods and standards for each operation.

Accounting—Uses B.O.M. to cost the product and obtain variances from standards.

B.O.M. accuracy is then essentially a function of how well manufacturing and engineering have done their jobs. It is an audit of the correct parts to be used in manufacturing. In the typical B.O.M. accuracy audit, literally hundreds of bills, such as those seen in Figure 4-9, are examined for errors, and a B.O.M. accuracy rate is derived.

Figure 4-10 is a typical report on B.O.M. accuracy. Both counts and correct part numbers are examined as can be seen in the top half of the form. The bottom half lists the summary of results along with the type of errors found.

BILL OF MATERIAL

PART: TENSION BRACKET PART NUMBER: 136-72A		
PARTS DESCRIPTION	PART NUMBER	QUANTITY USED
Bracket Frame	136-72A1	1
Sprocket	136-72A2	1
Spring	136-72A3	2
Set Screen	136-72A4	1
Holding Screen	136-72A5	3

Figure 4-9   Typical Bill of Material

B.O.M. AUDIT
WEEK OF SEPT. 7, 1989

COUNT

PARTS AUDITED	SPECIFIED	ACTUAL	COMMENTS
136-72A1	1	1	
136-72A2	1	1	Wrong part no. should be 136-72AC.
136-72A3	2	2	
136-72A4	1	1	
136-72A5	3	2	Should be two parts

SUMMARY OF RESULTS

$$\frac{\text{No. of parts incorrect}}{\text{No. of parts audited}} = \frac{4}{354} = 1.0\% \text{ error}$$

SUMMARY OF ERRORS

2 Excess parts specified
1 Insufficient parts specified
<u>1</u> Wrong parts specified
4

Figure 4-10   Measuring Bills of Material Accuracy

METHOD 9: CONTROL QUALITY COSTS

A textile mill in South Carolina was experiencing severe quality problems and high associated quality costs. In 1987 its COQ (Cost of Quality) was running about 8 percent with much of its costs deriving from warranty. Because of poor quality in customers' hands it was beginning to lose repeat sales.

Computing Quality Costs. A new quality manager was hired and installed a quality cost report, shown in Figure 4-11.

The quality cost report lists these items:

- *Warranty*—Contractual costs arising from product failures in customers' hands.
- *Rework*—Product rejected by inspectors and salvaged in the mills.
- *Scrap*—Products rejected by inspectors and scrapped.
- *Inspection*—Cost of inspectors' salaries.
- *Support*—All other overhead expenses of the quality control department.

The bottom of the report compares total quality costs to total sales, with the derived ratio indicating that percentage of the sales dollar needed to support a quality effort. Notice that, from a high of 8 percent in 1987, COQ during 1990 is at 3 percent, a 63 percent improvement. The change from 8 to 3 percent generated a savings of over half a million dollars, based on January through October results:

$$5.0\% \times \$10,750,000 = \$537,500$$

The calculation of quality costs, along with its attendant pressure to closely examine its components, soon enabled the textile mill to achieve these significant savings.

TEXTILE MILL
QUALITY COSTS
OCT., 1990

	1990 OCT.	1990 YTD	1989 TOTAL
Warranty	$5,000	$62,000	$78,000
Rework	3,000	26,000	29,000
Scrap	1,000	7,000	16,000
Inspection	19,000	188,000	225,000
Support	7,000	39,000	41,000
TOTAL:	$35,000	$322,000	$389,000
SALES:	1,110,000	10,750,000	8,061,000
COST OF QUALITY:	3.2%	3.0%	4.8%

Figure 4-11   Computing Quality Costs

METHOD 10: IMPLEMENT COST REDUCTION MEASURES

Through assignment of cost reduction goals to each segment of the manufacturing organization, and with the agreement of key managers in each of those functional areas, a textile machinery company was able to eliminate $1.7 million in costs from its operating budget. Each year, commitments were made and forecast based on specific plans to reduce costs. A large board with posted results was hung outside of the plant cafeteria for everyone to see. Such a board is pictured in Figure 4-12.

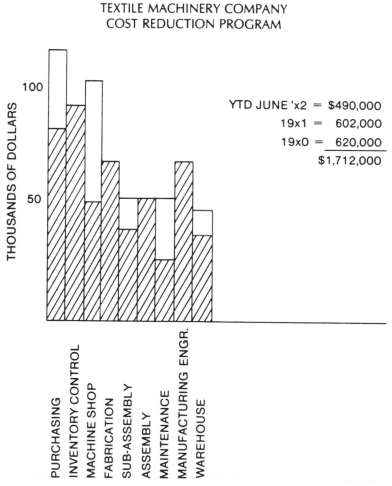

Figure 4-12 Cost Reduction Program Board

Typical areas of attack for cost reduction, as used by the textile machinery company, are listed as follows:

- Opening up engineering tolerances
- Low cost designs
- Increasing feeds and speeds
- Cheaper materials
- Standardized production methods
- Reduction of paper work
- Improved materials handling
- Replacement of slow and obsolete equipment
- Scrap and rework reduction
- Reducing downtime
- Selling scrap
- Elimination of production operations
- Mechanizing manual operations
- Curtailing utilities usage (fuel, etc.)
- Damage and corrosion protection
- Traffic rate reductions
- Implementing work standards
- Improved material flow
- Employee training
- Quality cost reduction
- Reduction of indirect labor
- Combining salaried jobs
- Reducing overtime
- Reducing supply usage
- Reducing inventory balances
- Shrinking lead times
- Using economic lot sizes
- Renegotiate vendor prices
- Control over obsolete blueprints

METHOD 11: CUT MAINTENANCE COSTS

Maintenance costs are easily forgotten in manufacturing. There is a tendency to bury them in the overhead account and focus instead on direct labor costs for cost reduction.

The targeting of maintenance costs for reduction, however, is an imperative for a well-run manufacturing company; otherwise those costs will grow unimpeded year after year and can damage even the most productive program for reducing direct-labor costs in two ways. First, an ever-burgeoning maintenance budget is a cost that offsets any gain made in other areas. Second, out-of-control maintenance costs reflect an out-of-control maintenance department. That hinders the cost-reduction efforts of production departments due to machine downtime.

There are six major ways to measure the effectiveness of the maintenance department. These are:

1. Maintenance Labor Ratio $= \dfrac{\text{No. of Maintenance Workers}}{\text{Total Direct Labor}} \times 100$

This demonstrates the control of the number of maintenance workers as a portion of all direct labor workers. It is a key indicator.

2. Maintenance Dollars $= \dfrac{\text{Total Maintenance Expenditures}}{\text{Cost of Sales}} \times 100$

This is the same type of indicator as the first one but uses dollars as the yardstick instead of number of people. It is a better reflection of the effectiveness of maintenance because it takes into account the higher cost of maintenance workers as opposed to direct labor workers.

3. Perishable Tools $= \dfrac{\text{Perishable Tool Expense}}{\text{Cost of Sales}} \times 100$

This ratio shows how efficiently maintenance workers are using expendable tools in their everyday jobs. Perishable tools are expensive and must be controlled or else their costs can zoom out of sight.

4. Machine Uptime $= \dfrac{\text{Machine Operating Time}}{\text{Total Operating Time Available}} \times 100$

This measurement comes from the production department. It is a key indication of how maintenance is doing its job. What better indicator than the percentage of time production machines are actually being used? This ratio must be interpreted with some discretion. Obviously, it is possible that factors other than maintainability, factors such as high absenteeism or low production orders, may be affecting this ratio.

5. Machine Maintenance $= \dfrac{\text{Maintenance Cost of Machines}}{\text{Machine Hours Available}} \times 100$

In this case, unit maintenance costs are based on machine hours available. This method is preferred over #2 or #4 only when delays other than maintenance have been subtracted from machine hours.

6. Maintenance Overtime $= \dfrac{\text{Maintenance Overtime Dollars}}{\text{Total Maintenance Labor Costs}} \times 100$

Maintenance departments in most plants have worse records than other departments when it comes to overtime. Nowhere is it easier to lose control because of the normally non-repetitive type of work maintenance does—work that is hard to measure. So nowhere is it more important to measure and control overtime than in maintenance. This ratio helps accomplish that.

METHOD 12: REDUCE CAPITAL EXPENDITURES

Although capital expenditures occur less frequently than other categories of manufacturing costs, they must be controlled as closely as other costs because each capital expenditure is generally high. There are two ratios in common use for that purpose:

1. Capital Intensity $= \dfrac{\text{Capital Equipment Costs}}{\text{No. of Direct Labor Workers}} \times 100$

This ratio is an indication of the relative expenditure made per worker. As such, its value is comparative. That is, there are no absolute good or bad ratios. Companies can observe whether or not capital expenditures are increasing proportionately from one financial period to another.

2. Capital Replacement Costs $= \dfrac{\text{Capital Equipment Costs}}{\text{Depreciation}} \times 100$

Here, the purpose is to determine how many times depreciation costs are covered by new capital expenditures. When the ratio is less than 100 percent, machinery productivity is lagging and is a sure sign that the company does not have an adequate capital expenditure program. A ratio greater than 100 percent indicates the company is investing in new equipment to keep machine productivity advancing.

METHOD 13: KEEP GRIEVANCES AND DISCIPLINES TO A MINIMUM

Grievances and workforce discipline, like other areas of concern in a plant, need to be adequately measured and controlled. In this area, particularly, trends can be discerned that will allow management to prevent serious labor problems before they occur. Four ratios are used. All of these ratios are self-explanatory and are best used as comparative measurements:

1. Grievances $= \dfrac{\text{Number of Grievances}}{\text{Month}}$

2. Grievances $= \dfrac{\text{Number of Grievances}}{\text{Employee}}$

3. $\text{Discipline} = \dfrac{\text{Number of Disciplinary Actions}}{\text{Month}}$

4. $\text{Discipline} = \dfrac{\text{Number of Disciplinary Actions}}{\text{Employee}}$

METHOD 14: CONTROL ABSENTEEISM

Like grievances and discipline, absenteeism is a reflection of trouble brewing. Therefore, absenteeism trends need to be monitored carefully to avoid gradually slipping into a condition where absent employees disrupt the production schedule. There are three monitors in widespread use:

1. $\text{Absenteeism} = \dfrac{\text{No. of Labor Days Lost}}{\text{Month}}$

2. $\text{Absenteeism Costs} = \dfrac{\text{Cost of Labor Days Lost}}{\text{Total Labor Costs}}$

3. Reasons for Labor Days Lost: sickness, death in family, jury duty, other explained absences, or unexplained absences. Reasons for labor days lost must always accompany the two ratios provided.

METHOD 15: LOWER ACCIDENT FREQUENCY

Accident frequency needs to be monitored carefully at all times. A rash of small accidents is often an indication of safety rules being ignored, which usually results in a catastrophic accident where a worker is maimed seriously. Manufacturing and safety professionals watch these trends closely; as soon as a series of accidents is evident, you should quickly conduct a safety investigation of all the recent accidents and review whether safety rules are adhered to throughout the plant. This must be done periodically, since it is all too easy for supervisors and workers alike to gradually ignore safety precautions.

There are two basic methods to monitor accident frequency. First, and foremost, is

$$\text{Accident Frequency} = \dfrac{\text{Number of Lost Time Accidents}}{\text{Total Labor Hours Worked}}$$

This is the key monitor. The other way is to track workers' compensation costs. Although too far after-the-fact, it is a good way for financial managers to prevent their compensation rates from going through the roof.

5

How to Save
$1 Million or More
in Plant Costs

Every manufacturing manager in every business everywhere faces one inevitable law of survival—cut costs or perish!

The pressure for cost increases is unrelenting. Labor costs rise almost every year; purchased materials, parts, tools, supplies, and equipment postannual (sometimes semiannual) increases; and other related costs of manufacturing exhibit their own upward spiral. Yet, general managers in all businesses *demand* ever-improving gross margins from manufacturing managers.

The atmosphere for improvement is intense. While this book is dedicated to showing manufacturing people how to cut costs, this particular chapter explains those organized methods needed to tap the potential of members of the organization. It shows how to take advantage of the good ideas of a manager's most precious asset—his or her people.

A well-organized and carefully thought-out cost reduction program can go a long way in reducing costs and helping to maintain the competitive viability of the manufacturing organization. This effort is best handled by manufacturing, although it can be company-wide. It should reside in manufacturing simply because the life blood of that department is cost reduction, and every employee must understand that his or her role is important to the collective success of manufacturing.

LAUNCHING A COST REDUCTION PROGRAM

Ideally, a cost reduction coordinator should be appointed to administer the program and should report directly to the manufacturing manager. The coordinator's job would involve evaluation of each cost reduction proposal, assurance that each accepted proposal was implemented by the right people, estimation of cost savings, and summary reports of progress of the program.

Several years ago a large textile machinery manufacturer in New England began such a cost reduction program. (See Chapter Four, Method 10). It began by having each major function of manufacturing (production, materials, quality, and manufacturing engineering) establish cost reduction goals for the coming fiscal year. The individual goals for the program's third year of operation can be seen in Figure 4-12, Chapter Four. These goals represented projected annual savings. Actual savings for the year were calculated and posted on the chart shown. Those savings are called "effective savings."

Effective savings are those portions of annual savings achieved during the calendar year. If, for example, a cost reduction proposal to substitute a cheaper material for a more expensive, existing material was projected to have an annual savings of $10,000, and if that savings was implemented halfway through the current year's production, then effective savings would amount to $5,000.

HOW TO EVALUATE COST REDUCTION PROPOSALS

An example of the cost reduction proposal used by the textile machinery company can be seen in Figures 5-1 and 5-2. This was the standardized form distributed among employees for the evaluation of all proposed cost reductions.

The top of side 1 of the form (Figure 5-1) is devoted to basic information regarding identification of the proposal as well as its originator. The next section describes the current method, and the following section explains the cost reduction proposal.

The next section, "Savings Calculation," relates exactly how the savings are derived.

The bottom of the first side of the proposal is reserved for sign-offs. In this case all major functional heads of the manufacturing department are asked to approve the adoption of the proposal. This is sound procedure, basically because all managers must evaluate the proposal's effect on their own operations.

The back side of the proposal in Figure 5-2 shows how savings are calculated.

"Capital Expenditures" describes the tooling cost necessary to get the vendor started producing plastic hoods.

"Annual Overhead Costs" relates any running costs needed to keep the cost reduction in effect. Here, there are none.

The payback description is essentially an indication of how long it will take before the cost reduction starts saving money. In this case, it will take almost six months.

The rest of the page is self-explanatory.

TEXTILE MACHINE COMPANY
COST REDUCTION PROPOSAL

COST REDUCTION PROPOSAL	**PART NAME** _Hood Cover_
NO. _117_	**PART NUMBER** _136 – 81A6_
DATE _5/10/x1_	**DEPARTMENT** 1) _Purchasing_
SUBMITTED	**AFFECTED** 2) _Assembly_
ORIGINATOR	
g. Mason	

CURRENT METHOD

Steel hood covers are being used in current production to cover winding spools – An OSHA requirement dictates some method of covering this moving part.

PROPOSED CHANGE

Use H-32 molded plastic hoods which can be supplied by Plastics Company of Boston, Inc.

SAVINGS CALCULATION

The difference in cost amounts to $5.50 per hood; annual need is 2400 hoods; total savings is $13,200 ($5.50 × 2400).

APPROVED BY:		DATE
MANUFACTURING MANAGER	_R. Jones_	5/25/x1
MATERIALS MANAGER	_S. Thompson_	5/23/x1
OPERATIONS MANAGER	_P. Major_	5/23/x1
QUALITY CONTROL MANAGER	_g. White_	5/20/x1
MANUFACTURING ENGINEERING MGR.	_B. Smith_	5/20/x1

Figure 5-1   Cost Reduction Proposal (Side 1)

ANNUAL PRODUCTION: 2400

CAPITAL EXPENDITURES: $6500 *Tooling for plastic company molds.*

ANNUAL OVERHEAD COSTS: *None*

PAYBACK: $\frac{\$6500}{\$13,200}$ × 12 = 5.9 *months*

ANNUAL SAVINGS NET:

    1ST YEAR: $6700 $\left(\begin{array}{c}\$13,200\\\$6500\end{array}\right)$

    THEREAFTER: $13,200

IMPLEMENTATION DATE: 7-1-x1

EFECTIVE COST SAVINGS: *None till 19x2. Effective savings of $6600 (½ × $13,200) & almost eliminated because of capital expenditures of $6500 in current year.*

Figure 5-2   Cost Reduction Proposal (Side 2)

MOTIVATING EMPLOYEES TO MEET COST REDUCTION GOALS

Figure 4-12 in Chapter Four is a reproduction of a large 6′ x 10′ board posted conspicuously at the plant's cafeteria door. Its value is that posted results leave all employees open to examination by their peers. This creates a subtle pressure to get the job done and to look good in the eyes of peers, bosses, and subordinates alike. The textile machinery company found it to be an effective tool for motivating most employees to meet their cost reduction goals.

Additionally, monthly lists were published (but not posted) displaying the names of all manufacturing salaried employees, their jobs, and the dollar amount of their cost reduction ideas that were implemented. This report also worked as an incentive to employees to seriously consider accepted cost reduction proposals as a method of increasing their pay raises and opportunities for promotion. A portion of such a report is shown in Figure 5-3.

TEXTILE MACHINE COMPANY
COST REDUCTION PROPOSAL
EMPLOYEE'S CONTRIBUTIONS
JUNE 19X2

DEPARTMENT: MANUFACTURING ENGINEERING

19X2 Goal:	$100,000
YTD Goal:	50,000
YTD Actual:	70,000

CONTRIBUTORS

I.E.	—Jones	$12,000
	—Murphy	—0—
	—Peterson	—0—
	—March	18,000
Process Engineer	—Davidson	20,000
	—Smalley	2,000
	—Kozokowski	8,000
Tool Engineer	—Smith	—0—
	—Robertson	3,000
Estimating	—Bollinger	4,000
NC Programming	—Dickerson	3,000
		$70,000

Figure 5-3   Employee's Contribution to Cost Reduction

110 IDEAS YOU CAN PUT TO WORK TODAY TO CUT COSTS IN YOUR PLANT

Following is a list of fertile ideas published by the textile machine manufacturer to spur the imagination of its salaried employees and to suggest productive areas of investigation for cost reduction. This list can be used by just about any manufacturing operation to help stimulate ideas.

21 Ways to Cut Costs in Product Engineering

1. Make tolerances more flexible.
2. Reduce surface finish requirements.
3. Eliminate need for a specific part.
4. Substitute a cheaper material.
5. Reduce the number of parts needed.
6. Combine part functions.
7. Design for low-cost tooling.

8. Design for high-speed production.
9. Increase feeds and speeds.
10. Improve the print control procedure.
11. Reduce the number of design changes.
12. Design in quality.
13. Design to reduce scrap.
14. Design to standardize production processes.
15. Use standard hardware in place of custom hardware.
16. Design to reduce manual production operations.
17. Design to reduce material content.
18. Design to reduce number of fasteners required.
19. Specify alloys to enable faster machining.
20. Specify alloys to cut tool wear.
21. Design the cheapest finish feasible.

26 Cost Reduction Ideas for Shipping, Receiving, and Warehousing

1. Use conveyors for moving operations.
2. Use reusable pallets and storage boxes.
3. Keep warehouse locked.
4. Minimize travel distances.
5. Group similar parts together in warehouse.
6. Use hydraulic lifts instead of ladders.
7. Ship and receive in unit loads.
8. Protect product from damage and corrosion.
9. Use maximum height for warehouse storage.
10. Speed handling by improving scheduling.
11. Use proper storage containers.
12. Prearrange movement of materials.
13. Replace obsolete equipment.
14. Combine clerical operations.
15. Place fastest moving items near dock.
16. Mechanize all movement of material.
17. Keep aisle space down to minimum needs.
18. Practice first-in, first-out.
19. Properly identify all stock.
20. Check all freight rates.
21. Audit freight bills.

22. Use economical small package ship methods.
23. Keep less than truckload to a minimum.
24. Minimize demurrage costs—unload promptly.
25. Keep bills-of lading legible.
26. Count number of parts received.

32 Ways to Slash Expenses in Production Planning and Control

Reduce inventories:

1. Reduce number of product lines.
2. Reduce size of purchased lots.
3. Reduce size of production lots.
4. Improve forecasting techniques.
5. Convert obsolete parts to current production.
6. Keep inventories organized.
7. Keep inventory records accurate.

Reduce number of salaried people needed:

8. Keep overtime low.
9. Keep warehouse space filled.
10. Reduce office space.
11. Reduce overhead expenses.
12. Improve package design.
13. Keep written procedures current.
14. Keep work standards up to date.
15. Shrink lead times.
16. Reduce emergency orders.
17. Keep product routings up to date.
18. Provide fast access to stock.
19. Use effective communication systems.
20. Minimize material flow.
21. Maintain fork trucks in good order.
22. Improve inspection techniques.
23. Improve vendor performance.
24. Guard against incorrect engineering drawings.
25. Provide for scrap/rework when planning.
26. Schedule to minimize waiting time.
27. Renegotiate vendor prices.

28. Keep production overruns to a minimum.
29. Recognize production bottlenecks, then eliminate them.
30. Keep accurate records.
31. Load work centers to minimize setups.
32. Minimize sales changes to master schedule.

19 Tips for Reducing Plant and Production Engineering Costs

1. Correct wrong bills of material.
2. Reduce average earnings.
3. Curtail use of fuel and electricity.
4. Correct loose work standards.
5. Keep 90 percent of all production jobs on standard.
6. Keep 80 percent of all indirect labor jobs on standard.
7. Use allowances in standards sparingly.
8. Ensure use of proper feeds and speeds.
9. Issue frequent labor performance reports.
10. Combine production operations.
11. Change standards to reflect improved methods.
12. Sample production counts for accuracy.
13. Analyze and reduce machine downtime.
14. Standardize equipment parts.
15. Combine or reduce machine setups.
16. Simplify tooling, jigs, and fixtures.
17. Keep accurate and up-to-date equipment records.
18. Lease rather than buy equipment.
19. Mechanize manual operations.

12 Ways to Improve Quality Control

1. Reduce scrap levels.
2. Reduce rework levels.
3. Reduce warranty.
4. Improve tool and gauge inspection.
5. Reduce vendor quality problems.
6. Calibrate testing equipment.
7. Prohibit use of marked-up prints.
8. Scrap all makeshift tooling.
9. Segregate defective stock.

10. Modernize inspection equipment.
11. Review packaging quality.
12. Investigate sales of plant scrap.

Following are some examples of how some companies used these ideas to reduce costs.

Case Study #1: A Consumer Appliance Company Eliminates a Production Bottleneck

After the conclusion of a methods study by industrial engineers, a rearrangement of parts bins at a series of subassembly stations cut cycle time 30 seconds. Since component subassembly was a 3.0 minute cycle, the 30-second reduction resulted in a 16 percent productivity improvement. This operation, using eight subassembly operators, was formerly a bottleneck. The productivity improvement helped it to keep pace with surrounding operations. Cost savings amounts to $20,500 per year.

Case Study #2: A Packaging Plant Improves Packaging

A rearrangement of packaged parts within a certain size of standard cartons allowed one additional package to be placed within the carton. The number of packages increased by 10 percent, from 10 to 11. This amounted to a carton savings of $5,400 annually.

Case Study #3: A Car Assembly Plant Substitutes Materials

Several years ago an enterprising process engineer conducted studies showing how the radiator shroud surrounding the radiator fan could be converted from steel to plastic and how the sheer bulk of it could be reduced. The resultant cost savings for the entire company amounted to $1,380,000 annually.

6

A Four-Step System
for Cutting Quality Costs
in Half

Quality is much more than designing, manufacturing, and servicing a product that meets company specifications. Ask any manufacturing manager. Quality, today, is the final frontier for reducing costs in manufacturing.

Every other aspect of cost reduction has been approached: design, production, purchasing, inventory, manufacturing engineering, and production planning and control. What's left is quality. Quality has the potential to strip millions of dollars of costs given the right perspective, a good and effective operating plan, and aggressive execution. Although it is hard to accurately assess cost of quality for most companies that do not have an effective quality program, it is *not* unusual to see figures at 10 percent of the sales range. If a company sells $20 million, for instance, quality costs in an uncontrolled situation could *easily* be as high as $2 million. Quality costs, for many different reasons, remain undiscovered and unchallenged in the overwhelming number of manufacturing companies operating today.

Effective quality practices, then, have the potential of slashing manufacturing cost significantly. To be considered in this category, the manufacturing quality program must include the following four steps:

1. *Conduct a painstaking and thorough analysis* of the capability of the manufacturing quality program. Assess its effectiveness honestly.

2. *Develop a quality plan* that describes all of the fundamental techniques which must be adopted to improve the effectiveness of manufacturing quality.

3. *Establish audit systems* capable of characterizing, on a timely basis, all of the

strengths and weaknesses of the quality effort. These should help you spot poor quality and respond quickly with corrective action.

4. *Audit the quality of product* being delivered from manufacturing into customers' hands. Manufacturing can use this tool to launch a well-targeted quality improvement program.

STEP 1: USE THE QUALITISCORE™* TO ANALYZE YOUR MANUFACTURING QUALITY SYSTEM

The first step is to assess the capability of the quality function in manufacturing. To do this, you should answer many detailed questions and evaluate the effectiveness of the quality function. The evaluation can take the form of a rating technique called THE QUALITISCORE,™ which should help you assess strengths and spot weaknesses by evaluating the following areas:

- organization and administration
- receiving inspection
- operator workmanship
- manufacturing quality
- packing and shipping
- gauge control and calibration
- warehousing and delivery
- quality reporting
- purchasing
- quality planning
- new product quality
- process audit
- product audit.

About 2000 companies in the United States, Canada, and Europe have used the QUALITISCORE™ to improve their quality. This system has been described in such periodicals as *INC. MAGAZINE* and *INDUSTRY WEEK*. It was developed in 1983 by Management Sciences International, Inc., a quality improvement consulting firm, and has been applied extensively in manufacturing operations since.

The QUALITISCORE™ is composed of questions regarding the effectiveness of a company's quality system. Each answer is assigned a numerical point value. When the checklist is completed, all points are totaled. Then the final sum is compared with industry standards that have been developed over a number of years.

The QUALITISCORE™ was designed so that any company manager with the

---

* QUALITISCORE is a registered trademark of Management Sciences International, Inc.

slightest knowledge of quality could answer the questions listed on the checklist. For example, one question asks the following: *Is quality assurance actively involved in the design of new products by establishing quality characteristics for those new products?* The possible answers are *actively involved, somewhat involved, and not involved.*

Each answer has a numerical point score; all you need to do is use your judgment regarding the answer to each question. The questions are very specific and there are no data involved, no mathematics needed.

Answers to the questions reveal weaknesses. For example, in the question previously given, if Quality Assurance does not participate in the design of new products by assessing the quality characteristics needed to assure customer satisfaction, then the way to improvement is clearly indicated (i.e., Quality Assurance should be involved in new product design).

One company that used the QUALITISCORE,™ Culbro Machine Systems, of Kingston, Pa.—a manufacturer of shrink tubing application machinery for tamper-resistant packaging—applied the QUALITISCORE™ to its operations. The results of the initial QUALITISCORE™ evaluation were about average for the company's industry, according to the quality control and test department manager. The company's outgoing quality was very good, but its rejections for vendor parts and in-house operations was higher than desired. The QUALITISCORE™ checklist, however, showed the company where its weaknesses were. These weaknesses pointed the way to improvements.

Six months later, both vendor and in-house quality at Culbro Machine Systems had improved dramatically. The results of a second QUALITISCORE™ were close to the superior range, the highest level achievable, and the company's quality levels had risen accordingly. The QUALITISCORE™ helped Culbro become the number one quality producer in its industry.

The QUALITISCORE™: 100 Questions for Evaluating Manufacturing Quality

The QUALITISCORE™ is composed of questions regarding the effectiveness of a company's quality system. Each answer is assigned a numerical point value. When the checklist is completed, all points are totaled, and the final sum is compared with industry standards that have been developed over a number of years. The rating system is shown below.

EFFECTIVENESS QUARTILE	POINTS	RATING EXPLANATION
85–100%	10	Highly Effective
50–84%	6	Acceptable Results
25–49%	3	Marginal Results
Under 25%	0	Poor Results

For each question on the QUALITISCORE™, assign points based on the rating shown here. Notice that the ratings are based on *results*; this tends to rate the activity realistically rather than on any apparent degree of sophistication.

A complete scoresheet for using the QUALITISCORE™ in your company follows on pp. 84-102.

The results of the QUALITISCORE™ culminate in a numerical rating that assesses the strength of the quality system. A review of the system's maximum points is given below (of course, the minimum point would be zero):

FUNCTION EVALUATED	NO. OF QUESTIONS × 10 =	MAXIMUM POINTS
Organization and Administration	4	40
Receiving Inspection	7	70
Operator Workmanship	8	80
Manufacturing Quality	15	150
Packing and Shipping	6	60
Gauge Control and Calibration	9	90
Warehousing and Delivery	8	80
Quality Reporting	8	80
Purchasing	6	60
Quality Planning	8	80
New Product Quality	5	50
Process Audit	6	60
Product Audit	10	100
Total	100	1000

Finally, total points are correlated to the following ratings:

RATING	POINTS
Highly Effective	840–1000
Acceptable	491–840
Marginal	251–490
Poor	0–250

Organization and Administration

1. Is the quality function organized properly to assure accomplishment of its mission?

Most companies have "after-the-fact" quality organizations. These quality organizations are geared to stopping defective work from reaching customers but do little to prevent its occurrence in manufacturing. Figure 6-1 is such an organization. It stresses day-to-day involvement and can be quite fast in putting out fires. But those fires continue to recur because, in an after-the-fact quality organization, the *cause* of the fires has not been eliminated.

This type of organization knows how to deal with today's problems, but it is

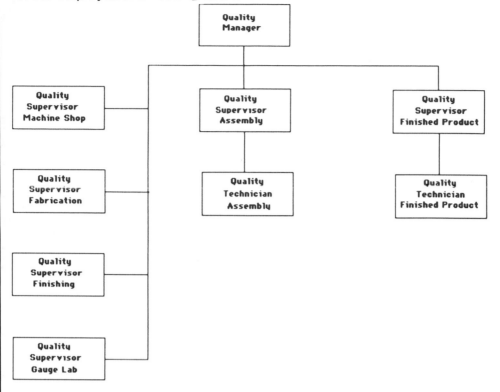

Figure 6-1   Typical Quality Organization

not organized properly to plan for tomorrow—for planning constant quality improvements. As time passes, this type of organization fails to deliver quality improvements and, in fact, may experience increasing defect rates in manufacturing. Problems that are not solved multiply. Also new problems are constantly occurring in manufacturing from new methods, new materials, new people, and new machines. These only add to the burden of existing problems.

An improved form of quality organization is shown in Figure 6-2. In this example, line quality functions occupy one half of the organization as can be seen on the left side of the chart. This is the fire-fighting component of quality—a component that will always be needed. It is their presence in manufacturing that focuses attention on quality.

The right side of the chart reveals the quality improvement muscle of the improved organization. The quality engineering function provides the new methods, techniques, and systems that help a company resolve its quality problems and assure the constant flow of quality improvements.

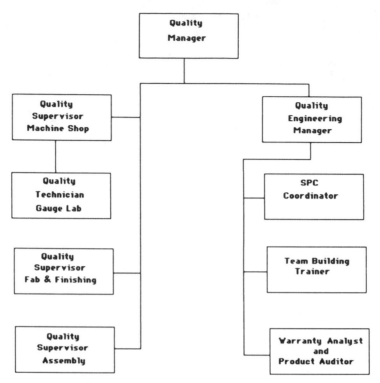

Figure 6-2　An Improved Quality Organization

The quality engineer has the following tasks:

- Works with design engineering to provide feedback on quality problems so that new designs and product modifications incorporate features responsive to customer complaints. Also works to improve manufacturing reproducibility and to reduce scrap and rework.
- Provides new and improved operator methods for reducing scrap and rework.
- Works with process engineering to improve tooling.
- Works with purchasing to correct vendor problems and improve vendor quality systems.
- Improves inspection methods and gauging.

The SPC coordinator is responsible for installing SPC tools (as discussed in Chapter 7) with the purpose of reducing customer problems and reducing failure costs.

The team-building trainer works with Human Resources to provide team-building techniques (e.g., those described in Chapter 8). These techniques are aimed at helping hourly and salaried employees to work together effectively to achieve common goals. This kind of training is essential because most employees in American factories have traditionally worked as individuals, with the focus on individual accomplishment and individual training. Very little has been done in the way of teaching people to work together in groups.

The warranty analyst and product auditor has two primary responsibilities (as the job title suggests). One responsibility is to analyze customer problems from warranty reports and feed back that information to the appropriate departments for corrective action. The other responsibility is to conduct audits of finished product; that is, product that has been manufactured and accepted into finished goods by the quality organization. This job allows all parties in manufacturing and quality to sharpen their performance.

2. *Is there a quality plan, and is it working?*

The proper execution of company and departmental objectives calls for drafting and implementing a quality plan that specifies what tasks must be performed to achieve objectives, who is responsible for segments of the plan, and when the tasks are scheduled for completion. This subject is covered in detail in Step 2.

3. *Is there a quality manual that explains all techniques, practices, and procedures used by Quality Assurance?*

Manuals are important, not only for training newcomers to the quality department, but also for assuring that the exercise of everyday quality techniques and practices remains consistent from employee to employee and from today to tomorrow. Drift is a very common fault among organizations that are not careful to specify, in writing, standard operating procedures.

4. *Are Quality Assurance employees trained well, and do they know their jobs?*

A common fault among quality organizations is to provide the latest testing equipment and up-to-date quality methods but fail to properly train inspectors, operators, engineers, and managers in their best use. A basic axiom to remember is *never let employees on their own until they fully understand what they are doing and feel comfortable handling the tools of their occupations.*

Receiving Inspection

5. *Are product drawings used up to date?*

This is not an incidental item. In all too many cases engineering changes may not have been reflected in new drawings. Naturally, this always generates needless scrap and rework in manufacturing. Very few companies face this problem squarely. Yet, following a well-developed engineering change procedure can save a lot of money and headaches.

6. *Are all tests performed written in a procedures manual?*

Over the course of the years many informal tests are developed by astute engineers and production supervisors, all of them designed to save time and money. Unfortunately, many of those same tests are never reflected in process and test instructions. When new test technicians are hired, the mistakes start all over again until somebody instructs the new testers. This inevitably results in excess costs and lost time.

7. *Are records maintained by vendors that prominently display a quality history for each batch or shipment?*

Batch record keeping is helpful when things go wrong. It allows vendors to trace problems in their processes and take corrective actions. It also permits the isolation of suspected batches of work without quarantining all materials.

8. *Is there rapid feedback of information regarding rejected material to vendors through the purchasing department?*

There are two points to consider here. First, when problems arise, fast corrective action based on rapid information flow from customers to vendors assures a minimum of disruption and cost. Second, the inclusion of the purchasing people helps obtain their cooperation in assuring quick vendor problem corrections since Purchasing is responsible for obtaining high quality parts and materials.

9. *Is there evidence of vendors correcting problems quickly and effectively?*

If the systems are in place for reporting and following-up on vendors' rejected materials, as reported in the previous question, then problems will be resolved expeditiously. If they are not, the system capability (or adherence to it) must be investigated promptly.

10. *Is rejected material separated from accepted stock, and is it locked-up?*

In a pharmaceutical or medical device plant, it's a matter of law. In other industries, it's a matter of common sense and smart operating practices. The separation and quarantine of unacceptable parts and material will prevent their use in production and the contamination of acceptable material.

11. *Are sample plans meaningful and easy to use by inspectors? In other words, will inspectors reject poor lots and accept good lots most of the time?*

This is essentially a matter of consulting an operating guide such as MIL STD 105-D, the standard and much used sampling plans developed for and used by the military. There are many textbooks on sampling plans for the quality practitioner.

The sampling plans must also be easy for inspectors to use. Unfortunately, too many sampling plans are complex and hard to use. MIL STD 105-D is probably the best place to start.

Operator Workmanship

12. *Are production operators well trained in quality techniques?*

Statistical Process Control (SPC) (See Chapter 7) is one of the basic and easy-to-use tools that allows operators to monitor the machines they are operating and to *prevent* defects before they are produced. The following chapters detail outstanding SPC techniques that have been proven to assure employee involvement and reduce scrap and rework costs up to 80 percent if installed properly.

13. Do operators sample inspect their own production?

Whether or not SPC is used, it is always a good idea to have operators sample inspect their own output. There are two basic reasons for this. First, it keeps them involved with the process and induces a sense of responsibility regarding the quality of their output. Second, their current knowledge of quality levels will reduce the amount of scrap and rework generated, because problems can be detected before they get out of hand.

14. Do operators have adequate gauges for measuring their own work?

In too many cases, operators do not have all of the measuring tools needed to adjust and control their machines. Gauge availability is an important ingredient for keeping quality high.

15. Are there written inspection procedures and quality standards for operators to use?

If there aren't, then operators will be unable to fully control quality. Written instructions are necessary to assure the consistent application of quality standards. The very presence of written instructions further assures attention to the importance of performing the job using approved methods.

16. Are inspection results told to operators?

They should be informed of the quality of their output; not only what they produce today, but the effect of the quality of their output in subsequent operations and, more important, the quality of their work as seen by customers. Without this feedback, they are flying blind and will be unaware of developing problems.

17. Are operators given the necessary training and guidance to help them constantly focus on quality improvement?

Quality improvement is a journey, not a destination; the job never stops. Quality must be constantly improved or it will slip backwards. There are just too many variables that push quality down: poor material, worn tooling, inadequate instructions, outdated methods, and so on. The fight to maintain quality levels is a fight to improve those levels to compensate for the presence of so many variables. The path to quality improvement is through proper and thorough operator training.

18. Are operators who produce faulty work given additional guidance and counseling to improve their performances?

Some people learn more slowly than others. The slower learners (they will always be present) must be accorded the time and attention necessary to bring their performance up to the level of other operators. This entails extra training tailored specifically to those poor performers. Without it, operators could get the impression that management does not really think quality is important. When this occurs, group morale will sag and quality levels will then drop even further.

19. *Does each operation have adequate process instructions and product drawings?*

Scrap and rework are often generated because of incomplete or wrong instructions and drawings. This is one of the main causes of quality problems. It is only reasonable to assume that high quality work can only flow from operations that are clearly delineated and specified.

Manufacturing Quality

20. *Are tests and inspections in the form of written instructions for inspectors?*

Inspectors are just like operators; they also need the most clearly spelled-out instructions concerning sampling plans, quality standards to be applied, measuring gauges and equipment to be used, and the most effective method for performing tests and inspections.

21. *Is first-piece inspection practiced on operations where the setup of the machine determines the quality of the parts, such as metal stampings?*

When the shape, dimensions, and tolerances of a part are established during the setup, and when that same part will not vary significantly thereafter, then inspection efforts must be concentrated upon first-piece inspection.

22. *Is roving inspection used to gather quality data rather than to control operations?*

The full responsibility for quality must always be vested in the production organization. This makes good sense; production people will only pay attention to what they are responsible for. If they are told to get every piece possible at the lowest cost, then their focus will be on quantity and cost. But if they are told they will be held accountable for the quality of the parts they produce, their boundaries of interest will broaden to include quality.

23. *Do all production batches funnel through a tollgate?*

A tollgate is an inspection station where all goods must be accepted by inspectors before passing on to the following operation. In actual practice this point should be at the end of the production process, since it is Quality Assurance's job to make sure that all parts passed on to stock and customer shipment meet company specifications and standards. Before appearance at the tollgate, manufacturing has full responsibility for the quality of parts produced.

24. *Are the inspections made sensitive enough to detect shifts in the production process?*

Here is where the value of SPC is most noticeable. Control charts, a prime SPC tool, are sensitive enough not only to detect changes in the production process, but also to determine whether or not that process is headed in the direction of producing defective pieces *before the pieces are produced*. This allows the operator to adjust the process before scrap or rework is generated.

25. *Is corrective action of substandard operations timely and effective?*

The most productive tools in the world for controlling quality are only as good as the corrective actions applied by operators and managers once the process needs fixing. The process doesn't fix itself; nor do tools such as SPC have built-in automatic problem solvers.

26. *Is defective material subjected to material board review prior to disposition?*

The material review board (MRB) consists of production, Quality Assurance (QA), purchasing and engineering people who review defective material to determine its disposition. The most effective method of disposition arises out of such a review, as well as an awareness of existing quality problems for production and engineering management. The MRB becomes a major avenue for problem correction.

27. *Are production operators made aware of defective parts that they produce?*

What could be more basic than to be notified when a mistake is made? How can operators be aware of a problem if it isn't reported to them? Unfortunately, this type of feedback should not be taken for granted. A reporting system must be in place to assure timely feedback of information to operators before the pipeline becomes choked with defective work.

28. *Are routine investigations by Quality Assurance made of recurrent defective parts and operations?*

The vast number of problems that face QA every day tends to discourage the routine investigation of the root causes of defective parts. Yet, if those problems are not eradicated they will return with deadly regularity along with other, newer problems until the organization is truly swamped with problems that it can no longer possibly attend to. The time must be found to handle such problems.

29. *Is defective material reworked by the same operator who produced the bad parts?*

As a matter of principle, this should always be done. In no more dramatic fashion can problems be resolved. When people are faced with the problems they cause, those problems will eventually be resolved.

30. *Are inspection buy-off stamps used for accepted products?*

These should be used to assure that bad parts don't get mixed in with good parts. An inspection stamp, traceable to a particular inspector, will also have the beneficial effect of assuring his or her attention simply because the inspector's "name" is on that product being shipped to a customer.

31. *Does the combination of operator and inspector sampling provide the needed quality protection?*

The number of sample sizes needed to rigidly satisfy the mathematical requirements of most sampling plans are so large as to drive most companies out of business. In practical terms, however, strict adherence to mathematical formulas is unnecessary. The combination of samples taken from the process for both operator and inspector should normally be enough to detect trends in time to take corrective action. With an active corrective action program and the use of statistical techniques (described in following chapters), quality should start improving.

32. *In assembly operations, is analysis made of defective parts to determine which depart-ment and operation is the cause?*

This analysis, along with the feedback to responsible departments, must be done religiously to assure prompt and effective resolution of problems.

33. *Are quality standards the same throughout the company?*

Physical separation always results in "drift." Employees in the fabrication department, for example, may interpret subjective quality standards differently than employees in assembly. This condition becomes worse when the operations are in different plants. The obvious answer is to provide visual standards for all locations and to agree on rejected parts and materials when more than one party is involved in the same inspection in different areas.

34. *Do inspections and tests simulate, when possible, the end use of the finished and assembled product?*

Why not find the defects in-house? When the customer becomes your last inspector, sales always nosedive.

Packing and Shipping

35. *Are written packing and shipping specifications available and used?*

The same comments that apply to written process specifications and instruc-tions apply here equally. (See Question 19.)

36. *Are packing and shipping containers adequate to prevent corrosion, spoilage, and damage?*

If they're not, customers are liable to be extremely unhappy when they receive melted ice cream, for example, because the dry ice was located in the wrong location.

37. *Are picked parts checked against master parts shipping lists to assure the right parts and correct quantities are being shipped?*

Nothing gets customers more upset than receiving the wrong parts or the wrong quantity. Their operations may have to be shut down and sales may be lost. The straightforward process of checking that the right parts are being picked pays dividends in fewer customer problems.

38. *Are shipping cartons well identified to prevent mix-ups in deliveries?*

Different colored or different shaped tags are strongly recommended to prevent delivery mix-ups.

39. *Are all appropriate documents included with the shipment?*

Again, customers can get incensed when the proper billing isn't received or the bill of lading is for oranges when the container has apples in it. This type of error makes vendors look awfully foolish.

40. Is release to ship authorized by Quality Assurance?

The final authorization to ship must always reside with QA. They are not responsible for designing, producing, and servicing the product, but they are responsible for assuring that any product shipped to customers fully meets company specifications and quality standards.

Gauge Control and Calibration

41. Are gauge masters traceable to the National Bureau of Standards (NBS)?

If they're not, then throw away the gauge program. The program will not be under control, and factory gauges are likely to be reading incorrectly. NBS traceability is the foundation of any gauge program.

42. Is there a written system for gauge control and calibration?

Once again, written instructions assure the consistency of methods and techniques needed for gauge control and calibration.

43. Are production gauges calibrated as well as Quality Assurance gauges?

If they're not, the gauge control program will be meaningless, because production uses their gauges for accept/reject decisions, just as inspectors do.

44. Are the frequencies of calibration adequate?

For a large piece of equipment, such as a coordinate measuring machine, a daily calibration may be necessary. For a micrometer, it could be every week. Frequency schedules should be specified and maintained by the gauge calibration supervisor.

45. Are gauge calibration records maintained for each gauge?

Historical records are helpful tools in determining when gauges should be rebuilt or discarded. Using such records carefully will help retire faulty gauges before they result in increased scrap and rework of production parts.

46. Are all gauges marked with the last date of calibration?

This will let the gauge calibration supervisor know when to make the next check.

47. Are all new gauges calibrated before their use in production?

Just because they're new doesn't mean that gauges have been calibrated. Sometimes, in the transportation process gauges are damaged or knocked out of calibration. Or they may have been set incorrectly at the factory that made them. Anything, usually unforeseen, could have happened to cause misreadings. It is prudent to calibrate all new gauges before they are put into use.

48. *Are calibration tests conducted under the proper environment of temperature and humidity?*

Temperature and humidity affect the readings of gauges. Calibrations should always be conducted in a temperature and humidity-controlled environment.

49. *Are employee-owned and subcontractor gauges calibrated?*

Sometimes companies do a great job of monitoring their own gauges but forget to check the gauges of outsiders used to inspect their parts. This problem can be prevented through the use of gauge calibration schedules that include outside gauging.

Warehousing and Delivery

50. *Are handling methods for stock such that little or no mixing and minimum damage occur?*

Separation of accepted from rejected stock, clear and distinguishable product tags, computer location tracking, inventory audits—all of these and more are important ingredients for keeping inventories pure and uncontaminated with other materials.

51. *Are all part bins and storage locations adequately marked to identify stored parts?*

As in Question 50, clearly marking storage locations is a necessary step to prevent mix-ups.

52. *Are export packaging requirements identified?*

When products are shipped overseas, extra protection is needed to keep damage at a minimum and to provide for special transport conditions to protect against corrosive salt air during shipment by sea, for example.

53. *Are handling, storage, picking, packing, and delivery operations specified in writing?*

Here, once again, the need for written instructions to assure consistency in applications is warranted.

54. *Are receiving and shipping operations adequately separated to prevent mix-ups?*

The best work flow has receiving at one end of the plant and shipping at the other end of the plant. But that is not always possible, particularly in small plants. When both functions are physically together, separate paths for the flow of material must be developed to prevent mix-ups from occurring.

55. *Is defective stock quarantined?*

If it isn't, you can bet on one thing: It will find its way into the production stream along with good material. The chance for error is just too great while everybody is engaged in the press of everyday business. Defective stock should always be kept in a cage to prevent contamination.

56. *Is accepted stock kept under lock to prevent contamination, pilferage, and loss of control?*

The latter point is the most significant. In any manufacturing operation one of the greatest problems is inventory loss. Inventory loss normally occurs when the inventory books fail to balance with usage. This almost always happens when parts are moved from inventory into production but are not signed out of inventory due to the lack of proper inventory control procedures (or brought into inventory from production without the accompanying paperwork to reflect that transaction). Placing good inventory under lock and key is the best way to prevent inventory loss and insist on the right inventory procedures being adhered to.

57. *Is release to stock authorized by Quality Assurance?*

In many plants parts are manufactured in fabrication and machining and then moved into inventory prior to assembly. When this happens, Quality Assurance should take responsibility for checking the parts and being sure they are acceptable. The responsibility for manufacture of those parts belongs to the production organization, but acceptance into stock is a chief responsibility of Quality Assurance.

Quality Reporting

58. *Is cost of quality (COQ) information published on a timely basis and does it identify all major costs?*

COQ should identify failure costs (such as scrap and rework, warranty), appraisal costs (mostly the cost of the inspectors), and prevention costs (such as quality engineering). How to prepare a COQ report was discussed in Chapter 3 and a sample of its power is reported through an example described later in this chapter. Its publication should be at time intervals that permit corrective action to be applied without a large scrap or rework or customer correction loss. In actual practice, the COQ report is a supplemental tool published monthly. SPC and sampling inspection are the day-to-day tools needed to control quality costs along with effective corrective action programs.

59. *Are performance reports (batch acceptance and sample percent defective) reported at all locations?*

Step 3 in this chapter discusses the value and use of performance reports as does the following chapter on SPC. In the context of the question asked here, performance reports should be used at all production locations, large and small. Quality problems can, and do, erupt anywhere, and performance reports are a management tool to control quality, attack problems, and reduce quality costs.

60. *Are quality records retained for sufficient lengths of time to satisfy all regulatory, statutory, and company requirements?*

The Food and Drug Administration's Good Manufacturing Practices, for example, require the retention of batch processing documents for several years. In other industries, customers and governmental agencies may require the retention of different records for a different period of time. The QA manager must be aware of all of these requirements and assure proper record retention.

61. *Are quality reports used effectively for quality improvement?*

The best designed quality reporting system is absolutely useless if nobody is using the data for corrective action. The chapter on SPC as well as Step 2 of this chapter and Chapter 4 describe some of the quality improvement tools available.

62. *Are records maintained in a protected area?*

If records are kept in the warehouse and the sprinkler system goes off, will the records be ruined? Most record retention systems call for storage in a closed room that is fire protected. Protection of records, in a large part, depends on how much material must be retained.

63. *Are the records of inspections and tests recorded in a manner suitable for defect analysis?*

In practice this means that inspection and test information must be summarized daily, weekly, and monthly. Then it must be used as raw data for quality improvement efforts. But that information must first be recorded on forms such as SPC control charts, defect tallies, and so forth, and the completed forms must be gathered daily for summarization.

64. *Are scrap and rework data summarized and then used to reduce defect levels?*

Again, information must be used to be productive. Daily summaries of scrap and rework by operator, machine, product, defect type, and shift are essential for problem analysis and traceability to responsible areas.

65. *Are suitable summary reports prepared for top management so they can monitor and control quality?*

Top management needs summary statistics that indicate overall progress of a department—or the lack of progress. For example, management should know that the machining department's quality slipped from 90.5 percent year-to-date to 83.1 percent for the current month. That will trigger investigations and correction of this quality problem.

Purchasing

66. *Does purchasing have the latest drawing revisions to give to vendors?*

One of the most common sources of error in the vendors' production operations is generated by information that is not up to date. When engineering drawing revisions trail the actual changes, scrap and rework dollars head skyward.

67. *Are vendors aware of the company's quality standards for purchased parts and materials?*

When they're not, the same inevitable increase in defects occurs as does in production when operators and inspectors do not have the information they need to work with.

68. *Are quality standards included in purchasing contracts?*

If they're not, expect quality costs to rise significantly. When vendors are pressured for fast deliveries and low unit prices (and they always are), quality will drop unless it is made a firm part of the contract.

69. *Do vendors submit their test results with shipments?*

There are several good reasons for doing this. First, it makes the vendor more conscious of only supplying acceptable products. Second, it provides a record for traceability when rejects occur. Third, it keeps quality standards from drifting; it assures that both the vendor and the customer are looking at quality standards from the same viewpoint.

70. *Are vendors made aware of rejections promptly?*

The rapid feedback of problem information to the responsible vendor will reduce the number of rejects in the pipeline.

71. *Do vendors move quickly to correct their mistakes?*

There is no excuse for not eliminating problems quickly and effectively when vendors are made aware of them. Vendors that don't eliminate problems should be immediately told by purchasing agents (not by Quality Assurance; Purchasing is responsible for vendor performance) that their continued substandard performance will result in a loss of business.

Quality Planning

72. *Are written test and inspection methods prepared for all new products and processes?*

The best time to develop quality procedures for a new product is during its planning and developmental stages, not after it's in production. The planning process will help spark ideas that result in improvements in testing and sampling methods. This, in turn, will result in improved product quality at lowered costs.

73. *Does quality engineering plan the inspection stations in the manufacturing process?*

As a standard protocol, quality engineering should develop the sampling plans to be used, the gauges to measure the product, quality standards and specifications to be applied, inspection methods, and reporting practices. This planning will ideally take place before production operations begin for the product.

74. *Does manufacturing engineering review all new tooling in the plant to assure its ability to produce acceptable products consistently?*

This review is not a function of the quality engineers, but of the manufacturing engineers, because it is the responsibility of manufacturing engineering to have tooling that produces products of consistently high quality. The job of quality engineering is to make sure that manufacturing engineers are performing that important task.

75.   Is the production of acceptable quality products recognized as a factor in work standards?

It must always be recognized so (a) operators can sample their own output without being penalized for the time needed, and (b) recognition is given to good output only; incentive payments should never be paid for the production of defective work.

76.   Does the paperwork process allow for the traceability of defective work to individual operators and work stations?

If it doesn't operators will simply not pay as much attention to it as they should, and quality will deteriorate.

77.   Does quality engineering train inspectors, operators, and foremen in effective work habits aimed at producing a top quality product?

Not enough words can be written about the benefits derived from the proper training at the right time. Operators, inspectors, supervisors, and others thoroughly trained in the performance of their jobs deliver a better service than do employees without that same training. To be meaningful, the training must focus on practical methods directly affecting the performance of employees.

78.   Has quality engineering determined the best testing equipment and gauging to be used in the product within the limits of the capital budget?

The determination of testing equipment is a basic function of quality engineers. Their knowledge of what's available in the market makes a big difference when trying to produce a high-quality product with a minimum of defects.

79.   Has quality engineering assured the availability of test and product specifications, visual standards, models and samples for production employees?

This is also the prime responsibility of quality engineers. A thorough and detailed approach to this crucial duty can make the difference between acceptable and non-acceptable product, between a stream of high-quality goods and a pile of scrap, between delivery promises made on time and good piled up at the dock with rejection tags all over them.

New Product Quality

80.   Are critical quality characteristics specified on engineering drawings?

When critical characteristics are identified, they receive more attention in the manufacturing process and, consequently, attain higher levels of quality. Some proponents argue that all characteristics are equally critical, but if that were the case they would all have the same potential for scrap and rework (which they don't), and customers would complain about different defects equally (which they don't). Critical characteristic identification, developed by engineering, sales, Quality Assurance, and manufacturing employees, is one of the more important quality functions begun early in the new product development cycle.

81. *Have quality standards and inspection requirements been planned for the new product, along with tooling and gauging?*

The more quality planning in the very early stages of design, the better the quality output from manufacturing later. One of the very real advantages of early quality planning is the opportunity to try out and to discard methods, techniques, tooling, design changes, and so on *before* production begins. Trying to work out the bugs during early production, however, inevitably translates into spending more money and having dissatisfied customers.

82. *Have potential quality problems been identified and corrected?*

When QA engineers and design engineers sit down together during the inception of new products and later on during the developmental stages, a focus on customer quality problems results in improved quality through design changes before the product reaches production.

83. *Are design reviews made sufficiently ahead of time to allow QA to prepare for manufacturing quality requirements?*

A common fault of the new product development cycle is the inevitable time compression it experiences when plans aren't achieved. (It is a certainty that problems will occur during the design and development of new products.) When participants hurry through the balance of the cycle to gain back some of the time lost, quality suffers. When that occurs, managers must be determined to assure that adequate quality planning takes place regardless of the initial time lost. Anything else is foolhardy. If the new product comes out faulty and customers being complaining, huge losses in sales can result. Better a small increase in costs now than a large loss in sales and quality costs later.

84. *Are prototypes run in production so manufacturing and quality capability can be improved?*

A pilot plan run in a laboratory is not a production run. What happens on the production floor cannot always be anticipated. It is always prudent to have "first runs" of sufficient quantity ahead of actual production at the planned work stations on the production floor to work out the bugs.

Process Audit

85. *Are process audits made to evaluate the capability of the manufacturing process to provide a consistently high-quality product that meets company specifications?*

A process audit is a periodic review of the adequacy of manufacturing methods, machinery and tooling used, materials, techniques, sampling plans, work standards, process instructions, gauging, and other relevant aspects of the manufacturing process. It is important because over time everything changes: Raw materials are improved or altered, new equipment and tooling become available to do a better job, new work methods are introduced within the work cycle (many times by operators, supervisors and engineers without respective changes in the drawings or process instructions) and a host of other factors occur. The sweeping nature of the process audit nets all of the major changes and formalizes their use within the written process specifications.

86. *Is the process audit conducted by employees outside of the production organization to assure its impartiality?*

It is human nature to cover one's tracks and that results in "buried" costs (inefficient costs that become an accepted part of the cost structure because they have been accepted for a long period of time). The full integrity of the process audit can be preserved only if some disinterested party conducts it.

87. *Are the audits made at random so no false preparation can cloud the results or hide the problems?*

When people—any people—know they are being audited, they will attempt to cover all of their mistakes and many of the problems. The same principle holds true here as in the previous question.

88. *Are reports of problems made to the functions that are in the best position to eliminate the problems?*

Engineering problems must be reported to engineering, vendor problems to purchasing, work standard problems to industrial engineering, and so on. While this is the common sense thing to do, many companies fail miserably at communication and feedback of quality problems. It cannot be taken for granted. *A system needs to be devised and followed.*

89. *Is corrective action timely and effective?*

The best system known to corporate managers will fall flat on its face if it isn't accompanied by the rigorous and fast application of corrective action. Managers must always be on the alert to prevent slippage. It takes a constant and sustained effort.

90. *Are steady improvements being made?*

Watch the quality cost and performance reports to monitor improvements. If improvements in the numbers have stalled out, that is the time to step in and reinvigorate the process by whatever means are appropriate at the time.

Product Audit

91. *Are audits made of completed and approved products ready for shipment?*

Many are surprised by what they find. This is a prime spot to catch the deficiencies of manufacturing, quality, and engineering. If used properly, fast and complete problem correction can become a routine practice.

92. *Are the auditors apart from the regular QA organization to assure their impartiality?*

The same answer applies here as for Question 86.

93. *Do field service and marketing employees participate in the audit so the view is tilted toward customer satisfaction?*

The worst possible move is to exclude them. That would guarantee that the main purpose of the product audit would be to assure conformance to company specifications rather than customer acceptance. Inevitably, specifications have a tendency to favor the design and manufacture of a product as opposed to the hard realities of what the customer wants which, at times, will run counter to what the manufacturing and engineering people want. Inclusion of marketing and field service people, those parts of the organization that face customers day-to-day, will guarantee the consideration of customer needs.

94. *Are prepared checklists made that list quality characteristics desired by customers?*

Examples are shown in Figure 6-4. This figure illustrates that these quality characteristics describe the functional and esthetic parts of the product considered important by customers using the product.

95. *Are those characteristics weighted to show the differences among critical, major, and minor defects?*

Failure to differentiate among varying degrees of quality will result in failure to establish priorities for attacking problems. Since there will always be quality problems, and many, many of them to contend with every day, and since most companies have limited people and dollar resources, a plan of attack with attendant lists of priorities must always accompany the plan. Obviously, all of the horses must be put behind the resolution of critical defects, less on major defects, and still less on minor defects.

96. *Is the final numerical rating achieved so that comparisons among audits and trends can be readily observed?*

The purpose of the numerical rating is to indicate those quality characteristics that are becoming problems. Timely use of the numerical rating will trigger corrective actions.

97. *Do manufacturing employees from diverse functions participate in the audit so they can learn the importance of quality in relation to customer satisfaction?*

In addition to engineers, operators, supervisors, and the like, inventory clerks, accountants, customer service reps, top managers, and eventually all departments of the company should also participate in product audits. Quality is everybody's business.

98. *When defects are discovered, are they quickly corrected in the manufacturing and design process?*

Defects simply must be corrected or the entire purpose of the product audit will come to nothing. Employees rally behind an effort that is successful; they want nothing better than to do what works and helps them do their jobs. When an effort, such as the product audit, is perceived as not contributing, employees will not give it the attention it needs to work. So, corrective action must be followed to assure that audits are timely and effective.

99. *Are product audits summarized for management review?*

They must be; without the needed information, management will be unaware of whether or not the system is working and will not be able to help out when problems arise.

100. *Do all Quality Assurance employees rotate turns in conducting product audits so they can keep in touch with customer expectations?*

Quality Assurance employees, like everybody else, must be attuned to customer needs. It's too easy for them to become enmeshed in the everyday details of their jobs and miss this critical ingredient. Their periodic participation in the product audit will focus the proper attention on the customer.

STEP 2: DEVELOP A QUALITY PLAN

Once the capability of the quality system has been evaluated, the weaknesses of the function must be addressed to improve quality results. The plan prioritizes needed action, establishes key events, sets timetables, and shows specific individuals responsible for corrective action. Figure 6-3 is a page from the quality plan of a machining subcontractor.

MACHINING SUBCONTRACTOR
QUALITY PLAN

PROBLEM	KEY EVENT	COMPLETION DATE	RESPONSIBILITY
High in-plant failures of vendor material	Establish effective receiving inspection system	3/X3	J. Barnes, Quality Engineer
High rejection rates in automatic chuckers and screw machines	Implement a statistical Bar $\bar{X}$ & $\bar{R}$ program	5/X3	M. Jones, Quality Engineer
Many false readings of inspection gages resulting in rejection of acceptable parts	Train inspectors to read and handle testing gages	6/X3	P. Shore, Assistant Quality Manager
Management complaining about poor quality reports	Start improved quality reporting system	7/X3	S. Pauley, Quality Control Manager

Figure 6-3   The Quality Plan

A quality plan can be made for almost any period of time, but in the opinion of a great many users it should cover a period of two to three years, normally an optimum period. Anything shorter will probably not be inclusive enough to cover the many key events that need to happen. Anything longer is speculative. Too many things can change in four or five years; the planning of events that far down the road is vague, at best.

STEP 3: WRITE QUALITY REPORTS THAT STIMULATE ACTION

Reports are the communication tool which spurs management to action. Without reports, management would not have knowledge of where its problems lie, along with their severity.

There are two dangers associated with reports—too little or too much information. With too little information, management will not be aware of the full extent of seriousness of the problems; with too much information, the significant information is buried in a swamp of words.

When reporting on quality, two types of reports have been found to do the job, and do it well: cost of quality and performance reports.

Cost of quality was discussed in Chapter Four. A typical report was shown in Figure 4-11.

A performance report for an oilfield coupling producer is seen here in Figure 6-4. It is segmented into two parts. The first, "Lots Defective," shows the number of lots (batches) rejected. This number is a measure of the level of quality being manufactured. It is a meaningful number to production people simply because production operations are geared to lot rejections which will be sorted and repaired. Production forepeople are responsive to lot rejections because the more that are rejected, the higher the cost penalty is in sorting and repair time.

The second number, "Process Defective," is a reflection of the quality level of the individual manufacturing operations. It can be found by dividing all of the rejected pieces discovered in all of the samples of the process checked by the inspectors.

Process defective is a number of particular significance to the quality control supervisor. That number demonstrates the basic capability of the process to sustain a quality product. It reflects, on a composite basis, the ability of the tooling, material, and operator to produce an acceptable product. Shifts in the process average indicate changes in these elements, and therefore signal the quality control supervisor that one or more of the elements have shifted.

Performance reporting spots poor quality early, hopefully before it has a chance to cause severe cost and customer problems, thereby allowing the organization *to respond with early and aggressive corrective actions.* Only in this way can all

OIL FIELD COUPLING COMPANY
WEEKLY QUALITY REPORT
WEEK OF SEPT. 28, 19X1

LOTS DEFECTIVE

DEPARTMENT	LOTS INSPECTED	LOTS REJECTED	PERCENT REJECTED
Saws	62	5	8.1
Boring	70	12	17.1
Automatic Chuckers	58	2	3.4
Screw Machines	64	4	6.3
Tapping Machines	66	7	10.6
Packing	68	5	7.4
TOTAL	388	35	9.0%

PROCESS DEFECTIVE

DEPARTMENT	SAMPLES INSPECTED	SAMPLES REJECTED	PERCENT REJECTED
Saws	193	16	8.3
Boring	210	48	22.9
Automatic Chuckers	403	29	7.2
Screw Machines	712	60	8.4
Tapping Machines	355	32	9.0
Packing	290	21	7.2
TOTAL	2163	206	9.5%

Figure 6-4   Quality Reporting Technique

involved employees have the information necessary to focus on the real purpose of *quality performance reporting—quality improvement.*

The way this information is presented to different levels of the organization is important because it determines how well the information is used. Either too much information or too little information is self-defeating. Of similar importance is the frequency of review of the information. The *right* information reviewed at the *right* time will result in its proper use.

The matrix in Figure 6-5 illustrates these points. Each succeeding level of the organization has timely information available to spot quality trends and patterns. Notice how the frequency of reporting grows at each successively lower lever of the organization. As we get closer to the line of fire, there is a need for more frequent control to assure the attainment of ever-improving quality.

The actual performance reports for a textile machinery are shown. These are:

REPORT	**USED BY**	**FREQUENCY OF USE**
Control Chart	Operator	Hourly*
Daily Quality Summary	Foreperson	Bi-Hourly
Dept. Quality Summary	Plant Mgr.	Daily
Weekly Quality Summary	General Mgr.	Weekly

* This particular chart is a daily recap derived from an hourly posted chart.

PERFORMANCE REPORTING*

REPORTING LEVEL	REPORTING FORMAT	FREQUENCY
General Manager	Quality Performance (Percent defective and major defects) for the plant	Weekly
Plant Manager	Quality Performance (Percent defective and major defects) for each department and each shift	Daily
Supervisor	Quality Performance (Percent defective and major defects) for each operator	Every 2–4 Hours
Operator	Control chart	Hourly

* Does not include COQ or Warranty.

Figure 6-5   Performance Reporting Matrix

STEP 4: IMPLEMENT THE BEST EARLY WARNING SYSTEM[1]

Early warning systems are designed to do just that—provide an indication of your product's outgoing quality level as well as highlight current quality problems. In most cases it is months, and sometimes even years, before products reach customers' hands. If companies rely mostly on warranties and complaints to assess customer satisfaction, the pipeline between the factory and the customer might be clogged with products that have a multitude if defects, undiscovered by the factory and inordinately costly in terms of repair costs and irritated customers.

Many firms conduct product audits to assess product quality levels, but few conduct them properly. They are seeking the best early warning system to suit their particular needs but, for one reason or another, they fail to do the right things.

Five Steps Toward a Well-Designed Product Audit

A well-designed product audit is the best method yet devised to provide early warning of outgoing quality levels and problems. To be successful, however, it should contain the following elements:

1. *Select products randomly* after they have been accepted by the line quality assurance organization and are ready for shipment to distributors or customers. The product audit is, after all, an indication of the effectiveness of the quality assurance organization as well as the manufacturing effort.

2. *Make the product auditor independent of the line quality assurance organization* that accepts the product. Ideally the product auditor should work directly for the general manager, but in practice that arrangement would be too cumbersome. Not enough direction would be provided by the general manager, who is too busy. There is nothing wrong with having the product auditor report directly to the top quality person in the organization. It is important, however, for the product auditor to be independent of the line quality assurance organization responsible for product buy-off and free from any pressure from it or from manufacturing people.

3. *Make sure the quality characteristics being rated during the product audit are the same characteristics that are important to the customer.* This is an extremely critical point that is most often missed by the majority of early warning systems.

Most quality systems are geared to product specifications; acceptance is based on whether or not the product meets specifications. What the customer wants is a product that functions properly, is aesthetically pleasing, and is safe to use.

---

[1] From the author's book, *Qualitysense: Organizational Approaches to Improving Product Quality and Service* (New York: American Management Association, Inc., 1979). Reproduced with permission.

While product specifications are generally defined in terms of customer needs, that is not always the case. As products mature they become subject to all sorts of compromises and modifications. Engineering changes, for example, are made to reduce costs. These changes may substitute materials that may not be acceptable to some customers; or part functions may be modified to accommodate manufacturing operations, and those changes might affect product function in customers' hands. All kinds of changes occur. Eventually, some product specifications become monsters on their own. They become self-perpetuating with no consideration of their intended purpose—that is, to consistently produce customer satisfaction.

Quality characteristics for product audits, therefore, should be established *jointly* by quality assurance *and* marketing. Salespeople and service representatives, in particular, will be most sensitive to customer wishes and customer needs. Many times the listing of quality characteristics important to customers will come as a surprise to quality assurance people simply because they have been trained to think in terms of specifications and, as we have come to see, specifications drift over a period of time. The exercise of establishing meaningful quality characteristics will generate positive changes in product specifications.

4. *Rate the quality characteristics according to their importance.* As Figure 6-6 shows, there are four classifications of defects ranging from "very serious" to "incidental." Each class is assigned a weight in points, with the most points assigned to the most serious classification of defects. During the product audit (see Figure 6-7) each characteristic is evaluated and actual points are assigned. Should the product auditor decide to assign partial points to a 50-point characteristic, the auditor should also ensure that some, but not all, of the quality characteristics have been attained.

At the conclusion of the audit, standard points and actual points are totaled and divided to establish the rating. In Figure 6-7, 815 standard points are divided into 754 actual points; the answer is multiplied by 100 and a rating of 92.5 percent is obtained.

5. *Trace and eliminate defects found during the product audit.* This is the most important segment of the audit. While it is relatively easy to reinspect the finished product for defects found in the audit, it is more difficult—but more necessary and more rewarding—to eliminate the cause of defects. The constant recurrence of the same defects signals higher rework or scrap costs, more defective products finding their way to customers, and, most importantly, a discouraged and dispirited management team that becomes increasingly frustrated watching the same defects recur.

A product audit constructed with the elements just described will be a powerful tool for management to use to upgrade quality levels and assess the effectiveness of the organization. A smart management team will take full advantage of this early warning system.

Points

100 CLASS A—VERY SERIOUS

(a) Will surely cause an operating failure of the unit in service that cannot readily be corrected in the field.
(b) Will surely cause intermittent operating trouble, difficult to locate in the field.
(c) Will render unit totally unfit for service.
(d) Is liable to cause personal injury or property damage under normal conditions of use.

50 CLASS B—SERIOUS

(a) Will probably cause an operating failure of the unit in service that cannot readily be corrected in the field.
(b) Will surely cause an operating failure of the unit in service that can readily be corrected in the field.
(c) Will surely cause trouble of a nature less serious than an operating failure, such as substandard performance.
(d) Will surely involve increased maintenance or decreased life.
(e) Will cause a major increase in installation effort by the customer or service representative.
(f) Has defects of appearance or finish that are extreme.

10 CLASS C—MINOR

(a) May cause an operating failure of the unit in service.
(b) Is likely to cause trouble of a nature less serious than an operating failure, such as major degrees of substandard performance.
(c) Is likely to involve increased maintenance or decreased life.
(d) Will cause a minor increase in installation effort by the customer or service representative.
(e) Has major defects of appearance, finish, or workmanship.

1 CLASS D—INCIDENTAL

(a) Will not affect operation, maintenance, or life of the unit in service (including minor deviations from engineering requirements).
(b) Has minor defects of appearance, finish, or workmanship.

Figure 6-6   Product Audit Classifications

CUSTOMER __CHARLTAN, INC.__ RATING = $\dfrac{\text{ACTUAL}}{\text{STANDARD}}$ = __92.5%__

TOTAL STANDARD POINTS __815__ ORDER NUMBER __WO45671-Z__

TOTAL ACTUAL POINTS ____754____ AUDITOR ____A. Marasco____

QUALITY CHARACTERISTICS	STD. POINTS	ACTUAL POINTS	REMARKS
Traverse	100	100	
Rest Plate	1	1	
Cone Holder	100	100	
Package Indicator	1	0	#1 spindle setting $^1/_2''$ off
Spindle Holder	10	10	
Cone to Traverse	10	10	
Package Brake	50	50	
Rotary Valve	50	50	
Package Valve	50	50	
Traverse Setting	10	10	
Traverse Shaft	100	100	
Control Shaft	50	50	
Reverse Roll (two screws)	50	50	
Traverse Brushes	10	10	
Package Valve (for nicks)	10	10	
Slubber Actuator	10	10	
Control Unit to Right	1	1	
Supply Rail Welded	100	50	cracks in welds
Supply Gears	10	10	
Supply Front Cam	1	1	
Trip Rods	10	10	
Supply Rear Cam	10	10	
Bobbin Ejector Cam	10	10	
Central Balloon Control Tubes	50	40	two tubes out of clips
Supply Reed Bail	10	10	
Separator Bail	1	1	
	815	754	

Figure 6-7 Product Audit

HOW THREE COMPANIES IMPROVED QUALITY AND CUT COSTS

Case Study: A Medical Supply Manufacturer Cuts Quality Costs 50 Percent

A company producing both natural and synthetic surgical sutures found itself with out-of-control quality costs and increasing problems with defective sutures in operating rooms and doctor's offices. Quality costs were running this high:

NET SALES	$62,600,000
COST OF QUALITY	
Warranty	4,800,000
Scrap and rework	1,700,000
Support	1,200,000
	$ 7,700,000

COQ/SALES = 12.3%

A new quality manager instituted the following controls and improvements:

- Strengthened receiving inspection function
- Improved control over manufactured sutures by installing a tight tollgate inspection
- Established finished goods testing program using a small sample to pass or reject every finished goods batch
- Improved gaging techniques
- Set up inspector training programs
- Pay incentives for production operators to produce high quality work

Within two years, COQ dropped dramatically:

NET SALES	$80,000,000
COST OF QUALITY	
Warranty	2,200,000
Scrap and rework	800,000
Support	1,900,000
	$ 4,900,000

COQ/SALES = 6.1%

Case Study: A Gear Manufacturer Slashes Scrap Costs

A company producing gears in the Midwest found its internal scrap costs soaring when it embarked upon a major capital equipment program which bought many new and complex gear cutting tools. Management people were not familiar with the new types of gear cutters, and scrap costs started to mount heavily. A loss of $600,000 for a three-month period alone was sustained. Quality control improvements were obtained through:

- Capability studies of the new gear cutters and subsequent corrections to the tools, materials, and operator techniques causing the problems
- Training of production operators on the equipment by representatives of the companies that manufactured the tools
- Strengthened roving inspection techniques aimed at monitoring the process more frequently
- A quality improvement group (with representatives from production, process and tool engineering, quality, and materials) aimed at identifying problem areas and correcting them

Within a six-month period, following installation of these steps, scrap costs dropped 80 percent.

Case Study: A Machinery Manufacturer Cuts Vendor Rejections 25 Percent

A manufacturer of plastics machinery in New England found its rejection rate of purchased parts increasing at an alarming rate in its assembly plant. Soon, the rejection rate had almost tripled with most of the increases attributable to defective purchased parts not being properly screened at receiving inspection, and passing through unhindered to assembly operations.

A strengthened receiving inspection activity was started with emphasis on:

- Complete engineering drawings, inspection instructions, and sample plans for all receiving inspectors
- Insisting that all vendors with over a 5 percent rejection rate establish a corrective action program and have that program approved by the machinery manufacturer's quality control manager
- Feedback of vendor problems found at assembly to receiving inspection so that corrections could be made
- Strengthening the ability of sample plans to contain defective product at receiving inspection. That involved assuring the statistical validity of each sampling plan.

7

How to Reduce Quality Costs Using the Employee Involvement SPC System*

The Employee Involvement (EI) SPC (Statistical Process Control) System has been regarded by quality professionals worldwide as one of the finest statistical process control systems ever devised.

Developed by Bell Labs and later perfected by such companies as ITT and General Electric, it has been widely applied by those companies and others, usually with spectacular results. It has also been used by many different industries and businesses across the United States, Europe, and Japan, improving product and service quality and reducing quality associated costs. Typical cost savings produced by the system have ranged from 25 percent to 80 percent of existing quality costs (scrap, rework, warranty, etc.).

One of the great advantages of this unique approach is the use of derived tables to remove all of the mathematics normally associated with SPC. There are no calculations needed by employees applying the system to determine control limits. The system is easily practiced by workers on the production floor, clerks in the office, as well as managers and supervisors.

The EI SPC System has been used in both manufacturing and service businesses. Its principles can be applied in any situation where an improved product or service is the desired result. Typical industries where the system has been applied include manufacturers of compressors, textiles, hardware, electronics, and lamps. Services include clerical operations of many kinds such as banks, parts depots, and insurance companies.

Please note that it generally takes experienced quality professionals to tailor-make EI SPC systems to individual companies. This chapter is intended primarily to give manufacturing managers an overview of the steps involved in such a system.

SIX STEPS THAT VIRTUALLY GUARANTEE QUALITY COST SAVINGS

The basis of the EI SPC System is the Number Defective Control Chart, popularly referred to as the "NP" chart (the result of multiplying the sample size "N" by the process average percent defective "P" to obtain the number defective).

Following is an outline which describes the basic steps that need to be taken to install the EI SPC System. The section after this uses a company-based example, illustrating step-by-step how the installation proceeds. For now it is enough that a framework be established to understand the integration of the entire SPC process.

STEP 1. Conduct a Defect Analysis

First, analyze your production processes to define the existing type of defects prevalent, from receiving inspection to shipping. Draw frequency distribution of defects using the Pareto methods. Then, write cause and effect diagrams to identify major defect causes.

STEP 2. Get Workers Involved

Devise a method to enable workers to participate in the SPC system. The EI SPC System is designed specifically to encourage, and even rely on the efforts of workers to improve quality.

STEP 3. Identify Process Averages for Defects

Determine defect levels by type, operator, machine, shift, and any other meaningful category that will help define problem areas and point toward the solutions to problems.

STEP 4. Develop Control Charts

Establish the "NP" chart system with charts established for all pertinent levels and functions of the organization. Use pre-determined tables to establish control limits.

STEP 5. Create a Reporting Structure

Install a dynamic method to report operating results as obtained by the control charts. This method is geared to highlighting problem areas, thereby focusing management's attention automatically on trouble spots.

STEP 6. Make Action Assignments

Establish a system to assure fast corrective action and response to quality problems.

CASE STUDY: ONE COMPANY THAT SAVED $500,000 BY IMPLEMENTING AN SPC SYSTEM

Twin-Turrets (a fictitious name) is a New England manufacturer of packaging machinery. Several years ago it installed the EI SPC System in its machining, fabrication, and assembly operations. By following the six basic steps, Twin-Turrets was able to drastically reduce its quality costs.

Step 1: How Twin-Turrets Conducted a Defect Analysis

In most companies, the possibilities for defects are virtually endless. At Twin-Turrets, for example, defects can be categorized by defect type, machine, department, shift, and part number. The EI SPC System uses attribute control charts to measure quality performance when many defect categories are present. Within this array of defect categories that produce defects a cause and effect relationship can be established. Many defects are causal; they produce many other defects. It is important to identify these causal defects since their elimination or, at least, reduction will generate a large reduction in many other defects. The leverage provided by reduction of causal defects is key to significant quality improvement. An abbreviated example of cause and effect is shown in Figure 7-1 from an analysis of defects found by Twin-Turrets' quality assurance department.

The matrix shown illustrates the relationship between defect causes and defect effects. The defect cause "Oversize," for example, generates "Poor Fits" in the machining and fabrication departments and assembly, as well as "Mandrel Spinning" (a defect in the completed packaging machine) in customer usage.

This particular analysis shows that 11 defect causes produce 9 *types* of defect effects. The summary at the bottom of Figure 7-1 identifies the number of times each defect cause results in defect effects in machining and fabrication, assembly, and customer use as well as the total of all three of these areas. In this case, the 11 defect causes produced 36 *instances* of defect effects (the summation of the "Total Losses" line). It is evident from this example that the incidence of defect effects generated by just a few defect causes can be quite significant in its impact on quality performance.

Zeroing in on the Problem. The defect cause and effect analysis gives the organization the opportunity to zero in on those few defect causes that are creating most of the problems. For example, the most prevalent defect causes in this case are:

- Undersize   6
- Angle Wrong   6
- Defective Material   6

DEFECT CAUSE AND EFFECT ANALYSIS

EFFECTS	Oversize	Undersize	Hole Depth	Angle Wrong	Burrs	Weld Marks	Warpage	Defective Tools	Defective Mtl.	Poor Finish	Fixture Problem	
CAUSES												
LOSSES – MACHINING AND FAB POOR FITS	X	X		X					X			
SCRAPPED PARTS		X	X	X			X	X	X		X	
GRINDING REPAIR				X	X	X						
LOSSES – ASSEMBLY POOR FITS	X	X		X					X			
FINISHING REPAIR					X	X			X	X		
SCRAPPED PARTS		X	X	X			X	X	X			
LOSSES – CUSTOMER USE MANDREL SPINNING	X	X										
ACCESS DOORS STUCK					X							
INOPERABLE PARTS		X		X			X	X	X			
SUMMARY LOSSES – MACHINING AND FAB	1	2	1	3	1	1	1	1	2	0	1	
LOSSES – ASSEMBLY	1	2	1	2	1	1	1	1	3	1	0	
LOSSES – CUSTOMER USE	1	2	0	1	1	0	1	1	1	0	0	
TOTAL LOSSES:	3	6	2	6	3	2	3	3	6	1	1	

Figure 7-1   Defect Cause and Effect Analysis

Using a Pareto diagram to identify areas for SPC attack. Another way to look at priorities in attacking and reducing quality problems is through use of a Pareto diagram. This is a ranking of defects in descending order to magnitude. Figure 7-2 displays the defect causes from Figure 7-1, ranked according to their impact on defect effects. Notice that the highest 3 of the 11 causes contribute to half of the problems (adding the top three = 18; the total number of defects is 36; 18/36 = 50 percent).

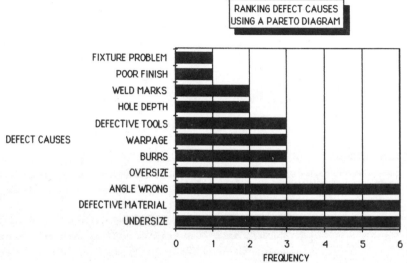

Figure 7-2   Ranking Defect Causes Using a Pareto Diagram

Since this is an abbreviated example, the full impact of the Pareto diagram is only hinted at. In most industrial or clerical applications here will be about 70-100 defect causes, and the top 20 will generate 80 percent of the defects found.

The purpose of the cause and effect analysis and its accompanying Pareto diagram is to identify areas of attack for the SPC program. After the NP attribute charts are installed (described in the following sections) special statistical tools, more powerful than the NP control charts, will be needed to control the defect causes enumerated. This may be variables control charts, Pre-Control, or some other method.

Step 2: What Twin-Turrets Did to Get Workers Involved

It is common knowledge among consultants that operators are to blame for poor quality only about 20 percent of the time. Most quality problems relate back to poor management systems and lack of appropriate techniques. Substandard raw material, machine malfunctions, inadequate methods and, many times, even poor worker performance are invariably a reflection of inappropriate management practices.

While management must attend to its problems, it must also provide the right environment to motivate workers and take full advantage of those good ideas workers have about improving quality.

As you'll see in the following discussion, the EI SPC System nurtures employee involvement. Employees' active participation in the control chart process is an integral part of the system. As part of the company team, workers need to be informed of the results of their work, just as managers and supervisors are. They also need to be involved in measuring the results of their work and be part of the corrective action process along with management.

Steps 3 and 4: How Twin-Turrets Used the Control Chart System to Monitor Quality and Performance

The NP chart system uses control charts to measure and control quality performance. Workers are provided with daily control charts to apprise them of quality progress—or lack of it—and areas most in need of improvement are pinpointed. Forepeople, superintendents and plant managers are provided with summaries of their progress.

The Number Defective (NP) Control Chart   At Twin-Turrets, the Chuckers and Lathe department forepeople used the control chart shown in Figure 7-3 to reduce defect levels of parts machined in thier area of responsibility. The form exhibited is called a "Number Defective" control chart. It is a type of statistical process control using attributes. Operators record and plot all defects found, regardless of their type on the chart.

The first two columns show the names of each operator in the Chuckers and Lathe departments and the operator's process average defective (P%). The process average defective is a percentage reflecting each operator's share of the total number of defects produced by the department during the previous month.

The numbers under the days of the month opposite each operator's name are the number of defective pieces found at his or her work station for that day. The line marked "Total Defects" is a sum of all the defective pieces produced for that day for all operators in the department. The "Number Inspected" line is the sum of all pieces *inspected* for all operators for that same day. It is not all pieces produced, unless all of them were inspected.

The circled numbers represent defects that exceeded the operator's upper control limit, and the diamonds are for those operators whose number of defects were under the lower control limit. In actual practice, circles are written in red and diamonds in green.

Using NP charts, statistically derived upper and lower control limits are calculated for each operator and for the entire department. Sanchez, for example, exceeded his upper control limit on Sept. 1, 3, 5, and 8. On Sept. 8 the "Total Defects" exceeded the department's upper limit and was circled in red accordingly.

Detecting stable performance.   At the bottom of Figure 7-3 the control chart with plotted points can be seen. The average number defective for the whole department

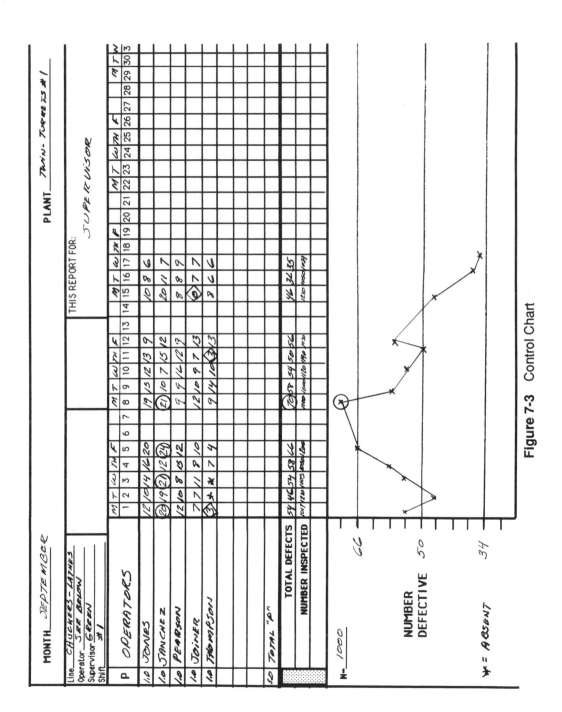

Figure 7-3 Control Chart

during the previous month was 50 defects per day. Control limits were calculated at 34 defects and 66 defects (explained in the following section on how to calculate control limits). These control limits constituted stable performance as determined by the department's quality performance in August. During September, the month this chart was written, the department's "Total Defects" was posted to the control chart every day and resulted in the plotted line seen.

Uncovering an out-of-control conclusion. From Sept. 2 to Sept. 8 there was a daily increase in the total number of defects culminating in an out-of-control condition on Sept. 8. Here the value of the control chart can be observed. If the foreperson, Green, had taken prompt corrective action on Sept. 5, the out-of-control condition on Sept. 8 may never have happened. Although the rule for an alarm to sound is when four points are heading in the same direction, familiarity with the system and its operations should have prompted Green into action. But Green did take corrective action on Sept. 9 and the defect level for the department began dropping thereafter.

Control limits for operators and departments are recalculated monthly. Control limits are never increased. They may, however, be tightened and, if the system is working properly and corrective actions are taken promptly to resolve quality problems, control limits will automatically tighten as operator performance improves from month-to-month.

How to Calculate Control Limits. In Green's chart, control limits for numbers defective were calculated for operators and the Chuckers and Lathe department as a whole. The beauty of these values is that no mathematical calculations, using laborious formulas are necessary. The Number Defective—NP—Tables, containing both upper and lower control limits already calculated are available from the author.*

Look at operator Sanchez's number defectives in Figure 7-3. We already know that during August, the previous month, the department average a 5 percent defective rate, and that Sanchez averaged 1 percent (20 percent of the total department; 1 percent/5 percent = 20 percent. The percent defective for operators is cumulative, the total of which results in the process average defective, P, for the month for the entire department. In other words, each operator's number inspected, the denominator of the process average fraction, is the *total number inspected* for the entire department).

Now, let's examine step-by-step how the NP tables are used.

1. Look at Figure 7-4, which represents part of an NP table. Go to the column marked N and find 1200 (N is the number inspected, the sample size).
2. On that same line at P (P is the process average defective), find the value 0.01.
3. Multiply that figure by 100 to determine the percentage, in this case 1 percent.

---

* Contact M. Smith, Management Sciences International, Inc., 2120 Lebanon Road, Lawrenceville, GA 30243.

N	P	UPPER	LOWER	P	UPPER	LOWER	P	UPPER	LOWER	P	UPPER	LOWER
940	0.01	16	2	0.02	29	9	0.03	40	16	0.04	52	24
950	0.01	17	2	0.02	29	9	0.03	41	16	0.04	52	24
960	0.01	17	2	0.02	29	9	0.03	41	17	0.04	53	24
970	0.01	17	2	0.02	30	9	0.03	41	17	0.04	53	25
980	0.01	17	3	0.02	30	9	0.03	42	17	0.04	53	25
990	0.01	17	3	0.02	30	10	0.03	42	17	0.04	54	25
1000	0.01	17	3	0.02	30	10	0.03	43	17	0.04	54	26
1200	0.01	20	4	0.02	35	13	0.03	50	22	0.04	64	32
1400	0.01	23	5	0.02	40	16	0.03	57	27	0.04	73	39
1600	0.01	25	7	0.02	45	19	0.03	64	32	0.04	82	46
1800	0.01	28	8	0.02	50	22	0.03	71	37	0.04	91	53
2000	0.01	30	10	0.02	55	25	0.03	78	42	0.04	100	60
2200	0.01	33	11	0.02	59	29	0.03	85	47	0.04	109	67
2400	0.01	35	13	0.02	64	32	0.03	91	53	0.04	118	74
2600	0.01	38	14	0.02	69	35	0.03	98	58	0.04	127	81
2800	0.01	40	16	0.02	73	39	0.03	105	63	0.04	136	88
3000	0.01	43	17	0.02	78	42	0.03	112	68	0.04	145	95
3200	0.01	45	19	0.02	82	46	0.03	118	74	0.04	154	102
3400	0.01	48	20	0.02	87	49	0.03	125	79	0.04	163	109
3600	0.01	50	22	0.02	92	52	0.03	132	84	0.04	171	117
3800	0.01	52	24	0.02	96	56	0.03	138	90	0.04	180	124
4000	0.01	55	25	0.02	101	59	0.03	145	95	0.04	189	131
4200	0.01	57	27	0.02	105	63	0.03	152	100	0.04	198	138
4400	0.01	59	29	0.02	110	66	0.03	158	106	0.04	206	146
4600	0.01	62	30	0.02	114	70	0.03	165	111	0.04	215	153
4800	0.01	64	32	0.02	119	73	0.03	172	116	0.04	224	160
5000	0.01	66	34	0.02	123	77	0.03	178	122	0.04	232	168
5200	0.01	69	35	0.02	127	81	0.03	185	127	0.04	241	175
5400	0.01	71	37	0.02	132	84	0.03	191	133	0.04	250	182
5600	0.01	73	39	0.02	136	88	0.03	198	138	0.04	258	190
5800	0.01	76	40	0.02	141	91	0.03	204	144	0.04	267	197
6000	0.01	78	42	0.02	145	95	0.03	211	149	0.04	275	205
6200	0.01	80	44	0.02	150	98	0.03	217	155	0.04	284	212
6400	0.01	83	45	0.02	154	102	0.03	224	160	0.04	292	220
6600	0.01	85	47	0.02	158	106	0.03	230	166	0.04	301	227
6800	0.01	87	49	0.02	163	109	0.03	237	171	0.04	310	234
7000	0.01	89	51	0.02	167	113	0.03	243	177	0.04	318	242
7200	0.01	92	52	0.02	172	116	0.03	250	182	0.04	327	249
7400	0.01	94	54	0.02	176	120	0.03	256	188	0.04	335	257
7600	0.01	96	56	0.02	180	124	0.03	263	193	0.04	344	264
7800	0.01	98	58	0.02	185	127	0.03	269	199	0.04	352	272
8000	0.01	101	59	0.02	189	131	0.03	276	204	0.04	361	279
8200	0.01	103	61	0.02	194	134	0.03	282	210	0.04	369	287
8400	0.01	105	63	0.02	198	138	0.03	288	216	0.04	378	294
8600	0.01	107	65	0.02	202	142	0.03	295	221	0.04	386	302
8800	0.01	110	66	0.02	207	145	0.03	301	227	0.04	395	309
9000	0.01	112	68	0.02	211	149	0.03	308	232	0.04	403	317

Figure 7-4 Number Defective (NP) Tables

4. On that same line, after 0.01 locate the upper and lower control limits of numbers defective, 20 and 4 respectively. These limits are valid for Sept. 5 only, the day when the department's "Number Inspected" was 1200 pieces for the entire department. On that day, Sanchez had 24 defective pieces, exceeding the upper limit of 20 pieces, an out-of-control condition. Therefore, the 24 was circled in red.

Without using the calculated NP tables, you can calculate control limits directly by using the following formula for determining upper and lower control limits for number defective attribute charts.

Where:

$$\text{Upper Control Limit} = \text{UCL}$$

$$\text{Lower Control Limit} = \text{LCL}$$

$$p = \text{Process Average Defective} = \frac{\text{Total Number of Rejects}}{\text{Total Number Inspected}}$$

$$n = \text{Total Number Inspected (Sample Size)}$$

Then:

$$\text{UCL} = np + 2.37 \ np(1\text{-}p)$$

$$\text{LCL} = np - 2.37 \ np(1\text{-}p)$$

Note: In most cases, three standard deviations are used to calculate control limits; here 2.37 standard deviations are substituted. The tighter standards assure earlier indication of adverse trends in the manufacturing process; trends that will, if left alone, lead to rejects. The tighter standard deviation band helps manufacturing employees spot problems faster and correct them *before* defective work is produced.

In Sanchez's example just described:

$$\text{UCL} = 1200(.01) + 2.37 \ \ 1200(.01) \times (1-.01) = 20$$

$$\text{LCL} = 1200(.01) - 2.37 \ \ 1200(.01) \times (1-.01) = \ \ 4$$

How the system capitalizes on superior performance. When an operator exhibits a succession of diamonds, management is advised to investigate and discover the reasons for his superior performance. Whatever steps that operator has taken to reduce his number of defects may be passed on to other operators to improve their performance also.

The following indicate out-of-control trends on the control charts' plotted lines:

• Any point either above the upper control limit or below the lower control limit.

• Any four consecutive points going in the same direction.

• Any seven consecutive points on the same side of the average (X) line.

When any of these conditions exist, workers and management must take corrective action to restabilize the process. The entire EI SPC System is geared to finding problem areas and correcting the process. Simple use of the control chart without taking effective corrective action will not result in improvements.

Step 5: How Twin-Turrets' Reporting Structure Highlights Trouble Spots

Out-of-control conditions that have been described above trigger responses of forepeople and operators to correct the process and return it to a state of control. But how about superintendents and plant managers? What tool do they have to participate in the system?

One of the advantages of the EI SPC System is that defect information is pyramided so that each organizational level has its own information, reflective of the operations directly under each person's control.

Figure 7-5 is the summary of defects for Riley, the superintendent who supervises Green, the foreperson whose chart is shown in Figure 7-3, and two other forepeople. This form is a summary of the quality level for the day and month and prior year.

This report contrasts the performance for each day against the month-to-date as well as last year's performance, expressed as the number of defects per machine per shift. Notice that for Stevenson and Green there has been evidence of improvement from last year to this month while Brown's quality has leveled off. All three forepeople, however, have excellent records for today (in the report, Sept. 17). In summary, total defects shown at the bottom of the form reflect consistent improvements.

Defect types are summarized in the right-hand column. The purpose of this abbreviated summary is simply to alert top managers concerning the overall effectiveness of their efforts to improve quality. Further, more detailed, summaries should be available at the foreperson level.

The plant manager's summary report on quality levels is shown in Figure 7-6. Superintendents Riley and Foster report to Sorenson, the plant manager, and their performances are shown here.

Notice the circles drawn around Foster's defect levels for both today and month-to-date. This indicates deteriorating performance. Since the month-to-date defect level is 165, appreciably above last year's 151 level, that poor performance is circled to highlight it. Similarly, today has 197 defects, way over even the month-to-date number of 165 and is circled accordingly. Total defects do show an improvement for the current month and for today's performance because of Riley's good showing. Obviously, corrective action is in order for Foster to improve.

Step 6: How Twin-Turrets Makes Action Assignments to Ensure That Quality Problems Are Corrected

Let's look at what happened at Twin-Turrets on one of the other days of the month of September. As can be seen in Figure 7-7, operator Sanchez's red circled performance triggered corrective action by his foreperson, Green. Now, moving up one

TWIN TURRETS				
MONTH SEPTEMBER TODAY 9-17	DEPARTMENT MACHINING	THIS REPORT FOR: MANAGERS_____ SUPERVISORS X RILEY - SUPERINTENDENT		
SUPERVISORS	NUMER OF DEFECTS PER MACHINE PER SHIFT			
	TODAY	MONTH TO DATE	LAST YEAR	DEFECT TYPES
STEVENSON 1ST SHIFT	15	23	29	FINISH HOLE DEPTH
GREEN 2ND SHIFT	35	56	62	BURRS FINISH ANGLE WRONG HOLE DEPTH
BROWN 3RD SHIFT	15	20	21	FINISH BURRS
TOTAL DEFECTS:	65	99	112	

Figure 7-5 Summary of Defects: Superintendent Riley

TWIN TURRETS				
MONTH *SEPTEMBER* TODAY 9-17	DEPARTMENT *MACHINING, FABRICATION,* *ASSEMBLY*	THIS REPORT FOR: MANAGERS __X__ SUPERVISORS_____ *PLANT MANAGER - SORENSON*		
SUPERINTENDENTS	NUMER OF DEFECTS PER MACHINE PER SHIFT			
	TODAY	MONTH TO DATE	LAST YEAR	DEFECT TYPES
RILEY *MACHINING*	65	99	112	*FINISH* *BURRS* *HOLE DEPTH*
FOSTER *FABRICATION &* *ASSEMBLY*	(197)	(165)	151	*POOR FITS* *FINISH* *WELD MARKS*
TOTAL DEFECTS:	262	264	263	

Figure 7-6   Report on Quality Levels: Plant Manager Sorensen

REPORTING PYRAMID

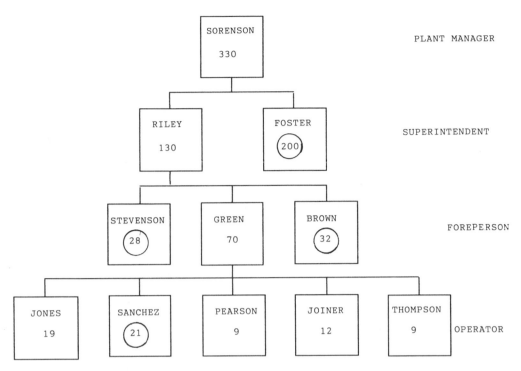

Figure 7-7   Reporting Pyramid

level, forepeople Stevenson and Brown had red-circled performances. This caused superintendent Riley to step into the picture and apply corrective action. Finally, the other superintendent, Foster, at the next level, had a bad day and plant manager Sorenson discussed with Foster the steps being taken to resolve the problems.

Why action assignments must be handed to specific individuals.   It is this constant review of operating results on a daily basis, coupled with effective and timely corrective actions, that causes the EI SPC System to succeed. Using this system, action assignments for correction of problems must be assigned to specific individuals. If the problems are within the control of line managers, they must assume responsibility for their correction. If the problems are outside of their control, say a vendor quality problem, then the appropriate person in the organization must be assigned specific responsibility for correcting that problem and be asked to report back at a given time to specify the actions he or she has taken for problem resolution. While Number Defective (NP) charts are sensitive to developing problems, just using them cannot resolve the problems. Aggressive management action is ultimately the answer.

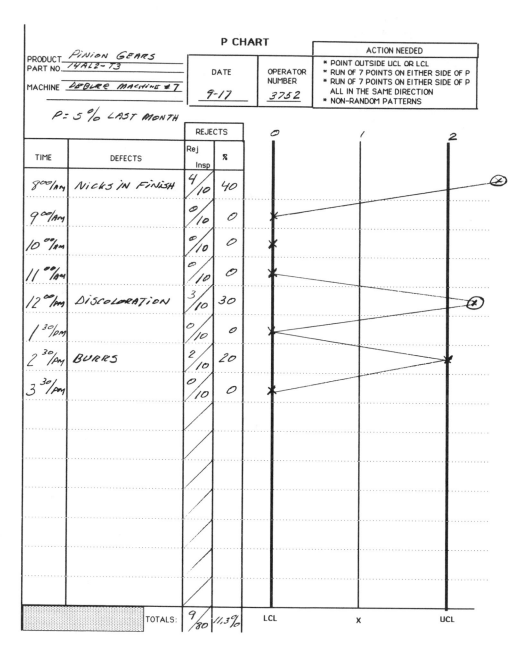

Figure 7-8 Number Defective Control Chart for Operator 3752

How to use an alternate quality control system based on individual operator performance. Some managers feel uncomfortable working with number defective control charts where the operator's performance is based on the defects he or she reports related to the total number of pieces reported for all combined operators, the total department.

It is possible to use an alternate form of the number defective control chart where each operator's reported defects are related to the number of pieces he or she inspects, not to those of the entire department. This Is illustrated in Figure 7-8, a number defective control chart for each operator based on his or her solo performance, without regard to other operators.

In this example, Operator 3752 inspected 10 pieces per hour, 80 for the shift. He found a total of 9 defective pieces in this inspection at those hours shown on the chart. His number defective control chart limits are based on the 5 percent process average defective he experienced the previous month and the sample size of 10. From the NP Tables it can be seen that his control limits for each of the samples taken is 2 for the upper limit and 0 for the lower limit. He therefore ran out-of-control at 8:00 a.m. and at noon, when the defects he produced exceeded his upper control limit.

For the day his defect level of 9 pieces matched the upper control limit of 9 defects as can be seen in the NP Tables for P = 5%, and N = 80.

Conclusion

Within six months of the installation of the EI SPC program, quality levels had improved by 20 percent, yielding a savings in scrap and rework of more than $500,000.

The EI SPC program is designed to offer quick savings by defect reduction and to assure continued employee involvement well into the future.

8

How to Make Your Employees Key Players in Reducing Quality Costs

Instituting an employee involvement SPC system represents a major step towards reducing manufacturing costs and improving product quality. Many companies, however, are going one step further to get each and every one of their employees involved at some level in quality cost reduction.

The productivity improvement team concept is a natural outgrowth of the SPC techniques described in Chapter 7. The workers' fast response system is an even broader approach to generating employee participation in cost reduction and quality improvement efforts. Properly implemented, both of these approaches can have a significant positive impact on your company's bottom line.

USING PRODUCTIVITY IMPROVEMENT TEAMS TO BUILD PROFITS

A productivity improvement team is a small *volunteer* group of employees who meet about once a week to discuss their productivity and quality problems, use predetermined methods to investigate causes, recommend specific actions to correct the problems, and finally shepherd the implementation of changes to bring about the improvements.

The volunteer aspect is crucial to the success of the program. People at any level of the organization cannot be forced into productivity improvement teams;

they will resist participation and the resulting poor performance of the teams will not encourage their continuation.

Productivity improvement teams are composed of machine operators and support members such as material handlers, inspectors, and maintenance workers along with salaried specialists such as manufacturing and design engineers. The composition should be mostly hourly employees and the group size should generally not exceed ten.

Normally the group leader is the production unit's supervisor, although this may not always work. If the supervisor is the type who chokes-off debate and imposes his or her will on subordinates, the supervisor cannot be permitted to sit in with the group, much less lead it.

SEVEN KEY CHARACTERISTICS OF A SUCCESSFUL PRODUCTIVITY IMPROVEMENT TEAM

A productivity improvement team must be nurtured to flourish, just like any other management program or effort. The following elements are essential:

1. *Top management support.* This doesn't mean that the plant manager gives approval; it means providing resources. It's easy to say, "Go ahead with my blessing." It's much harder to say, "Okay, here's $100,000 for your budget." But money is what it takes.

2. *Employee empowerment.* If the company has operated strictly or the line and staff principle and, as in the traditional plant of the past, hourly workers have not been given any voice in decisions relating to their workplaces, then it will be difficult, if not impossible, to foster an environment of teamwork without a lot of changes in the operating climate. And that doesn't happen overnight. But use of a productivity improvement team is a good way to start and will allow supervisors and operators to find ways to work together effectively.

3. *Participation by all group members.* Once the teams have been formed, trained in the techniques discussed later in this chapter, and are up and running, everybody must be encouraged to participate. It is necessary to recognize that many workers will find it difficult to speak up. Since giving their opinions may be such a radical departure from past practices, some team members may be reluctant to speak at first. Most, however, will warm up and relax enough to contribute their thoughts as time progresses. Patience and encouragement go a long way to assist in the transition.

4. *A team approach.* Members should be encouraged to help one another. One of the very fine benefits of this method is the team approach that it fosters among its participants. As the team develops over time, members will naturally encourage other members to express their views. Team bonds develop that carry over to the workplace.

5. *Creativity.* Creativity is a valued commodity whose effect is heightened in a productivity improvement team. Unusual solutions to problems are encour-

aged, even rewarded, so members become eager to discover different paths to the resolution of problems. Creative thoughts by one member spark creative thoughts by another member, and from this interchange many original solutions to problems occur.

6. *A scope limited to the workplace.* Only problems directly affecting the workplace of participants are discussed. It's certainly nice to know how the company will direct its marketing efforts for the next five years, but the team cannot contribute anything significant to that kind of discussion. Neither do team members feel comfortable trying to handle functions out of their range of knowledge and sphere of influence. When the talk turns to the workplace, however, everyone has something to contribute and the range of ideas expressed is usually broad enough to result in many improvements.

7. *Two types of training.* Training must follow two avenues; the first is a methodology that embraces the specific techniques described in the following pages. The second is more conceptual—how to work together to effect change. It is the second type of training that will need professional guidance. Behavioral training is supplied today by most consulting companies dedicated to implementing productivity improvements.

How to Find Out What Your Employees Really Think About Their Jobs And the Company

A successful productivity improvement team starts with what is called a "Productivity Climate Diagnostic." This is a survey of attitudes of team members taken before the teams are formed. The diagnostic measures the response of workers and salaried people to management's efforts to help employees do their jobs. Inevitably, the diagnostic reveals many surprises. It serves to wake up management to the realities of how workers perceive their jobs, management, and the relationship between both. In many cases what management thinks the attitudes of workers are differs substantially from what workers really think. The customary finding is that management must sharpen its ability to support the workplace with the proper resources and training. A sample diagnostic is shown in Figure 8-1.

How to Use Your Productivity Improvement Team to Solve Quality Problems

A productivity improvement team follows six steps to solve manufacturing quality problems. These steps are shown in Figure 8-2 and described briefly below.

Step 1: Identify quality problems. Since there are generally problems everywhere, this is probably the easiest step. Chances are you've already identified problems by a technique such as the Pareto method described in Chapter Seven. It is important, however, to aim your efforts at quality problems that are readily solvable, will reduce costs, and will improve quality substantially.

QUALITY CLIMATE DIAGNOSTIC

INSTRUCTIONS

Please read each of the follwing statements carefully. Then decide the extent to which you either agree or disagree with the statement as it applies to your situation. Indicate your choice by placing a check mark (✓) in the appropriate column to the right of each statement.

	STRONGLY AGREE	SOMEWHAT AGREE	SOMEWHAT DISAGREE	STRONGLY DISAGREE
1. The company is very dedicated to producing a high quality product.				
2. I am interested in participating in some sort of employee quality program.				
3. The company cares more about quantity than quality.				
4. Quality goals are clear for my job and my department.				
5. We have clear specifications.				
6. I have all the tools and equipment I need to do the job				
7. I have clear written instructions that show me how to do my job.				
8. I understand what my company means by the word "quality".				
9. I have enough time on my job to devote to quality.				
10. The different departments cooperate with one another to get the job done.				
11. The products we produce are of high quality.				
12. Our present efforts are focused on detection rather than prevention of quality problems.				
13. My work has an effect on quality.				
14. I understand customer quality requirements.				
15. When it comes to quality, management listens to my suggestions.				

Figure 8-1   Sample Productivity Climate Diagnostic

	STRONGLY AGREE	SOMEWHAT AGREE	SOMEWHAT DISAGREE	STRONGLY DISAGREE
16. I feel personally responsible for my work meeting company quality standards.				
17. When it comes to quality, the only time I hear anything is when there is a problem.				
18. We have good tools and techniques to measure quality.				
19. I am well trained in the techniques of solving quality problems.				
20. I always know when I am producing poor quality.				
21. If the company begins an employee quality program, I want to be included.				
22. The hourly employees are the most important group in the company affecting quality.				
23. The company spends a lot of money on quality.				

Figure 8-1 Sample Productivity Climate Diagnostic (continued)

Step 2: Gather data. Collect numerical data and explore conditions surrounding the quality problem.

Step 3: Analyze quality problem causes. The brainstorming and fishbone techniques described in the next section represent a highly effective approach to identifying and analyzing the causes of quality and cost problems.

Step 4: Recommend solutions. The capstone of each team's work is developing and recommending solutions to the quality problems it has uncovered.

Step 5: Eliminate the quality problem. The problem must be tackled and eliminated by managers and workers alike in well-planned, well-executed moves. Even if the first four steps are perfectly accomplished, failure to implement Step 5 will undermine the effect of the productivity improvement team.

Step 6: Follow up to make sure the solution is truly working. Examine performance data from the suspect operations to make sure that progress is being made and that quality is improving.

Once the quality problem has been addressed, the team can move on to tackle another problem using the same step-by-step approach.

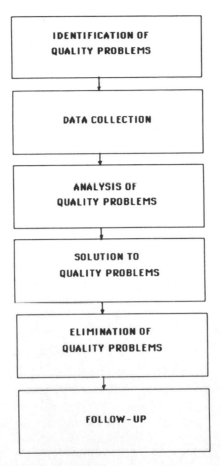

Figure 8-2   How a Productivity Team Works

Five Rules for Using Brainstorming to Generate Fresh Solutions to Problems with Manufacturing Quality

When the productivity improvement team is formed, the very first technique learned is brainstorming. Brainstorming is a freewheeling, say-what-you-will approach to generate ideas and fresh solutions to problems. The more ideas generated in a brainstorming session the better. The general rules for using brainstorming techniques are:

1. *Use brainstorming to spark ideas.* These ideas are used to fill out the fishbone diagram explained in the next section.
2. *Give everybody a chance to suggest ideas.* Rotating through the group in an orderly sequence gives all participants the opportunity to be heard.
3. *Don't dismiss any ideas.* The purpose is to generate new thinking about the

problem being discussed and to spark fresh ideas. The synergy of the technique is that one idea triggers another idea from somebody else, and eventually the problem's causes are identified.

4. *Don't force responses.* Anybody is permitted to pass when his or her turn arrives. People will sometimes be reluctant to express their ideas, particularly at the beginning. After a time, most people will normally loosen up. Many people will also run out of fresh ideas momentarily and pass until the next turn when something else said sparks another thought.

5. *Hold the group size to 10 people or less.* Any larger than this and the group will be too difficult to steer. Also, in a larger group, group pressures tend to interfere with the relaxed, restrained atmosphere that makes brainstorming productive.

How to Use Fishboning to Come Up With Solutions to Quality Problems

Figure 8-3 is a fishbone diagram. Its name is derived from the depiction of the technique which has the appearance of a fish skeleton. The scientific name for this is a "Cause and Effect" diagram. It is designed to discover the root causes of quality and productivity problems. At the head of the fishbone the problem is stated and defined with as much precision as possible.

Example of how to use fishboning. If, for example, you want to find out why your car is getting low gas mileage, stating that fact as the problem would not be sufficient. Rather, the problem might be stated this way, "Old 4-door Cadillac Seville getting low mileage." This further defines the problem, making it easier to solve. (Note: The low gas example is an ideal way to introduce fishbone diagramming to workers. They relate well to the problem and it gets their attention.)

Step 1: Define the problem. There are usually four defined variables that can cause the problem in a manufacturing setting: machines, staffing, methods, and materials. These are the fish's backbones radiating from its spine. (Some include as a variable the measuring instrument as a way to assure the proper gauge is being used and that it is being read correctly.) Figure 8-4 shows a completed fishbone diagram with all of the variables filled in. In the construction of the fishbone, the bare bones outline as shown in Figure 8-3 is plotted on the blackboard and the problem is stated clearly.

Step 2: Brainstorm to define causes. Then, using the brainstorming techniques already described, participants take turns guessing at the causes of the problem. A moderator, elected by the group, chalks in the ideas presented by individuals along the backbones where they belong. A machinery adjustment cause, for example, becomes a small spine along the "machine" backbone. In another instance, defective material goes into the "material" category.

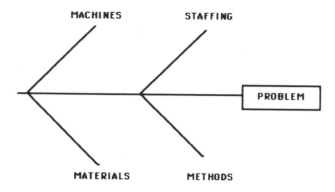

Figure 8-3 Outline of a Fishbone Diagram

Step 3: Establish the most probable causes. Ideas are gathered until the group runs out of steam. Then participants vote on those causes they consider the most probable as being the problem causes. Each person usually gets three votes, but this can be adapted for each individual case. In some instances, the problem causes may be only one or two; in other instances, there may be four or five *major* causes among fifty causes shown on the fishbone.

Step 4: Identify the probable causes. The moderator then tallies the vote and the dominant causes are identified.

Step 5: Determine solutions. In the next phase, brainstorming is used to determine probable solutions to the problem.

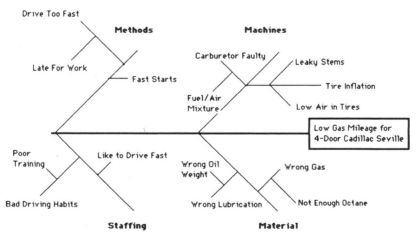

Figure 8-4 Completed Fishbone Diagram

Step 6: Develop and implement an action plan. An action plan for process improvements should be developed and presented to management for approval. Then both management and workers should work together to resolve the problems.

Figure 8-5 is an example of a fishbone diagram used by a team to reduce circuit board scrap in an electronics operation.

When constructing a fishbone diagram, the productivity improvement team should answer the following six questions:

1. What is the problem?
2. What are the many causes?
3. What are the most probable causes?
4. What are the solutions?
5. Who will implement them?
6. When will the implementation take place?

The fishbone diagram technique has been used by literally thousands of companies internationally to help resolve productivity and quality problems. When used sensibly, it can produce dramatic results at the same time it teaches all employees within a company how to work together.

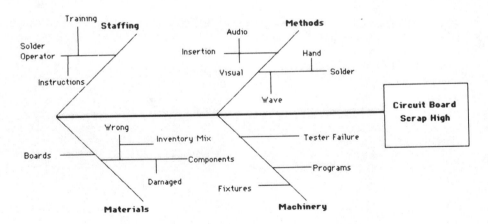

Figure 8-5   Fishbone Diagram for Reducing Circuit Board Scrap

Case Study: A Sock Manufacturer cuts waste 34 percent. A large sock manufacturer formed teams among its knitters and fitters (machine adjusters) and taught them the fishbone technique to combat high waste levels for some particular styles of socks. Within a matter of eleven weeks (with the individual teams meeting one hour every week) some 52 practical suggestions for improvements had been made and implemented. The amount of waste generated at the knitting machines dropped by 34 percent within the first year of the program.

USING THE WORKERS' FAST RESPONSE SYSTEM TO REDUCE COSTS AND QUALITY PROBLEMS

Once SPC control charts are set in place and running, and once a productivity improvement team has been formed and is operating, the question of how to resolve many problems not handled through the system still remains. SPC and the productivity improvement team will address only a finite number of problems, and that may not be enough to aggressively reduce excess costs and address all major customer quality problems.

Additionally, not everybody on the production floor will immediately participate in an SPC program or a productivity improvement team. For those who are not yet involved, the question still remains of how to elicit their participation and support in the company's efforts to reduce manufacturing costs and improve product quality.

The Fast Response System is a new channel of communication. It allows individual workers to tell plant managers of the problems affecting their job performance that they are experiencing. It is a way to attack problems that workers and first-line supervisors have been unsuccessful handling by themselves. Its purpose is to identify problems hindering productivity and quality; it does not require that solutions be presented along with the problems.

In a typical plant, the communication channel from top management to workers and back is shut off by middle managers who interpret the plant manager's instructions and relay them down the line. Although this usually works, the procedure many times shuts down when information flows back up the line. The Fast Response System re-opens that channel.

The Fast Response System gives workers the opportunity to express their concerns about impediments to high productivity and high quality. It addresses those day-to-day problems that plague every manufacturing organization. The fast response system's lasting value lies in its ability to improve communication between top plant management and workers, an essential link that is often missing in American manufacturing. Another of its strengths is the mutual bond it helps workers and managers alike establish when they, working together, focus on problem correction.

Six Important Points to Remember When Implementing A Fast Response System

There are certain premises that underlie full understanding of this system. These are:

1. *Every production organization has an almost infinite number of productivity, cost and quality problems facing it; all of those are correctable.* It's a matter of priorities and resources.

2. *The root causes of repetitive problems have not yet been determined.* Otherwise, they wouldn't be present.

3. *Everybody, up and down the line organization, must accept the presence of these problems* and know the magnitude of their impact on the organization.

4. *Top management must get involved.* Some of these problems can readily be handled, without the additional help of top management, by workers and supervisors, who have been trained in SPC or who belong to a productivity improvement team. Many problems cannot; these require the attention of the plant manager and his or her staff.

5. *The Fast Response System must attack problems without reprisals.* The Fast Response System is a tool for correcting those latter kind of problems that the production floor needs help with. It provides a way to attack problems without any accompanying personal fear of supervisors and workers being held accountable for their presence.

6. *Every worker and supervisor is responsible for identifying those problems* and bringing them to the attention of the plant manager in a systematic way.

How to Use the Fast Response System to Solve Manufacturing Quality Problems

The fast response system is a means of resolving problems that workers and first-level supervisors have been unsuccessful in handling by themselves.

Step 1: Report the problem. The core of the system is a report (see Figure 8-6) that originates with any person in the plant, regardless of his or her rank and position. Generally, these reports are submitted by workers and first-line supervisors with frequent participation by engineers and other support people assigned to the production operation. Problems that cannot be corrected within the production department itself are passed along in this program.

Essential information in the report includes:

• Specific location of the problem by work center.

• A brief description of the problem.

• Solutions to the problem, if any are known.

Step 2: Review the problem. After the report has been completed, it is given to the department clerk who gathers all reports weekly and submits them to an assigned secretary. The secretary can be anybody who the plant manager thinks will be a welcome addition to the plant manager's action group.

The plant manager's action group, which reviews all reports should meet weekly at a predetermined time. This group is usually composed of the plant manager and his or her immediate staff, including the production manager, mate-

```
┌─────────────────────────────────────────────────────────────┐
│                 FAST RESPONSE SYSTEM REPORT                   │
├─────────────────────────────────────────────────────────────┤
│ DATE: 5-7    DEPARTMENT: MACHINING    SHIFT: 4-12 P.M.        │
├─────────────────────────────────────────────────────────────┤
│ ORIGINATOR: BARBARA SANCHEZ        FRS REPORT LOG NUMBER: 91-247│
├─────────────────────────────────────────────────────────────┤
│ DESCRIPTION OF PROBLEM: PART NO. PQ-141R RUNNING 18%         │
│ SCRAP.                                                        │
│                                                              │
├─────────────────────────────────────────────────────────────┤
│ PROPOSED CORRECTIVE ACTION: RUN ON CHUCKERS INSTEAD OF       │
│ OLD LATHE WHICH CAN'T HOLD TOLERANCES, LATHE IS             │
│ SO WORN.                                                     │
│                                                              │
├─────────────────────────────────────────────────────────────┤
│ INVESTIGATOR: BRIAN FORBES   DATE DISCUSSED WITH ORIGINATOR: 5-12│
├─────────────────────────────────────────────────────────────┤
│ ACTION TO BE TAKEN: PART # PQ-141R TO BE SCHEDULED BY       │
│ PLANNING DEPARTMENT FOR CHUCKERS                            │
│                                                              │
│ ASSIGNED TO: STANLEY BRAUN                                   │
├─────────────────────────────────────────────────────────────┤
│ SCHEDULED COMPLETION DATE: 5-20   ACTUAL COMPLETION DATE: 5-20│
├─────────────────────────────────────────────────────────────┤
│ _____       DATE CLOSED: 5-28         │
│ ORIGINATOR'S SIGNATURE                                       │
├─────────────────────────────────────────────────────────────┤
│                                                              │
│                                                              │
└─────────────────────────────────────────────────────────────┘
```

Figure 8-6   Sample Fast Response System Report

rials manager, manufacturing engineering manager, quality manager and personnel manager and anybody else who the plant manager feels may contribute.

Each fast response system report is discussed along with any ideas anybody
has regarding appropriate corrective actions.

Step 3: Investigate possible solutions.   Next, an investigator is assigned to gather data about the problem reported and formulate an approach to resolve it. This investigator can be anybody at the meeting or somebody from that person's staff. A due date is set for the investigator to report back to the plant manager's action group (normally within the next meeting or two). *Key Action:* The investigator now sets up a meeting with the originator of the report. The investigator reviews the problem with the worker on the production floor right at the workplace where the problem is happening. This simple action is critical for two reasons. First, it demonstrates management's interest in resolving the problem to workers. Second, it provides an opportunity to personally investigate the problem, define it further, and discuss corrective actions with workers and first-line supervisors.

Step 4: Implement corrective action. Next, the report with investigative comments is returned to the plant manager's action group. The investigator reports the findings, and a discussion regarding corrective action ensues. When a recommended course of action is decided upon, one of the members present should be assigned the task of implementing the corrective action. A due date should then be determined.

Step 5: Report back to the worker. The original investigator now reports back to the worker who originated the report, relaying the decision of the plant mana-ger's group for corrective action, even if that decision is to take no action at the time. Again, the group is acting to keep the door open between worker and manager.

Assuming a decision has been reached to implement a specific recommendation, the person who was assigned the corrective action then reports back to the group when the implementation is complete, and also tells the worker involved. At this time, that particular report is closed.

The entire sequence of events—the fast response system workflow—is portrayed in Figure 8-7.

The value of the fast response system is in the support given workers. It shows them, in concrete ways, management's intentions to eradicate costly productivity and quality problems.

At the beginning of the program, if managers have truly encouraged workers to identify their problems, there will be a flood of fast response system reports flowing into the plant manager's action group. So many, in fact, that the task will initially appear overwhelming. But over time, as the problems are attacked and eradicated, the flow of reports will trail off. This is due, in part, to the nature of any new undertaking. People lose the original enthusiasm displayed at the inception of a program. That is to be expected. Also, as the SPC and productivity improvement team programs kick in, there will be less need for another channel of problem communication with management.

In most instances, the fast response system will last about one year. During that period, enormous contributions to improved productivity and quality can be garnered.

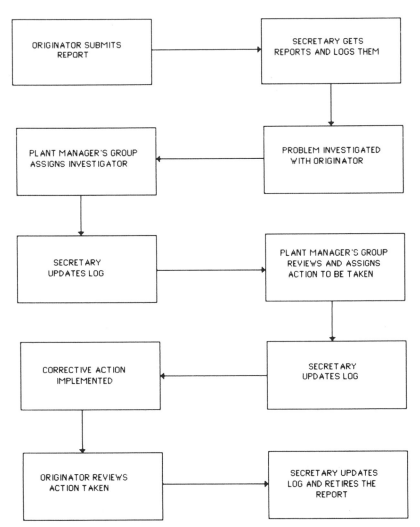

Figure 8-7   Flowchart of the Fast Response System

Case Study: How a Catheter Manufacturer Reduced Defect Levels

A case in point is a medical products manufacturer making catheters in Southern California. The defect rate for the silicone molding operation—the most critical operation in the entire department—was running at an unacceptable rate of 16 percent. Regardless of what production engineers did to modify the process, the defect rate stubbornly refused to budge.

When the fast response system was introduced, two of the silicone molding machine operators suggested certain modifications to the dies with a change in the silicone feed rate. The *combination* of these two ideas was the key to unlocking the puzzle. Within a matter of days, the defect rate had dropped from 16 percent to 2 percent.

Examples of this nature abound in manufacturing operations. The people who run the machines usually know how to improve their individual operations. Unfortunately, too many times their participation is ignored. The fast response system is a perfect way for them to ask for and receive the help they need to improve their operations.

9

How to Use Cycle Forecasting for Production Planning And Control

Production planning and control is the very essence of a manufacturing organization. The purchase and use of materials, the movement and control of parts in manufacturing, the warehousing and shipment of products to customers—these activities constitute the basic determinants of success in manufacturing. An effective production planning and control function enables a manufacturing organization to meet customer delivery requirements, maintain low inventories, and minimize production costs. And the core activity of production planning and control is forecasting.

Forecasting determines how much material will be purchased, stored, and manufactured, how large inventories will be, how well customer delivery commitments will be met, and how many people will be employed in manufacturing. Forecasting of orders is the first activity of the production planning and control system, and its successes—or lack of it—has made or broke the careers of many manufacturing managers.

THE TRADITIONAL FORECASTING METHOD AND WHY IT DOESN'T WORK

The most established procedure used to forecast orders is the weekly or monthly meeting between sales and manufacturing managers. It is usually at these meetings that forecasts are made based on sales expectations.

The problem with this method is universal; sales managers—invariably optimistic and concerned about satisfying customer commitments for fast delivery—almost always project greater sales levels than those which actually occur. They reason that an optimistic outlook on sales will keep the factories producing at high enough levels to satisfy the requirements of an avalanche of customers.

Of course, when the anticipated avalanche turns into a small trickle, the person holding the bag won't be the sales manager. Inevitably, the person who will be blamed for high inventories and overstaffed shifts will be the manufacturing manager. Regardless of fancy platitudes issued from above concerning the responsibility of sales for issuing realistic forecasts, it will *always* be the job of manufacturing management to hold down inventory and labor costs in relation to sales. Unfair as that might be, that's the way it really is! So it behooves every manufacturing manager to learn how to forecast realistically. One forecasting method that is relatively precise is cycle forecasting.

HOW CYCLE FORECASTING WORKS

Cycle forecasting, a technique developed almost 25 years ago by the Institute For Trend Research, recognizes that there will almost always be peaks and troughs in business orders, and that those peaks and troughs can be roughly predicted. Regardless of product or technology, cycles occur, and they appear to occur within all economic and political institutions.

Cycle forecasting predicts when those orders will expand and when they will contract. It is based on the fact that, throughout economic history, cycles have been artificially induced by businesspeople and consumers, through either their optimism or pessimism regarding the prevailing economic climate. Cycles occur, in other words, when people defer purchases because of fear, and later make those same purchases because of their belief that business conditions are improving.

Case Study: How to Use Cycle Forecasting

A Houston manufacturing plant has been using cycle forecasting for many years to predict inventory and labor requirements. The company follows a four-step cycle forecasting procedure.

Step 1: Compile monthly orders. The company starts by listing actual monthly order rates in dollars for the past several years, as seen in the first column of Figure 9-1.

Step 2: Accumulate 12-month order totals. The next column in Figure 9-1 "Moving Annual Total" shows the current twelve-month total. As these numbers are accumulated, the total for the current month is added and the total for the same month during last year is dropped. The moving annual total for January 1990, for example, was calculated this way:

Total for 1989:	$18.50 Million
Plus 1/90 Orders:	1.85 Million
Sub-Total:	$20.35 Million
Less 1/89 Orders:	1.13 Million
Moving Annual Total—1/90:	$19.22 Million

	ORDERS*	MOVING ANNUAL TOTAL*	ORDER LEVEL %	
1989 J	1.13			Note: All numbers marked
F	1.42			* expressed as millions of
M	1.66			dollars.
A	1.46			
M	1.50			
J	1.68			
J	1.58			
A	1.39			
S	1.66			
O	1.57			
N	1.64			
D	1.81	18.50		
1990 J	1.85	19.22		
F	2.03	19.83		
M	2.49	20.66		
A	2.06	21.26		
M	2.03	21.79		
J	2.11	22.22		
J	1.94	22.58		
A	1.91	23.10		
S	1.95	23.39		
O	2.44	24.26		
N	2.12	24.74		
D	2.50	25.43		
1991 J	1.88	25.46	132.5%	
F	2.59	26.02	131.2	
M	3.14	26.67	129.1	
A	2.91	27.52	129.4	
M	2.87	28.36	130.2	
J	2.95	29.20	131.4	
J	2.62	29.88	132.3	
A	2.60	30.57	132.3	
S	3.45	32.07	137.1	
O	2.90	32.53	134.1	
N	3.40	33.81	136.7	
D	3.38	34.69	136.4	

Figure 9-1   Sample Cycle Forecasting Calculations

Step 3: Calculate the sales order level. Each current moving annual total is divided by the year-ago moving annual total to derive the next column in Figure 9-1, "Order Level," as shown here for January, 1991:

$$1/91 \text{ Order Level} = \frac{1/91 \text{ Moving Annual Total}}{1/90 \text{ Moving Annual Total}}$$

$$1/91 \text{ Order Level } = \frac{\$25.46 \text{ Million}}{\$19.22 \text{ Million}} \times 100 = 132.5\%$$

The order level tends to reduce the impact of seasonal variations and other factors affecting incoming orders (such as order processing delays). The resultant order level trend clearly illustrates basic changes in the ordering cycle alone.

Step 4: Compare actual orders with order levels. Compare actual orders for 1991 with their corresponding order levels for the same months to see the differences. April and May, for example, show actual declines in the number of orders received, but their corresponding order levels are steadily increasing, signaling an upturn in the order cycle. This trend is verified by the higher number of actual orders received from September through December.

RESULT: If Houston had reduced its purchasing and staffing levels based on decreasing incoming orders experienced in April and May, the plant would have been in poor position to handle the larger influx of orders six months later. They conceivably could have failed to honor customer commitments, or they might have been forced to extend customer delivery dates while they built up inventories and hired and trained additions to the workforce.

Figure 9-2 graphs actual new orders vs. order levels for Houston during the period 1977-1988. Notice the major differences between the graphs. Quite obvi-

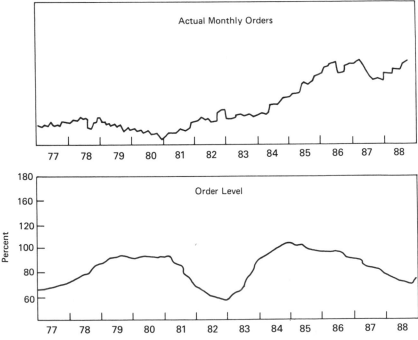

Figure 9-2 COMPARISON OF OPEN ORDERS AND ORDER LEVELS

ously, looking at actual new orders alone is not enough to discern sales trends. Cycle forecasting has helped Houston prepare for major shifts in the marketplace. Its plant manager has been able to match inventory and staffing levels with long-term market needs.

USING THE BUSINESS CYCLE TO DEVELOP A CYCLE FORECAST

Cycle forecasting is predicated upon the inevitability of peaks and valleys in the business cycle. As shown in Figure 9-3, there are six distinct phases, each recognizable, and each possessing its own unique characteristics.

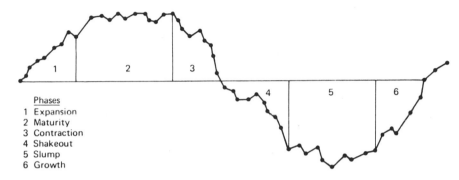

Phases
1 Expansion
2 Maturity
3 Contraction
4 Shakeout
5 Slump
6 Growth

Figure 9-3 The Business Cycle

Six Phases of the Business Cycle

1. *Expansion.* This phase occurs during a period of optimism. It is recognizable by gains in employment, business increases, and a rapidly improving gross national product. Productivity increases and purchasing agents contract for additional orders.

2. *Maturity.* The end of the expansion period is marked by narrower gains on the chart for a period of approximately three months and most gains thereafter are balanced by some downturns. The curve "flattens out." During this period employment and business activity remain high, demand triggers inflationary price increases, and plants are near full capacity.

3. *Contraction.* Three consecutive months of decline on the chart mark the start of a period of business contraction. Purchasing levels drop off slightly, inventories increase, plants stop hiring people, overtime is drastically reduced, and businesses curtail capital improvement plans. Business, though, continues to be good but not at the level of the preceding period.

4. *Shakeout.* When the order level drops below 100 and subsequent points on the chart continue to fall, the business cycle has reached its shakeout period. This phase is recognizable by plant layoffs, sales declines, inventory reductions, de-

creases in the prime rate, and a general sense of pessimism. Business plans are generally curtailed and unemployment levels begin climbing.

5. *Slump.* This is the roughest period of all; if business conditions are severe enough, a depression ensues. Plant layoffs continue, employment rates begin to alarm the politicians, capital improvement plans are virtually nonexistent, and inventories continue to climb to discouraging levels.

6. *Growth.* Usually three successive points of growth on the chart signal the faint beginnings of a period of economic growth and recovery. Plant layoffs stop and some companies begin to slowly rehire skilled employees. Purchasing agents see the first glimmer of hope through small increases in buying levels. Inventories begin to decline and business makes new capital improvement plans. The GNP begins to rise.

A normal business cycle lasts about four years with two-and-one-half years above the order level of 100, and about one-and-one half years below 100. Obviously, the duration of a business cycle is influenced by a great many variables such as whether the country is at war or peace, the strength of the dollar both at home and abroad, the type of product being manufactured, and literally dozens of other factors. The business cycle curve, therefore, must be individually interpreted by each company using its own product demand and in the context of its own situation.

USING THE BUSINESS CYCLE TO FACILITATE MANUFACTURING PLANNING

Manufacturing managers can use the business cycle curve described in Figure 9-3 to plan ahead. Listed below are typical actions which you can take during each of the six phases of the business cycle.

1. *Expansion.*

- Build or expand manufacturing facilities.
- Install new machine tools.
- Expand the labor force.
- Build inventory.
- Subcontract work.
- Write-off obsolete inventory losses.
- Develop new vendors.
- Start training programs.

2. *Maturity.*

- Sell surplus machinery.
- Maintain—but do not increase—inventories.
- Freeze all expansion plans.
- Freeze salaried hiring.

- Develop plans for business downturn.
- Plan to reduce subcontract work.
- Get machinery in top condition.
- Work overtime.

3. *Contraction.*

- Begin layoffs
- Start reducing inventories.
- Stop training programs.
- Reduce purchasing levels.
- Establish tight budgets.
- Avoid long-term purchasing contracts.
- Reduce fixed costs wherever possible.
- Begin cost reduction program.
- Stop all overtime.

4. *Shakeout.*

- Continue layoffs.
- Continue reducing inventories.
- Reduce purchasing levels further.
- Freeze capital improvement programs.
- Get tougher on customer returns.
- Reduce indirect labor activities.
- Reduce management deadwood.
- Combine functions.

5. *Slump.*

- Stop layoffs. Hold onto skilled people.
- Consider eliminating a shift.
- Set tighter budgets.
- Make new expansion plans.
- Begin purchasing capital equipment.
- Keep cost reduction programs moving.
- Locate better vendors.

6. *Growth.*

- Begin rehiring skilled employees.
- Build inventories.

- Move ahead with expansion plans.
- Place added purchasing orders.
- Prepare training programs.
- Hire new salaried employees.
- Introduce new products.

10

Shaving Purchasing Costs Twenty Percent or More

In most manufacturing companies the cost of purchased material represents the single largest category of total manufacturing costs (cost of sales). It is not uncommon to find purchased material costs running 50 percent to 70 percent of cost of sales. And it is in purchasing that a sizable amount of dollars can be saved to contribute to profitability.

Obviously, saving 10 percent of a very large quantity of dollars is preferable to saving 90 percent of a very small quantity of dollars. Assume, for example, that purchasing costs for a company are running at $10,000,000, labor at $1,000,000, and overhead at $2,000,000. It would take much greater savings in labor and overhead to equal a smaller effort with equal results in reducing purchased costs, as seen below:

COST CATEGORY	PERCENT SAVINGS	DOLLARS SAVED
Purchasing	20%	$2,000,000
Labor and Overhead	67%	$2,000,000

It would take a *combined* effort of labor and overhead at a *67 percent* rate to equal the 20 percent savings of the purchasing group. A 100 percent reduction of labor *alone* (if that were possible) would equal only half of the savings in purchased material.

151

A HANDY Q&A YOU CAN ADAPT TO ANALYZE YOUR PURCHASED MATERIALS BUDGET

A substantial manufacturing company in Ohio makes kitchen appliances such as dishwashers, garbage disposal units, and sinks. They follow a definite protocol when it comes to analyzing where savings are possible in purchased materials. A sample of this protocol follows. Notice that the questions asked follow a definite pattern aimed at uncovering potential cost savings. The answers are from the appliance company. The commentary following explains the significance of the question.

1. Question: What do purchased materials amount to in dollars and what portion do they constitute of cost of sales?

Answer
$38 million; 50 percent of cost of sales.

Commentary
Most manufacturing companies have purchasing material budgets amounting to about 50 percent of sales. Some manufacturing companies with extensive assembly operations and fewer preparatory (fabrication, machining, etc.) work have a much higher ratio, sometimes approaching 80 percent. In either case the amount of money consumed by purchasing is enormous; savings generated here can be substantial.

2. Question: What is the breakdown of purchased materials?

Answer

$14 million	Sheet metal and plate
10 million	Commercial components (pumps, valves, etc.)
6 million	Electrical (wires, controls, etc.)
5 million	Hardware (nuts, bolts, screws, fittings, etc.)
3 million	MRO (maintenance, repair, and operating supplies—materials
38 million	not used in the product)

Commentary
Obviously, the most fertile areas for cost savings investigation are the categories of sheet metal and plate and commercial components. Between them, they comprise almost 80 percent of purchased material dollars.

3. Question: Are standard costs higher or lower than actual purchase prices?

Answer:

CATEGORY	ACTUAL COSTS	STANDARD COSTS	VARIANCES
Sheet metal and plate	$14 million	$15 million	– $1 million
Commercial components	10 million	11 million	– 1 million
Electrical	6 million	7 million	– 1 million
Hardware	5 million	4 million	+ 1 million
MRO	3 million	3 million	0 million
Totals	$38 million	$40 million	– $2 million

Commentary

Standard costs are used to make the budget. When purchasing agents manage to beat those costs (through quantity discounts, price negotiations, etc.) they have effectively reduced costs by the amount of the savings generated. If, for example, a purchasing agent for the appliance manufacturer had negotiated a lower price for gas stove valves, a good deal of money could have been saved:

GAS VALVE STD. COST	GAS VALVE ACTUAL COST	SAVINGS PER VALVE	×	ANNUAL USAGE	=	TOTAL SAVINGS
1.80	1.40	.40		120,000		$48,000

4. Question: What percentage of purchased materials are from the same vendor? From other vendors?

Answer

32%	1 vendor
57%	2 vendors
6%	3 vendors
3%	4 vendors
2%	5 or more vendors
100%	

Commentary

A purchasing department that relies heavily on one source for a large proportion of its purchased materials is not in the most favorable position to negotiate reduced prices. When more than one vendor is supplying the same part, however, increasing the quantity of purchases from one vendor at the expense of another is a marvelous lever for price reduction. The company that gets more than 25 percent of its purchases from a single source is a company that has severely curtailed its ability to drive purchase prices downward.

5. Question: Are new purchases based on the competitive bidding of at least three vendors?

Answer

All purchases in excess of $10,000 annual cost are determined by the lowest of at least three bidders.

Commentary

More price concessions than most people realize can be achieved through competitive bidding. When one vendor charging $2.00 per part is aware that another vendor charging $1.75 per part is about to be awarded a purchase contract, it is amazing how quickly the price can drop to $1.60. Such is the power of competitive bidding.

6. Question: What is the ratio of purchased material prices to sales and what is its relationship to labor and overhead costs? What annual increases or decreases are taking place?

Answer

	1988	1989	1990	1991
$\dfrac{\text{Purchased Prices}}{\text{Sales}} \times 100$	45%	41%	42%	38%
$\dfrac{\text{Labor and Overhead}}{\text{Sales}} \times 100$	3%	3%	3%	3%

Purchased prices as a percent or sales decreased 15.6 percent from 1988 to 1991

$$\left[\frac{45\% - 38\%}{45\%} \times 100 \right]$$

Labor and overhead, for the same period remained constant, at 3 percent.

Commentary

The improving ratio of purchase prices to sales shows that the purchasing management is really doing a job. In these days of constant inflationary expectations, just holding the line requires exceptional management. The fact that purchase prices are consuming a smaller portion of the sales dollar indicates an effective purchasing function, particularly in a period when labor and overhead costs shows no improvement.

A 15.6 percent reduction represents a savings of *$5,928,000* based on 1991's $38 million purchase costs.

7. *Question:* What is the correlation between rush delivery purchases and high purchase prices?

Answer

A study by purchasing analysts revealed information shown in Figure 10-1. The sharply increasing curve shows that when a vendor supplies 40 percent of its

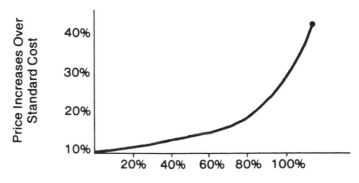

Figure 10-1   Percent of Rush Order Business Per Vendor

parts with rush deliveries, the cost to the appliance company increases by 10 percent. When the vendor must supply 80 percent of its orders well before contracted delivery dates it then costs the appliance company 20 percent more, with sharp increases thereafter to 40 percent when *all* of the parts need to be delivered ahead of schedule.

Commentary

Needless to say, rush deliveries are expensive. A company caught in that trap cannot possibly reduce net purchasing costs. Any reductions obtained through shrewd negotiations or through quantity discounts are soon wired out because of rush orders.

8. Question: What percentage of orders are made outside of the normal purchase requisition procedure?

Answer

The appliance company's records indicate that less than 5 percent of all purchase orders are made outside of established procedures. These are almost always the result of (1) call-in rush orders, (2) prototype materials requested by product engineering people, and (3) specialized machine tools ordered by manufacturing engineers.

Commentary

Purchases made by employees other than purchasing agents is a fertile area for cost savings. Almost invariably, these other people are engineers who do not have the necessary expertise to obtain low prices. Neither do they normally competitively price the parts they purchase. Funneling most of these requests through purchasing almost always results in lowered purchase prices.

9. Question: What percentage of vendor material is unusable?

Answer

The records of the appliance company are as follows:

	1991 RESULTS
Percent Rejected Receiving Inspection	4.7%
Percent Rejected Dollar Value	$1,786,000
Disposition of Rejections	
Return to Vendor	$1,000,000
Scrap	20,000
Rework	466,000
Use-As-Is	250,000
Total	$1,786,000

Commentary

The result of 4.7 percent is really not an unexpected or poor performance. The important point is that vendor rejections be classified and quantified continually. Most rejected material should be returned to the appropriate vendors so that all of the expense of sorting and repairing is borne by them. There are many times, however, when that cannot be done, particularly when the parts are needed to support production. In those cases the vendor should be charged with all of the costs associated with the scrapping, sorting, and reworking operations.

Note: "Use as is" refers to material which is very close to, but does not quite meet, the specifications. A judgment has been rendered by Quality Control to use the material "as is." Most often this occurs in esthetic rejections where a finish or color is slightly off standard.

10. Question: What percentage of purchased materials has cash discounts?

Answer

	1988	1989	1990	1991
Percent Orders with Discounts	12%	15%	22%	41%

Commentary

Cash discounts for quantity purchases or for early payment often amounts to considerable cost savings. Purchasing management should always be aware of this ratio and make plans to improve it.

11. Question: What percentage of purchased materials arrives ahead of scheduled delivery dates?

Answer

The appliance company has managed to hold this number down to 3 percent.

Commentary

Invariably, earlier arrivals of purchased materials equates to earlier payments to vendors. When that happens, two cost penalties are incurred. First, inventory swells, and since the cost of carrying inventory today approaches 40 percent of purchased value, this cost can not only be prohibitive, it can also be disastrous if allowed to occur frequently. Second, payments made earlier decrease cash flow which, if invested in short-term notes at high interest rates, generate a lot of cash for the company. That return is lost when dollars are used instead to pay for inventories not needed until sometime in the future.

12. Question: Does the company have a "make-buy" procedure?

Answer

Yes. The "make-buy" decision is routinely made on all new purchases by both industrial engineering and purchasing employees.

Commentary

Many times it is cheaper to manufacture parts in-house then it is to buy them from vendors. The relative costs can readily be ascertained by industrial engineers and purchasing people. In this case the savings can be quite large, although oftentimes the purchase of expensive capital equipment is first necessary.

REDUCING PURCHASING COSTS WITH THE VARIANCE CURVE

How well the purchasing department and its individual buyers do is best expressed through examination of the variance curve.

The variance curve is a reflection of actual purchase costs as contrasted to standard costs. Standard costs are established sometime before the start of the calendar year by buyers for individual parts and vendors. These standard costs are then used to forecast the purchasing budget for the forthcoming fiscal year. Because the approximate increase in the level of purchase prices for the next year is generally known ahead of time, buyers can roughly determine their course throughout the year. If, for example, a buyer plans the pricing level of needle valves during the year, he might see this trend:

	JAN-JUNE	JULY-DEC
Cost Per Valve	$0.65	$0.73

These numbers indicate that, while the average or standard cost for the next year will be $0.69 $\left(\dfrac{0.65 + 0.73}{2}\right)$ the second part of the year will have a higher rate than the first part of the year.

A typical variance curve used by a chemical company for commodity purchases of acids is seen in Figure 10-2. The vertical side of the graph plots unit costs while the horizontal side plots time. Average standard cost forecasted for acids is shown by the horizontal line midway on the graph. The curved line plots projected standard costs during the year. Notice that during the first six months of the year this curve (the variance curve) shows favorable purchase variances to standard cost while the last six months of the year shows unfavorable variances. If all twelve

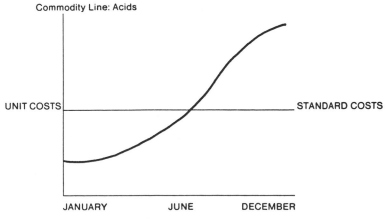

Figure 10-2   The XYZ Chemical Company Purchasing Variance Projections

months of the variance curve were averaged, the result would be equal to the standard costs for acids. So it is now easy to measure what the purchasing agent must do to meet and better standard costs for acid purchases. A monthly follow-up detailing actual purchased costs can be made to track performance.

Using Variance Curves to Assess Buyer and Vendor Performance

Variance curves can be successfully used to plot not only commodity purchases, but also buyer and vendor performance.

Figure 10-3 is an illustration of a variance report used by a fastener company to control both commodity and buyer performance. The columns are explained as follows:

- *FORECAST AT STANDARD COST.* This is the forecasted annual usage multiplied by forecasted standard costs, in this case screw machine rod and bar.
- *VARIANCE FORECAST.* These numbers are the monthly variance curve projections.
- *PLUS OR MINUS.* This is the difference between the forecast at standard cost and the variance forecast. It zeros out in December.
- *ACTUAL USAGE.* The actual purchase price multiplied by quantities bought are shown here.
- *PLUS OR MINUS.* This is the difference between the variance forecast and actual usage. The difference represents either savings or losses to the established variance curve.
- *PLUS OR MINUS CUM.* This number shows the cumulative effect of savings to the variance curve. In this case a savings of $3,000 was made for the entire year by the buyer for screw machine rod and bar.

COMMODITY: Screw Machine Rod and Bar   BUYER: P. Swanson

	J	F	M	A	M	J	J	A	S	O	N	D
Forecast at Standard Cost	5	5	5	5	5	5	5	5	5	5	5	5
Variance Forecast	4	4	4	4	4	4	6	6	6	6	6	6
Plus or Minus	−1	−1	−1	−1	−1	−1	+1	+1	+1	+1	+1	+1
Actual Usage	3	4	4	5	3	3	5	6	6	6	6	6
Plus or Minus	−1	0	0	+1	−1	−1	−1	0	0	0	0	0
Plus or Minus Cum		−1	−1	0	−1	−2	−3	−3	−3	−3	−3	−3

Figure 10-3   Fastener Company Variance Curve Report ($000)

FIVE NEGOTIATING TECHNIQUES THAT SAVE DOLLARS

Negotiation in purchasing is quite obviously of paramount importance. There are but few cases where clever negotiating tactics by purchasing agents will not result in lower unit costs.

A hardware manufacturer in the New York City area used these negotiating tactics to reduce purchased material costs almost 15 percent:

1. *Deal with Commission Salespeople Whenever Possible.* Sales representatives who earn all or a large part of their money on commission are more likely to press their company for price concessions to make a sale. They are hungrier than a sales rep on straight salary who doesn't have the same motivation.

2. *When Price Breaks Are Hard to Get, Deal with the Sales Manager.* If the regular sales rep has taken a firm stand and refuses to make any concessions, sometimes a talk with the sales manager will prove rewarding. Sales managers can make themselves look good back at the home office by walking away with orders their sales reps have had a hard time getting. Occasionally, they have the authority to issue price concessions on the spot while their sales reps don't have that same authority.

3. *Use Competitive Bidding and Make Other Buyers Aware of the Low Price.* This often acts as a stimulus to further cuts by salespeople anxious to close the order. Many times what started out as the low bid suddenly becomes the high bid when several sales reps attempt to beat the competition.

4. *Establish Payment Terms as Far in the Future as Possible.* Since the longer a company can hold on to its dollars the more short-term interest it will make, it pays to stretch out payments. Many companies, anxious to make sales, will allow sixty days, ninety days, or even longer. This is money in the company's pocket.

5. *Go for Quantity Discounts, Regardless of Quantities Purchased.* Again, companies wanting to deal, to sell their products, may allow the purchaser quantity discounts. Some will offer this in lieu of price concessions on the product. Either way, it's still a savings for the buying company.

11

How to Use MRP to Increase Productivity and Shrink Material Costs

One of the most powerful tools available to manufacturing managers today is Material Requirements Planning (MRP). MRP determines the plant's requirements for all of its inventory, from raw materials to the finished product; it does so by dates while specifying quantities. A schedule is produced that describes what all of those requirements are for a year or more.

MRP then considers inventory on-hand, outstanding purchase orders, and plots these against requirements to determine when additional quantities will be needed. It indicates when new orders should be placed and uncovers the need for rescheduling existing orders when schedules are changed.

MRP in manufacturing allows production planners the opportunity to eliminate inactive and surplus inventories, heavy work-center backlogs, excess capacity, and overreliance on expediters to move orders through the factory.

HOW THE MRP SYSTEM WORKS

The MRP system flow begins with the initiation of a production plan and ends with the execution of shop floor control as seen in Figure 11-1. The system is explained through the use of MRP by an elevator cab manufacturer in the East.

Step 1: Develop a Sales Plan

On a monthly basis the sales department of the elevator cab manufacturer specifies anticipated orders for the following twelve months; each month these orders are updated, the exception being that sales forecasts for the following three months are frozen because that represents the period of lead time for committed purchase orders. This document is called the "Sales Plan."

Step 2: Create a Production Plan

The production plan describes the production rate for the basic elevator cab product mix expressed in numbers of units of each of the different types of cabs to be manufactured over the period shown by the sales plan.

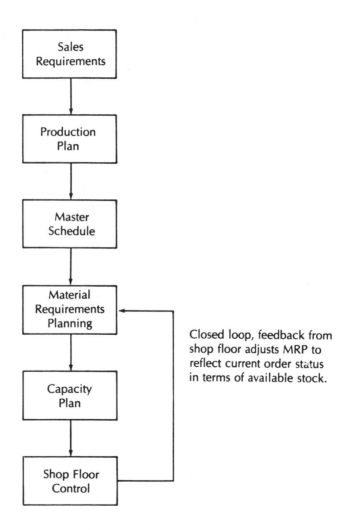

Closed loop, feedback from shop floor adjusts MRP to reflect current order status in terms of available stock.

Figure 11-1 MRP System Flow

A simplified version of the elevator cab company's production plan is shown here:

PRODUCTION PLAN ($000)			
MODEL: STANDARD CABS		DATE: 4/2/X2	
MONTH ENDING	PRODUCTION	SALES	ENDING INVENTORY
1/X2 — PLAN / ACTUAL	20 / 20	20 / 20	100 / 100
2/X2	25 / 25	20 / 15	105 / 110
3/X2	25 / 25	20 / 20	110 / 115
4/X2	30 / 30	20 / 25	120 / 120
5/X2	30	25	125
6/X2	30	40	115
7/X2	35	45	105
8/X2	35	50	90
9/X2	30	45	75
10/X2	30	45	60
11/X2	25	30	55
12/X2	20	20	55

The top of the diagonal line reveals planned quantities while the bottom of the diagonal line reveals actual quantities. Notice that at the conclusion of the fourth month, the actual ending inventory was equivalent to planned ending inventory, which shows the company's production plan is right on stream. Both sales and production are where they should be at the end of the first four months, although sales figures for individual months varied slightly.

Notice also that this particular production plan is for standard elevator cabs, just one model. In actual practice, a separate plan will be made for each model and revised monthly.

Step 3: Develop a Master Schedule

Once the production plan has been determined it is then necessary to forecast the demand for parts at each level of the manufacturing operation. This part level is based on the bill of material for the product. A bill for a standard elevator cab is shown in Figure 11-2. This bill of material lists all of the component parts, whether purchased or manufactured, for the standard model of elevator cabs. This bill forms the basis for the master schedule.

Figure 11-2 is referred to as an "indented bill of material." This means that the highest level assemblies are shown on the left while the next level of parts, which comprise the assemblies, are indented and shown to the right. The cab panel, for example, constitutes the highest level of assembly on the bill, and the handrails,

BILL OF MATERIAL
STANDARD ELEVATOR CAB

PART DESCRIPTION	QUANTITY	PART NUMBER
DOME	1	900600
Diffuser	3	900251
Fan	1	900347
Blower	1	900610
Fixtures	6	850135
Grilles	4	900380
Headers	4	850173
Safety Door	1	850102
Plate Brackets	12	900695
Door Opener	1	850176
CAB PANEL	1	960600
Handrails	3	900651
Frame	6	960322
Pad Buttons	24	960494
Posts	4	960491
Telephone Box	1	850333

Figure 11-2 BILL OF MATERIAL

frame, pad buttons, posts, and telephone box constitute the next level—the component parts that make up the assembly.

In actual practice there are as many as a dozen indented levels (or more) depending on the complexity of the assembly. This example has been simplified to describe the principle involved.

The quantities shown on the bill are those needed to assemble one standard elevator cab.

With accurate, well-documented bills of material in place the master schedule is ready to be prepared. At the elevator cab company the master schedule is prepared from data obtained in the production plan. It states the specific product mix for the forecasted production period.

The master schedule takes the production plan (what we are going to manufacture), explodes this through the bills of material (what it takes to manufacture this product), and compares those quantities with the inventory on-hand (what we have) to determine material requirements (what we need). A master schedule for the elevator cab company is seen, as follows:

PT# 900347 DOME FAN	ELEVATOR CAB COMPANY MASTER SCHEDULE					4/30/X2
	6/X2	7/X2	8/X2	9/X2	10/X2	11/X2
MASTER SCHEDULE REQUIREMENTS	30	35	35	30	30	25
ACTUAL DEMAND	20	25	25	30	35	30
AVAILABLE	10	20	30	30	25	20

The master schedule matches requirements to actual demand; the computer automatically subtracts demand from requirements to determine available parts inventory.

The schedule is generally updated every week and forms the link between the production plan and the MRP, which we will now investigate.

Step 4: Make an MRP Run

The MRP run shown in Figure 11-3 is for a purchased component of the standard elevator cab dome fan. The lead time for purchase of the brass bushings is three months and the order quantity (probably determined by an EOQ (economic order quantities) calculation—see Chapter Fourteen) is 100. The master schedule requirements are the same as for the dome fan, as seen previously, since one brass bushing is required for every dome fan. Scheduled receipts are every three months since that represents purchase lead time. When scheduled receipts are subtracted from master schedule requirements the results reflect the balance of brass bushings available for future requirements.

With MRP, users can get on-hand inventory by product group in both parts and dollars; they can see the number of dollars required to support the production. Inventory balances can be predicted by product line for months ahead; it is easy then to summarize what must be manufactured, purchased, and assembled to support the production plan. Comparisons of plan to actual are easily calculated.

ELEVATOR CAB COMPANY

MATERIAL REQUIREMENTS PLAN

DOME FAN BRASS BUSHINGS
PT# 900347-6

LEAD TIME = 3 MONTHS   ORDER QUANTITY = 100

	ON HAND	6/X2	7/X2	8/X2	9/X2	10/X2	11/X2
MASTER SCHEDULE REQUIREMENTS		30	35	35	30	30	25
SCHEDULED RECEIPTS			100			100	
BALANCE AVAILABLE	60	30	95	60	30	100	75

Figure 11-3   Material Requirements Plan

The entire effect from production plan through master scheduling and into MRP can be visually demonstrated by the following pyramid:

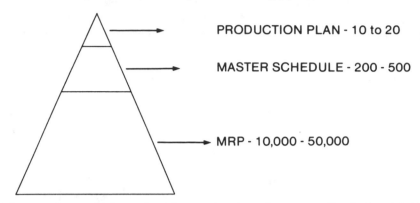

PRODUCTION PLAN - 10 to 20

MASTER SCHEDULE - 200 - 500

MRP - 10,000 - 50,000

The numbers tell the story. The production plan generally deals with 10 to 20 products; the master schedule explodes those products into 200-500 models, and the MRP further explodes the models into 10,000-50,000 individual part numbers.

Step 5: Create a Capacity Plan

When the MRP run has been made it is necessary to determine operational capacity needed to process orders through manufacturing in time to meet scheduled commitments to customers. This is accomplished by converting work orders into standard hours, as explained in Method 1, Chapter Four. Standard hours, once calculated, are compared to planned hours by work center and time periods to satisfy master schedule requirements as seen here:

ELEVATOR CAB COMPANY
SHOP CAPACITY REPORT
DEPT: FINAL ASSEMBLY
WEEK: 6/14/X2

CUSTOMER	STANDARD HOURS		
ORDER NO.	AVAILABLE	PLANNED	+/−
16040	320	330	− 10
16045	320	275	+ 45
16120	320	330	− 10
16162	320	280	+ 40
			+ 75

The final assembly area, then, has additional capacity of 75 standard labor-hours for the week of 6/14/X2, enough to handle all of the scheduled customer orders.

Capacity plans are made for all manufacturing departments every week.

Step 6: Implement Shop Floor Control

Shop floor control refers to that activity which executes and controls the implementation of MRP on the shop floor. It is an extension of the shop capacity report just described.

Shop floor control uses labor reporting techniques to determine the status of orders. This technique—labor reporting—is discussed extensively in Chapter Seventeen.

In essence, shop floor control, through its labor reporting arm, indicates the completion of orders through the manufacturing process. The critical ratio method, described in Chapter Fourteen, is a way to track and prioritize orders in manufacturing.

Shop floor control follows three basic steps:

1. Issue shop capacity reports that match planned vs. available standard labor-hours for specific customer (or job) orders.
2. Use labor reporting techniques to track the progress of individual orders.
3. Use the critical ratio method to prioritize all orders on the manufacturing floor.

GETTING THE RIGHT MRP SOFTWARE FOR YOUR COMPANY

Generally, when most companies install MRP, the computer (hardware) is in place and software selection becomes the issue at hand. Since software for MRP represents the type of programs available to govern the MRP system, its proper selection is paramount; it can, and many times does, spell the difference between success and failure of the MRP installation.

There are normally two options available to the software purchaser: (1) buy ready-made software from either computer manufacturers or independent software companies, or (2) develop your own with in-house specialists. Most companies opt to buy, from the viewpoint of many users and MRP professionals, buying from the computer manufacturer has the edge. The computer manufacturer will generally be around for a long time, while the independent may go out of business. It's essentially a matter of resources.

A NINE-POINT BLUEPRINT FOR IMPLEMENTING MRP

The following section illustrates the steps needed to install an MRP program in manufacturing. It is a framework of structural events necessary to apply the basic mechanics of the system. Although not comprehensive (it would take an entire book to do that job satisfactorily) the essential ingredients of a successful program are described. The serious user will use this section to gain some insight into MRP, and will then go ahead with further research.

1. Make Sure That Bills of Material Meet Accuracy Requirements

Whoever structures bills of material for the company[1] must assure themselves of minimum accuracy levels of 98 percent. Since the purchase and manufacture of parts is based on bill of material (B.O.M.) accuracy, any accuracy level below 98 percent could easily result in either missed deliveries or excess inventories.

1. Measure 50 to 100 bills at random for accuracy. This sample will indicate the degree of accuracy of the total population of bills of material, and it will permit the user to access the extent (and type) of problems encountered.
2. Verify all bills where problems are apparent on a line-by-line basis, correcting both part number and quantity errors.
3. Assure that bills of material are structured to reflect the actual flow of work in the manufacturing process.
4. Assign *one* group the responsibility for handling bills of material. In manufacturing this group is either industrial engineering or manufacturing planning.

2. Take Steps To Establish Inventory Accuracy

1. Measure 100 to 200 parts at random in the warehouse to determine accuracy of (a) quantity, (b) part number, and (c) location. If the accuracy level is below 95 percent, then corrective action must follow.
2. Assure that the warehouse has limited access to (essentially) warehouse workers and supervisors. If necessary, fence in the warehouse. This will prevent unauthorized removal of parts into production which generates inventory accuracy problems.
3. Provide for adequate paper transactions that reflect, on a timely basis, the movement of parts into and out of the warehouse.
4. Begin a daily count of parts in the warehouse to verify (and correct problems found with) inventory accuracy. This is called "cycle counting." As a general rule, all "A" items can be included in the count four times per year, "B" items twice per year, and "C" items once annually.

3. Develop a Master Scheduling System and Methods of Handling Changes

1. Develop a master scheduling system, decide on report formats, and implement procedures to start the master schedule.

---

[1]   Bills written by product engineers are usually restructured to represent the sequential processing of production operations. This task is generally performed by industrial engineers.

2. Develop methods of handling changes to the master schedule, including:

- who can implement a change
- criteria for allowing changes
- approval process

4. Establish an Ordering Policy

1. Check all parts ordered for correct lead times; investigate lead times to assure that they are neither inflated nor short.
2. Establish safety stock policies.
3. Establish order quantities based on economic lot sizing *and* good judgment.

5. Select Software

(Refer to previous section of this chapter.)

6. Install Support

1. Establish systems to support all of the critical phases of the MRP program just described.
2. Train users and materials people (probably the most neglected get the most critical phase of the entire MRP implementation process).
3. Write (or buy) programs to support systems requirements.

7. *Establish capacity planning* module.

8. *Implement shop floor control* procedures.

9. *Develop control reports* to monitor the system and report on:

- size of inventories
- delivery performance
- B.O.M. accuracy
- inventory accuracy
- parts shortages

12

Scheduling for On-Time Delivery at the Lowest Possible Cost

If forecasting is the first essential step of effective production planning and control, then scheduling—the drafting of the production plan—is the second essential step. Scheduling takes the information from the forecast and changes it to specific planning for shop operations.

The objective of scheduling is to plan factory operations to meet customer delivery dates and to do so with commitment of a minimum of inventory at the lowest possible operating costs. Poor scheduling results in either low inventory and missed customer delivery promises or high inventory and high operating costs. An effective scheduling system falls somewhere between those two conditions and optimizes resources.

FIVE FEATURES CRITICAL TO A GOOD SCHEDULING SYSTEM

A comprehensive scheduling system has these factors in common:

1. Anybody can understand it and work with it. Its simplicity is proved through its usage.
2. It establishes obtainable goals. Those goals are neither too loose nor too tight.

The schedule provides time to respond to the unexpected—a common and anticipated problem in *all* manufacturing operations.

3. It provides reliable information to users. Manufacturing people can depend on its accuracy and use the information to make decisions regarding changes in the schedule in response to problems as they arise.

4. Deviations to the schedule are highlighted in time for responsible supervisors to make needed changes. Since deviations are the prime reasons for failure to achieve schedules, they must come to the immediate attention of supervisors as soon as they occur. Time is always critical.

5. It must be flexible enough to allow for changes to be made without disrupting the schedule itself.

THE KEY ELEMENTS OF SCHEDULING

All scheduling systems have certain elements in common. Whether the production planning system is done manually or by computer makes no difference; all scheduling systems must consist of the following:

• The machines and other work centers to be scheduled.

• The routing of parts through manufacturing.

• The length of time it takes to manufacture and assemble the product (lead time).

Let's examine each of these in more detail.

How Machines and Work Are Scheduled

For each individual machine or assembly operation, a schedule must be developed for every different part they handle which identifies:

• Machine number.

• Part number of product being manufactured.

• Standard hours to produce the part.

The Houston plant (discussed in Chapter Nine), for example, has a master schedule of its two heat treat furnaces which shows the following information:

		PART NUMBERS		
	WEEKLY	**500 PCS**	**270 PCS**	**160 PCS**
	AVAILABLE			
MACHINE NUMBER	CAPACITY	**PMD 1-263**	**264-495**	**496-1007**
H.T.-1	72 hours	1.0 hours	1.8 hours	2.2 hours
H.T.-2	70 hours	1.1 hours	1.9 hours	2.4 hours

The first heat treat furnace, H.T.-1, operating two shifts, five days per week, is available for a weekly load of 72 hours while the other heat treat furnace, H.T.-2, has shown an historical availability of 70 hours per week. Under "Part Numbers," the number of pieces and heat treat times are listed by part number groups. Above those numbers is the maximum quality which can be heat-treated at one time. If, for example, Houston schedules 250 pieces of part number PJMD-6 and 250 pieces of PMD-204 to be heat treated, they will be loaded into the furnace together and will take 1.0 hours to process in H.T.-1 or 1.1 hours in H.T.-2.

Using this chart, the scheduler can then fully load the heat treat furnaces to the extent of their available capacity.

In similar fashion, the master scheduling system keeps cards (or computer files) for each part number and operation in the plant.

How Parts Are Routed Through Manufacturing

While the master schedule identifies work to be done at individual machines, routings describe the flow of parts through the shop. A routing is in essence, the road map of the parts being manufactured in the plant. A routing will describe the operation to be performed, the machines and assembly lines where they will be performed, and the standard hours needed to complete the schedule at individual work stations.

A typical routing for manufacture of a 3.5" line coupling is shown in Figure 12-1, Houston's routing for that part.

The top of the routing describes order data: part name and number, customer, quantity, and delivery date.

The bottom of the routing shows department, operation number (the cost

---

ROUTING TICKET   Houston

Part: 3.5" Line Coupling   *Part Number:* PMD—37
Lot Number: 2066   *Customer:* Richards Supply, Galveston
Quantity: 2500   *Delivery Date:* 4/18/92

DEPARTMENT	OPERATION	OPERATION NUMBER	STD.HOURS PER PIECE	TOTAL STD. HOURS	COMMENTS
Stocking	Stock	106	—	.2	
Saws	Cut to size	219	.05	125.0	
Boring mills	Taper bore	305	.03	75.0	
Chuckers	Chamfer and tap	412	.01	25.0	
Heat treat −1	Temper	533	1.00	5.0	500 pcs.
Assembly	Assemble caps	640	1.00	10.0	250 pcs.
Pack	Carton parts	718	3.00	7.5	1000 pcs.

SPECIAL INSTRUCTIONS: USE MASTER CARTONS WITH TYPE # 3 CORRU-
GATED SEPARATORS. SHIP ON TRUCK # 2 DESTI-
NATION GALVESTON.

Figure 12-1   Houston Plant: Routing Ticket

center of the operation), the operation to be performed, standard hours per piece, total standard hours, and comments. Set-up times are factored into the standards.

For the operations heat treat, and pack, the comments display 500, 250, and 100 pieces respectively. Those numbers are related to the standard hours/piece, heat treat, for example, shows 1.0 standard hours needed to process 500 pieces. For 2500 pieces the total is five standard hours:

$$\left(\frac{2500 \text{ pieces}}{500 \text{ pieces/hour}} \right)$$

How Lead Times Are Established

This is not simply a matter of adding standard hours from routings to determine how long it takes parts to travel through the plant.

Lead times must include *all* time spent in the plant, and not only time spent in operations. Normally, the disparity is amazing. Time spent during machining or assembly is termed "In-Process Time" as contrasted to time spent waiting (for any number of reasons) which is called "Total Process Time."

Houston decided to identify total process time vs. in-process time to establish realistic lead times for meeting customer commitments. That was done by flagging a group of orders going through the plant. Times of arrival and departure for each order were recorded on a work ticket for each operation. Since standard hours had been determined for each part and operation, Houston management already knew in-process time. Using the work tickets, they were then fortified with total process time.

A chart was drawn (Figure 12-2) illustrating the relationship. The sequence of operations is listed on the left side of the chart. The next columns describe in-process time, total process time, and idle time.

From this a formula can be expressed:

Total Process Time = In-Process Time + Idle Time

From Figure 12-2 the small number of in-process hours—247.7—is in sharp contrast with idle time of 493.4 hours. This is not unusual. In fact, in many operations, idle time constitutes up to 90 percent of total process time compared with 67 percent seen in Figure 12-2 (493.4 hours ÷ 741.1 hours).

Lead time, then, is comprised of several elements. These follow:

* Operation time (machining, assembly, etc.)
* Setup time
* Queue time (waiting to be worked)
* Delay time (machine problems, etc.)
* Wait time (finished operation, waiting to be moved to next operation.)
* Transit time

Determination of lead times must take all of the elements described above into account to be realistic.

	TOTAL PROCESS TIME vs. IN-PROCESS TIME		
Product: 3.5" line cplg.	Quantity: 2500	Lot Number: 2066	
	HOURS		
OPERATION	**IN-PROCESS TIME**	**TOTAL PROCESS TIME**	**IDLE TIME**
Stock	.2	26.4	26.2
Saw	125.0	175.5	50.5
Bore	75.0	128.6	53.6
Chuck	25.0	78.8	53.8
Heat-treat	5.0	143.2	138.2
Assemble	10.0	63.5	53.5
Pack	7.5	125.1	117.6
Total	247.7	741.1	493.4

Figure 12-2 Houston Plant: Lead Time Analysis

HOW TO CUT PROCESS TIME BY REVERSE LOADING

Most production planning systems load the plants from front to rear. Loading is accomplished by scheduling each subsequent plant operation. Inevitably, this practice swells total process time.

Reverse loading reduced total process time. This happens through scheduling the last operation first, and then loading all prior operations in reverse sequence. Let's observe reverse loading at work.

Case Study: How to Cut Three Shifts Out of Process Time

At one time Houston scheduled all of its operations from front to back. A typical operation was production of ½" standard couplings. Total process time for 1000 of these couplings averaged eight shifts. They could be sized and shaped on screw machines in one shift, and finished on chuckers in four shifts. Chamfering and tapping would average two shifts. The final steps, plating and packing were accomplished in one shift. Several thousand couplings jammed the manufacturing process during the eight-shift span, and delivery dates were constantly missed.

Houston management found two major problems upon analyzing the production planning and control system. First, all orders were loaded from beginning operations, and second, all orders were processed in discrete lots. Before a lot could move from one operation to another, every piece of that particular order had to first be completed. This factor alone created large gaps in the work flow. Large lots would take days to process, and subsequent departments would not start work on them until every last piece was completed in the prior operation. Because of this labor practice, labor efficiencies suffered and missed customer delivery dates were the order of the day. The 1000 pieces of 1/2" standard couplings moved through manufacturing like this:

PIECES PROCESSED	OPERATION	TIME TO PROCESS
1000	Screw machines	8 Hours Monday
1000	Chuckers	32 Hours Tuesday–Friday
1000	Chamfers and taps	16 Hours Monday–Tuesday
1000	Plating line	2 Hours Wednesday
1000	Packing	6 Hours Wednesday

Reverse loading was established to reduce the total process time, and lot tickets were printed to allow movement of partial orders between departments. The two changes reduced total process time (lead time) from eight to five shifts:

PIECES PROCESSED	OPERATION	TIME TO PROCESS
1000	Screw machines	Monday
1000	Chuckers	Monday–Thursday
1000	Chamfers and taps	Tuesday–Thursday
1000	Plating line	Friday
1000	Packing	Friday

THE PRODUCTION PLAN: SCHEDULING PARTS WITHIN A DEPARTMENT

The scheduling activities described thus far have been directed at movements between departments and throughout the entire plant as a whole. When scheduling within a given department, however, another tool needs to be developed to schedule parts on the many machines each department has. That tool is called the "Production Plan."

Figure 12-3 is the production plan for Houston's Grinding Department. The left side of the plan shows work scheduled to be run in the Grinding Department the week of April 14, 1992. It details lot number, product tooling number for that order, quantity ordered, and pieces per hour required by established work standards for the lot's product.

The right side of the plan lists all twelve grinding machines available for use as well as the available hours for each machine during the week. Available capacity for the grinders on a two-shift basis has been calculated to be 60 hours.

Underneath each machine, scheduled hours are listed based on the particular lot to be run. The first lot, 2135, calls for a run of 4000 pieces; at a standard of 100 pieces per hour there are 40 hours needed to complete the lot (4000 pieces ÷ 100

HOUSTON PLANT PRODUCTION PLAN			GRINDING MACHINES						WK. ENDING 4/14/92					

MACHINE HOURS AVAILABLE (TWO SHIFTS)

					60	60	60	60	60	60	60	60	60	60	60	60	TOTAL DEPT.
LOT NO.	PRODUCT	TOOLING NO.	QUANTITY	PIECES PER HOUR	1	2	3	4	5	6	7	8	9	10	11	12	
2135	6" Studs	A143Z	4000	100	40												40
2243	1" Cplgs.	A443T	30000	300	20	60	20										100
2692	½" Plugs	A672V	100000	400			40	60	60	60	30						250
2204	5" Liners	A152R	25000	125							30	60	60	50			200
2725	8" Studs	A142N	4000	80										10	40		50
																Open	0
TOTAL SCHEDULED LABOR-HOURS:					60	60	60	60	60	60	60	60	60	60	40	0	640

Figure 12-3 Houston Plant: Production Plan

pieces per hour). Scheduled hours for each lot are calculated in the same manner, and each grinder is then loaded to its capacity of 60 hours.

When scheduled loads exceed individual machine capacity, additional machines are added. Lot 2243, for example, needs 100 hours to run the needed 30,000 pieces (30,000 pieces + 300 pieces per hour). Since grinder #1 has only 40 of its available 60 hours scheduled, 20 hours of lot 2243 are added to grinder #1, then 60 hours to grinder #2, and the residue, 20 hours, to grinder #3.

The far right-hand column contains total scheduled machine hours (in this case machine-hours are equivalent to labor-hours) by lot number and for the entire department.

The production plan is projected weekly for the following week. Normally it is made on Wednesday or Thursday. By scheduling work ahead of time, management is in control of its own fate; any problems anticipated during preparation of the schedule can be handled before the schedule is implemented. This saves time and keeps costs down.

Six More Advantages

The production plan offers additional advantages:

1. Departmental workloads and individual machine workloads are readily observable.
2. Scheduled machine hours are planned ahead and are clearly depicted.
3. Scheduled machine hours are measured against capacity.
4. Work standards are listed for use by manufacturing foremen.
5. The production plan can be stepped-down daily schedule segments for control by foremen.
6. Machine overloads as well as underutilized machines are made apparent so the schedule can be altered accordingly.

13

How to Use Priority Control to Ensure On-Time Product Delivery

One of the most difficult and complex tasks for a production planning function is to assure that orders on the plant floor are being worked on in priority of shipment for customers. This is not as straightforward a job as it may appear to be. Orders are in a constant state of flux: customer due dates change and manufacturing problems arise constantly. When a plant has several hundreds or thousands of orders, as is normally the case, the necessary job of deciding which jobs must be processed first in all of the diverse manufacturing departments can be extremely difficult.

Priority control is an organized approach to resolving this problem. It assigns priorities to each and every batch or lot of work in the plant, thereby giving supervisors a way to schedule their operations in accordance with customer due dates.

Plants that do not use priority control are inviting the loss of customer orders, an increase in overtime (or the need to hire extra workers) to rush through production jobs that have been sitting in inventory unnecessarily while other, less pressing orders have been processed.

Priority control ensures that due dates are met and that operating costs are minimized; other factors remaining constant.

A textile machinery manufacturer in Rhode Island used this technique to improve fulfilling delivery promises from a terrible 76 percent to a more respectful 93 percent and, in the process, reduced its labor costs some $200,000 annually.

Forecasting and scheduling are the first two essential components of production planning and control. The third component is control—control to assure the schedule is being met, that inventories are adequate through manufacturing, that operators are achieving at standard production rates, that subassemblies are ready at the right time to achieve final assembly schedules, and that parts are being purchased in accordance with the production plan.

HOW PRIORITY CONTROL WORKS

One of the better control instruments at the command of production planning and control people is called "priority control." Priority control is a procedure which helps decide the status of orders in manufacturing and indicates which orders should be worked first. It establishes work priorities and helps production planning people decide which orders to review for rescheduling or even cancellation.

Priority control can be used with either manual or computerized scheduling systems, but it is easier and less expensive to use in computerized form. Often it is associated with MRP programs. Under MRP, forecasted and firm requirements for purchased parts, raw materials, and manufactured parts are scheduled by month into the future (usually twelve months). Orders for both purchased and manufactured parts are then prepared based on dates needed as determined from the MRP program. (See Chapter Eleven for a detailed discussion of MRP). At this stage the priority control program takes over. It adjusts schedules, production plans, and purchase order deliveries for changes in the requirements of purchased parts, raw materials or manufactured parts.

Requirements are constantly changing. This is a characteristic all production planning and control people must face. Customers cancel or modify orders all the time. This continual shuffling of order changes the requirements. Some parts may need to be advanced in the schedule while other parts must be canceled. To keep inventories current, all schedules for both purchased and manufactured parts must now be adjusted.

CALCULATING PRIORITY RATIOS

When the Houston plant (discussed in Chapter Nine) revises its production plans, a new MRP file (which lists all customers' orders) the priority of each order is calculated based on this information:

- Lead time by operation
- Date ordered is needed
- Standard hours by operation.

The measurement used in priority control is based on that information to obtain the following ratio:

$$\text{Priority ratio} \ = \ \frac{\text{Number of days till needed}}{\text{Number of days work to be done}}$$

An example of Houston's priority control ratio for 5" liners for part number PMD-62 follows:

Part PMD-62 has the following customer parts requirements for the first quarter of 1991:

	JAN.	FEB.	MAR.
Assemblies	3000	3000	2000
Service Parts	2000	0	4000

The MRP system shows the following inventory balances for PMD-62:

	JAN.	FEB.	MAR.
Beginning Balance:	8000	3000	0
Less: Requirements*	5000	3000	6000
Ending Balance	3000	0	6000

* Requirements are equal to the total of assemblies and service parts.

PMD-62 for January shows 8,000 available parts which will be depleted the end of February. There is an open order in manufacturing for 10,000 pieces which needs to be completed by March 1 to meet the requirements for parts. The priority ratio for this order would be calculated as follows:

The number of days till needed extends from January 1 to March 1, a period of 42 work (not calendar) days. This number is the numerator of the priority ratio.

The denominator, number of days work to be done, is 65 (Houston's lead time on each remaining operation for this particular order).

$$\text{Priority Ratio} \ = \ \frac{42 \text{ days till needed}}{65 \text{ days work to be done}} \ = \ 0.65$$

The priority ratio of 0.65 represents the percentage of lead time left until the order is needed. In this case, 65 days of work remain to be done but the order will be needed in 42 days; it is behind schedule. The ratio of 0.65 means that 65 percent of the work remains to be done if the parts are to be ready on the required date of March 1.

In priority control, there are three conditions which can exist for any given order in relation to the schedule: on schedule, ahead of schedule, and behind schedule. Examples are the following:

$$\text{Priority Ratio} \ = \ \frac{5 \text{ days till needed}}{10 \text{ days work to be done}} \ = \ 0.5 \ = \ \text{Behind Schedule}$$

$$\text{Priority Ratio} = \frac{10 \text{ days till needed}}{10 \text{ days work to be done}} = 1.0 = \text{On Schedule}$$

$$\text{Priority Ratio} = \frac{20 \text{ days till needed}}{10 \text{ days work to be done}} = 2.0 = \text{Ahead of Schedule}$$

Obviously, jobs behind schedule need to be expedited while jobs ahead of schedule should be delayed until the priority ratio is reduced to 1.0.

As a guideline, action to be taken on any given order depends on its priority ratio:

PRIORITY RATIO	ACTION TO BE TAKEN
0.00–0.99	Expedite. Run order with lowest rtio first.
1.00–9999	Delay manufacture until priority reaches 1.0 or below.

PREPARING THE PRIORITY CONTROL REPORT

Figure 13-1 shows a section of Houston's priority control report used by production planning expediters and forepeople to assign work and expedite orders behind schedule. As orders arrive in each department, forepeople check the priority ratios for all orders and assign them to machines accordingly. In Figure 13-1, for example, the following priorities would have been established:

RUN PRIORITY	LOT NUMBER	PRIORITY RATIO
1st	2622	0.00—If part arrives on time.
2nd	2162	0.13
3rd	2450	0.52
4th	2935	1.25

Forepeople, moreover, must take into account groupings of orders to minimize set-up time on machines. Set-up time can be minimized through careful scheduling, and forepeople should be given some flexibility in modestly rearranging priorities.

The priority control system is flexible and can handle exceptions easily. When machines break down or when changes are discovered by forepeople and expediters, orders can be reassigned on the spot to account for changes.

LOT NUMBER	PART NUMBER	START DATE	LOT SIZE	CURRENT LOCATION	PRIORITY RATIO	COMMENTS
2162	PMD-77	8/21/92	2000	Dept. 12	0.13	
2935	PMD 432	8/19/92	300	14	1.25	Hold
2622	PMD 129	9/26/92	4500	10	0.00	Part Shortage
2450	PMD 365	8/30/92	10000	15	0.52	

Figure 13-1   Priority Control Report

14

Nine Tested Methods For Lowering Inventory Costs

Inventories for many manufacturing companies represents the largest single item on the asset side of the balance sheet. They also constitute for most manufacturing companies the largest portion of manufacturing costs. Some typical cost-of-sales compositions are as follows:

COMPANY	PERCENT OF COST-OF-SALES		
	MATERIALS	DIRECT LABOR	OVERHEAD
CONSTRUCTION EQUIPMENT	65%	10%	25%
AUTOMOTIVE EQUIPMENT	55%	15%	30%
PHARMACEUTICAL	45%	20%	35%
ALUMINUM FABRICATION	70%	10%	20%
HOME TOOLS	60%	15%	25%

Not only do inventories constitute the largest single cost in terms of purchased material costs, as shown in the previous table, but they also create additional costs for carrying the inventory.

Typical inventory carrying costs follow:

- Insurance
- Taxes
- Storage and space
- Maintenance
- Obsolescence write-offs
- Deterioration
- Packaging
- Material handling
- Expediting
- Opportunity (money invested in inventories that could be invested in money market certificates)

These carrying costs today run up to 30 percent annually. For a manufacturing company, for example, averaging $10 million, carrying costs add $3 million to material burden costs (overhead). There are ways to reduce inventory costs, however, this chapter provides 9 methods.

METHOD 1: DEVELOP AN ANNUAL INVENTORY PLAN

The first step necessary to control and reduce inventories is to formulate an annual inventory plan. A manufacturing company producing electric motors uses the format in Figure 14-1. Their inventory is composed of three elements:

- *RAW MATERIAL*—All purchased materials in raw, semi-finished, or finished form. Examples are:
  - Raw—steel, chemicals
  - Semi-finished—fabrications
  - Finished—bearings, pumps, motors
- *WORK-IN-PROCESS—Commonly referred to as W.I.P., this category is composed of all materials used in the product that are in-process of being manufactured.*
- *FINISHED PRODUCT*—The finished product ready for shipment,

In the example shown in Figure 14-1, all three categories of inventory are planned by quarter, and the final annual average (19X2) is contrasted to the average inventory numbers from the previous year. Notice that while cost-of-sales have increased from 19X1 to 19X2 (as seen below the inventory numbers in Figure 14-1) total inventories are planned to decrease from $11.4 to $10.5 million, a substantial improvement.

Inventory turnover, the next part of Figure 14-1, is derived by dividing cost of sales by total inventory. The electric motor company hopes to improve turnover from 3.8 times in 19X1 to 4.1 in 19X2.

Caution: Inventory turnover numbers are relative indices. Their best usage is

	1ST QTR	2ND QTR	3RD QTR	4TH QTR	19X2	19X1
RAW MATERIAL	6.5	5.6	5.2	5.1	5.6	6.4
WORK-IN-PROCESS	2.0	2.0	1.8	1.7	1.9	2.0
FINISHED PRODUCT	3.0	3.0	3.0	3.0	3.0	3.0
TOTAL:	11.5	10.6	10.0	9.8	10.5	11.4
COST-OF-SALES:	44.2	45.2	43.0	43.0	43.4	42.8
INVENTORY TURNOVER:	3.8	4.3	4.3	4.4	4.1	3.8

SUPPORTING ACTIONS

Reduce obsolete inventory ($ million):
Raw Materials: .5
W.I.P.:   .1
Sub-Total: .6

Reduce safety stocks ($ million):   .3
Total: .9

Figure 14-1   Electric Motor Company Annual Inventory Plan 19X2   ($ million)

confined to individual companies where progress, or lack of it, can be easily measured. Industry averages are deceptive. Each company has its own unique policies, methods, and procedures which, collectively, make it difficult, if not impossible, to compare different companies in the same industry.

One company, for example, may elect to carry a very large finished inventory to service customers, while a competing company may not elect to do so. Factors such as this determine turnover rates and make company comparisons faulty.

The second part of Figure 14-1 explains the specific actions needed to support the inventory reduction planned by the electric motor company. In this example, reductions of $600,000 in obsolete inventory and reductions of $300,000 in safety stock are planned.

How to lower costs. The annual inventory plan permits a company's manufacturing managers to think through exactly how inventory reductions will take place.

Alternative plans can then be devised should conditions affecting the plan change. Without an annual plan it is very difficult to achieve significant improvements. Too many factors are left to chance.

METHOD 2: PUBLISH AN INVENTORY STATUS REPORT

Once the plan is up and running, it is necessary to periodically review the size of inventories by composite categories. This review is facilitated by publishing, normally every week or every month, an inventory status. The electric motor company's inventory status report is seen in Figure 14-2. Planned and actual inventories are compared every month. In the example shown, the actual meets the planned quantity but does not extend it.

How to lower costs. The inventory status report is a measurement that helps you ensure that inventory plans are being met; if they are being exceeded the monthly report permits effective corrective action to take place to reduce inventories so budgeted quantities will not be exceeded in future months.

	ACTUAL	PLAN	VARIANCE
RAW MATERIAL	5.7	5.6	+ .1
W.I.P.	2.0	2.0	0
FINISHED PRODUCT	2.9	3.0	− .1
TOTAL:	10.6	10.6	0

Figure 14-2   Electric Motor Company Inventory Status Report, June 19X2

METHOD 3: IDENTIFY INACTIVE INVENTORY

The designations of raw, work-in-process, and finished inventories constitute only the most rudimentary breakdown of inventory categories. For most manufacturing managers that is simply not enough information. It is necessary to further identify categories of active and inactive inventories. The three generally accepted categories are (1) active, (2) surplus or excess, and (3) obsolete. Definitions of these follow.

* *ACTIVE INVENTORY*—This represents all materials and parts of the current design with an anticipated usage of one year or less. If, for example, the electric motor demand for mounting brackets is 20,000 annually and the inventory records show 25,000 on hand, then 20,000 are considered active, while 5,000 fall within the category of surplus inventory.

- *SURPLUS INVENTORY*—This is all inventory of current design with a usage exceeding one year, as shown in the previous example.
- OBSOLETE INVENTORY—This final inventory category describes materials and parts no longer in usage due to obsoleted designs.

Figure 14-3 illustrates how the electric motor company accounts for these three classifications of inventory. The report is made monthly and shows where specific inventory values lie.

How to lower costs. This breakdown permits a more thorough analysis of inventory reduction possibilities and allows management to exercise control over inventory quantities.

ACTIVE INVENTORY

Raw Material	5.3
W.I.P.	1.9
Finished Product	2.9
TOTAL:	10.1

SURPLUS INVENTORY

Raw material	.1
W.I.P.	.0
Finished Product	.0
TOTAL:	.1

OBSOLETE INVENTORY

Raw Material	.3
W.I.P.	.1
Finished Product	.0
TOTAL:	.4

TOTAL INVENTORY:	10.6

Figure 14-3 Electric Motor Company Active/Inactive Inventory, June 19X2 ($000)

METHOD 4: CALCULATE ECONOMIC ORDER QUANTITIES

Large lot sizes minimize production setup costs but create huge inventories. Small lot sizes, conversely, minimize inventories but create havoc in production because of downtime costs created by excessive setups. A balance somewhere in between is needed. But where should that point occur?

The economic order quantity (EOQ) describes that specific point. It calculates the optimum trade-off between ordering costs and carrying costs. Carrying costs have already been described. Ordering costs include such costs as placing purchase order and production set-up time.

The EOQ is calculated using this formula:

$$EOQ = \sqrt{\frac{2 \ [Annual \ Usage \times (Setup + Order \ Cost)]}{Cost \ Per \ Part \times Carrying \ Cost}}$$

A manufacturer of oil field couplings computes EOQs for each of its major parts. One such part is:

Part Name	— 3" tapped coupling
Annual Usage	—20,000
Cost Per Part	—$11.50
Order Cost	—$70.00
Setup Cost	—$60.00
Carrying Cost	—$ 3.45

Calculation of the EOQ for the 3-inch tapped coupling is as follows:

$$EOQ = \sqrt{\frac{2 \ [20,000 \times (\$60.00 + \$70.00)]}{\$11.50 \times \$3.45}}$$

$$EOQ = \sqrt{\frac{5,200,000}{39.68}}$$

$$EOQ = \sqrt{131,048}$$

$$EOQ = 362$$

The relationship of ordering cost (including setup) to carrying cost can be determined from the chart shown in Figure 14-4. Point A is the EOQ since it represents the lowest combination of ordering and carrying costs.

A chart similar to this can be made for any part used in the manufacturing process. In reality, EOQs can best be handled through a simple computer program. Manual calculators are cumbersome and time consuming.

Remember that the EOQ represents costs for a given moment in time. The factors that comprise the EOQ change frequently. Neither ordering costs nor carrying costs are static. They should be reviewed semiannually and updated when significant changes are encountered.

Using economic order quantities allows a company to carry just enough inventory to meet production schedules and no more. It does away with the necessity to carry surplus inventory to meet emergency needs. Most companies going through the task of establishing economic order quantities for the first time can generally reduce their raw material and work-in-process inventory by ten to fifteen percent.

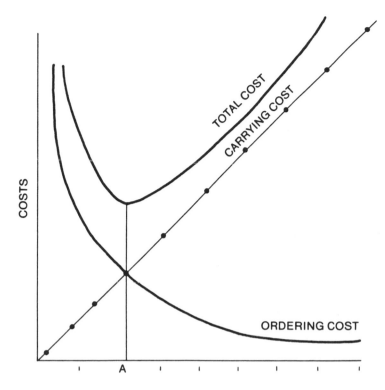

Figure 14-4 Economic Order Quantity

METHOD 5: MAKE AN ABC INVENTORY ANALYSIS

In almost every manufacturing company an analysis of parts used will indicate that a relatively small proportion of the different parts of the product constitute the overwhelming share of volume. In most of these cases, 10 percent or more of the parts will account for about 70 percent of inventory. These are referred to as "A" parts. A, B, and C parts volume are seen here:

TYPE	NO. OF PARTS	PRODUCTION $ VALUE
A	10%	70%
B	20%	20%
C	70%	10%
	100%	100%

In pictorial form, the relationship can be shown as follows:

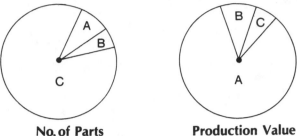

How to lower costs. ABC analysis is fundamental to the resolution of inventory control problems. Typical benefits are:

- Concentration of resources for inventory reduction of the significant few as opposed to the trivial many.
- Manual control of "A" and "B" purchase orders to assure that only the needed amounts of parts and materials are ordered to achieve the production schedule.
- Focus of attention on "A" and "B" parts in assuring inventory accuracy.
- Minimizing inventories on-hand through establishment of ordering policies, such as:

TYPE	NO. OF MONTHS ON-HAND
A	2 Months
B	3 Months
C	12 Months

- Use of larger safety stocks for "C" parts than for "A" and "B" parts to minimize stock-outs and improve customer service. The value of "C" safety stocks will be minimal since the value of "C" parts is generally low.

METHOD 6: REDUCE LEAD TIMES

Lead time can be defined as the time that elapses from the moment an order is placed until the moment it is delivered. Major events affecting lead time include the following:

- Order received
- Data prepared for computer
- Credit check of customer
- Engineering review of order
- Parts ordered from vendors
- Parts received from vendors
- Order manufactured

- Order packed
- Order shipped
- Order received by customer

Lead times in manufacturing are computed by the following formula:

$$LT = Setup + Run + Move + Queue + Delay$$

- *SETUP*—Parts are waiting to be manufactured while the machine is being setup.
- *RUN*—The actual time the machine is in operation.
- *MOVE*—Time spent moving parts or semi-completed or completed product from one operation to another or to and from storage space.
- *QUEUE*—The time parts await manufacturing while other parts are being manufactured.
- *DELAY*—Time lost for reasons such as machine adjustments and break-downs, personal time of operators, material not at operations, wait for crane, etc.

In most manufacturing companies queue time constitutes the overwhelming percentage of lead time, regardless of product line. Figure 14-5 displays the elements of lead time for a stamping manufacturer. Notice that queue time accounts for over three-quarters of total lead time; that percentage is not unusual.

Since queue time is essentially a function of the amount of inventory in-process (work-in-process) the obvious key is to keep work-in-process inventories at a

LEAD TIMES FOR COMPANY
MANUFACTURING STAMPINGS

AVERAGE ORDER

	HOURS	% OF TOTAL
SETUPS	3.5	3.1
RUN TIME	12.2	10.7
MOVE TIME	4.7	4.1
QUEUE TIME	86.8	76.1
DELAYS	6.8	6.0
	114.0	100.0%

Figure 14-5   Lead Time Elements

minimum level to sustain production operations without causing delays due to lack of parts.

The common method used to reduce inventory and, therefore, lead times is reverse loading. For example, suppose the stamping company has these sequenced operations and lead times:[1]

	DAYS
1. Pick order form warehouse	.5
2. Stamping operation	1.0
3. Anneal	.5
4. Inspect	.5
5. Pack	.5
6. Ship	.4
	3.4 Days

Reverse loading would initially load the last operation and work backward to fill previous operations. In this way a start date would be determined:

	1ST DAY	2ND DAY	3RD DAY	4TH DAY
PICK STAMP ANNEAL INSPECT PACK SHIP				

How to lower costs. Using reverse loading (and calculating standard time adjusted to actual performance), all operations can be loaded to planned capacity without jamming W.I.P. with inventory. The reduction in lead time will be quite large if this technique is handled properly. Work-in-process inventories will be reduced significantly and costs reduced accordingly.

METHOD 7: IMPROVE PRODUCTION FORECASTING

In forecasting production requirements the use of sales projections alone has serious drawbacks. Most sales projections are normally too high, too low, or the projection of product mix is drastically incorrect. In any case, forecasting must be accurate to assure that production schedules are met, and that inventories are minimized.

One of the simpler, yet more effective, techniques used is called exponential

---

1 In this case lead time is calculated *without* including queue time.

smoothing. This is really nothing more than a weighted moving average and it is quite easy to calculate. Production planning departments have used this technique effectively to supplement the sales forecast with historical performance.

In an *unweighted* moving average historical sales are added together for a given period of time (say, twelve weeks) and divided by twelve to derive weekly requirements. One week later the newest week is added to the total while the oldest week is discarded. For example:

WEEK NO.	SALES	WEIGHTED X
1	100	
2	120	
3	110	
4	90	
5	110	
6	100	
7	105	
8	115	
9	90	
10	80	
11	90	
12	75	92.5 (Weeks 1–12)
13	80	90.8 (Weeks 2–13)
14	60	85.8 (Weeks 3–14)

These data represent a simple weighted average. In this technique of forecasting, however, the latest week receives exactly the same weight as the previous week. It usually makes more sense to place greater significance on historical performance than on the latest week's forecast because the latest week's projection could represent a single—and large—departure from average sales.

Using the previous example of the simple moving average, a *weighted* moving average can be calculated where, from experience, it is determined to place 70 percent weight on the previous forecast and 30 percent weight on the new forecast.

Week 15

$$\text{Forecast } 60 \times 0.7 = 42.0$$

$$\text{Actual } 80 \times 0.3 = \underline{24.0}$$

$$\text{New Forecast} \qquad 66.0$$

The 66 would then be used to calculate the weighted average previously shown. It would represent the latest week, to be added to the total, and the oldest week would be discarded.

How to lower costs. Exponential smoothing will help reduce the peaks and valleys experienced in the sales forecast and will definitely help in keeping inventories low.

METHOD 8: USE THE CRITICAL ORDER RATIO

One way to move parts through production operations by priority, and thereby maintain delivery schedules while preventing inventory accumulations behind different machines, is called critical order ratio expediting.

Critical order ratio expediting focuses on those orders in manufacturing by these priorities:

- First—Orders behind schedule
- Second—Orders on schedule
- Third—Orders ahead of schedule

A hand tool manufacturer in Pennsylvania calculates its critical ratios using this formula:

$$\text{Critical Order Ratio} = \frac{\text{No. of days till needed}}{\text{No. of days till completed}}$$

One of their products, a small hand wrench, normally takes five days to process (including queue time). In that case, they have the following critical order ratios on three jobs in-process:

$$\text{Critical order ratio} = \frac{2 \text{ days till needed}}{5 \text{ days till complete}} = 0.4 \quad \text{Behind Schedule}$$

$$\text{Critical order ratio} = \frac{5 \text{ days till needed}}{5 \text{ days till complete}} = 1.0 \quad \text{on Schedule}$$

$$\text{Critical order ratio} = \frac{10 \text{ days till needed}}{5 \text{ days till complete}} = 2.0 \quad \text{Ahead of Schedule}$$

How to lower costs. A daily computer printout records all such critical order ratios for all orders in manufacturing. Using such a system, the hand tool company has estimated an annual work-in-process inventory reduction of $1 million.

Perpetual inventory control has been around a long time: as long as manufacturing plants themselves. The technique is simple and easy-to-use and lends itself readily to computerization. Its value is that it constantly exposes inventory levels to the scrutiny of management. It also compares current inventory levels with previous inventory levels so that trends can be spotted. When inventories begin growing, they are scrutinized by managers and planners for possible reductions. Without this simple but powerful tool, inventories can easily grow out of proportion to their actual need.

METHOD 9: ESTABLISH PERPETUAL INVENTORY CONTROL[1]

In most operations the use of the production plan and expediting methods will suffice for controlling backlogs. Because the supervisors plan their workload and must keep sufficient work ahead of their employees, they are constantly aware of the extent of this backlog. Some operations are more complex, and the use of the plan is insufficient to maintain the proper in-process inventory level. This usually occurs in operations that have a large product mix. While the forepeople will still be required to keep their eyes on backlogs, he will need some help in determining inventory counts during their shifts. This is the job of the perpetual inventory control. The task of preparing and maintaining it is usually assigned to the production office clerk or an indirect hourly worker. It can be taken at any significant interval of time, depending on the need. Generally, it is posted twice per shift.

Figure 14-6 is a simplified version of a perpetual inventory control form used in the buck shop of a door manufacturing plant. Across the top of the form the various types of door bucks are listed. Although the buck shop actually processes about twenty-five different types of bucks, the number has been reduced for this illustration to clarify the document. It is easy to guess, however, that with twenty-five product mix variables, some instrument of control is needed.

Flat trim bucks that were received on the date specified were entered in the column entitled "In" on the same line as the bundle number. Flat trim bucks that were assembled on the same day were recorded in the "O.H." (on-hand) column. To arrive at the on-hand figure, the number of bucks that went out during the day would be subtracted from the total bucks received on the same day plus the on-hand figure of the previous day. The same procedure would be repeated for the other categories of bucks.

When all balances had been recorded they would be totaled both horizontally and vertically. The totals then reflected daily production by type of buck and bundle number. The final entry in the "Total" column gave the total number of bucks received, total bucks produced, and the total number of bucks in the system.

---

1 Reprinted from the author's book, *Short-Interval Scheduling* (New York: McGraw-Hill, 1968).

PERPETUAL INVENTORY CONTROL

DATE	BUNDLE NUMBER	FLAT TRIM			TRANSOM			HOUSING			COVE			TOTAL		
		IN	OUT	O.H.	IN	OUT	O.H.	IN	OUT	O.H.	IN	OUT	O.H.	IN	OUT	O.H.
5-2	3210	4,000	2,000	2,000										4,000	2,000	2,000
5-2	4618				2,000	500	1,500							2,000	500	1,500
5-2	415-A							3,000	2,000	1,000				3,000	2,000	1,000
5-2	4503				1,000	1,000	—							1,000	1,000	—
5-2	3800										500	—	500	500	—	500
TOTAL	→	4,000	2,000	2,000	3,000	1,500	1,500	3,000	2,000	1,000	500	—	500	10,500	5,500	5,000
5-3	4605				2,000	2,500	1,000							2,000	2,500	1,000
5-3	3271	3,000	4,000	1,000										3,000	4,000	1,000
5-3	4240							4,000	3,000	2,000				4,000	3,000	2,000
5-3	4677										500	1,000	—	500	1,000	—
5-3	3772										500	—	500	500	—	500
TOTAL	→	3,000	4,000	1,000	2,000	2,500	1,000	4,000	3,000	2,000	1,000	1,000	500	10,000	10,500	4,500

Figure 14-6 Perpetual Inventory Record

15

Using Just-In-Time to Reduce Inventories by 75 Percent

Just-in-Time (JIT) is based on the assumption that a company should produce or buy and receive parts and materials only at the exact time they are needed for production and shipment. It is a manufacturing strategy aimed at full utilization of all of a company's assets, including the effective use of machinery and equipment, the delivery of materials to work stations at the time of manufacture, and the development of the company's employees ability to properly use the information and methods to manufacture the product. JIT is the prime motivator for reducing set-up times from hours to minutes, for example. It affects throughput time, work flow, inventory size, labor utilization and efficiency, and a host of other factors.

JIT is a technique that returns many lost dollars to the bottom line. All of the factors mentioned above contribute to reduced inventories, reduced lead times, and reduced labor expenditure. And, of course, those are the essential ingredients of cost. These will be examined shortly.

It is not uncommon for a company that has fully implemented JIT to experience inventory reductions in the neighborhood of 50–75 percent. This may take a few years to achieve simply because of the systems changes needed to make JIT work, but it is possible and it has been done.

The implementation of systems to reduce set-up times, for example, cannot be done overnight. The implementation of these systems takes a coordinated effort among the major plant functions, such as manufacturing engineering, production, quality, and materials management. Yet, when it does happen, the reduction of setup times will bring about reduced lead times, reduced inventories, reduced overhead costs (such as overtime), and reduced set-up allowances in the work standards.

Although Japanese manufacturers are credited with the development and widespread use of JIT, JIT is an American, not a Japanese, concept. JIT was first developed by Henry Ford for his mammoth production complex at Dearborn, Michigan more than 60 years ago. Ford brought together steel, glass, and part manufacturing to supply its car assembly plant at the same complex. Materials and parts flowed from one plant to another, just in time, for assembly. (It is interesting to note that modern Japanese assembly plants now locate their suppliers close to the point-of-assembly, as Ford did those many years ago.)

JIT was adapted by the Japanese and refined to the point that it became one of the best techniques for running an efficient manufacturing plant. In essence, the Japanese got the drop on Americans, but American manufacturers came back and have been using the technique since. In both Japan and the United States, JIT is composed of the following elements:

1. Reduce setup times.
2. Cut lot sizes.
3. Implement a manufacturing quality system.
4. Implement a Kanban system.
5. Move toward the use of manufacturing cells.
6. Eliminate buffer inventories.
7. Extend the JIT program to vendors.

HOW TO REDUCE SET-UP TIMES

It has been estimated that, depending on the type of machinery and equipment involved in the manufacturing process, set-up time constitutes from 15–40 percent of total machine cycle time (defined as the time work is being processed through production equipment, including set-up time but not including wait time behind machines or materials handling time). This creates extended lead times as inventory backs up behind production operations during set-up. The result is a rapid swelling of work-in-process inventories.

One of the major problems with set-up time is that manufacturing managers and supervisors view set-up time as fixed. Actually, long set-up times should be a target for analysis and improvement. More recently, this has been the case, and the rewards have been substantial. It is not unusual to see a reduction of set-up times from hours to minutes for many common pieces of machinery, including mills, lathes, drills, extruders, and screw machines.

The improvement of the set-up portion of the manufacturing cycle often requires the design of special conveyors, jigs, fixtures, and tools. It also necessitates the re-evaluation of what sometimes is called general-purpose machinery (i.e., machinery used for the processing of many different kinds of products that need their own tooling, which dramatically increases set-up time). More dedicated pieces of equipment are needed in this case.

When analyzing set-up times, standard work simplification techniques need to be applied. These techniques might be work flow analysis, time study, and work motion analysis—all are typical industrial engineering skills. Several excellent texts exist on the subject.

Probably one of the more significant tasks regarding set-up time reduction involves reorientation of the workers. As shown in Figure 15-1, the necessary type and levels of skills change when set-up times are reduced.

FORMER REQUIREMENTS	NEW REQUIREMENTS
Other workers (not production operators) set up machines	Production operators now set up machines themselves
Knowledge of set-up most crucial factor	Set-up simplification skills now of paramount importance
Set-ups performed by one worker	Set-ups now performed by two or more workers, including maintenance workers
General-purpose tools used	Special tools now used

Figure 15-1   Reorientation of Worker Skills in Setup Time Reduction Program

Case Study: Shelving Manufacturer Cuts Setup Times in Half.   A large shelving manufacturer in the Northeast established six productivity improvement teams to focus on set-up time reduction for its stamping presses. Each time was assigned a production supervisor, press operator, set-up persons, planner, and industrial engineer. Each team was given a clear direction regarding the specific piece of equipment, products, and process to focus on.

The team used the fishbone diagram, work flow analysis, and method studies, and met one hour per week for an eight-month period. Each team established proposed specific ideas for reducing set-up time; the ideas pertained to tooling, materials, operator methods, and gauging. Most ideas were quickly implemented by management direction. Within a year, set-up times had been reduced about 50% for the stamping operations.

HOW TO CUT LOT SIZES

Traditionally, lot sizes are a function of the cost of inventory vs. the cost and time it takes to set up and run. In recent years, machine tools have become more complex, more expensive, and capable of performing a multitude of jobs which, in the past, would have required several different pieces of equipment. For example, CNC equipment (computer controlled machinery) combines several functions in one machine. These more expensive machine tools need larger lot sizes; their very expense puts managers under a lot of pressure to keep the machinery operating.

Large lot sizes, however, create many costly problems:

- Work-in-process inventories increase.

- When inventories swell, lead times expand, because more work remains on the production floor waiting to be processed.

- More inventory means more backlog behind different production machines. When that happens, supervisors and workers become anxious—particularly when planners are yelling for work sitting in the pile—and that's when mistakes happen as anxious workers hurry. Defect rates increase greatly.

- Inventory sitting around is always subject to damage, rust, obsolescence, and the carrying costs associated with large unmoving inventories. It takes up valuable space.

- Planning becomes more difficult. The more work on the floor, the more work to be planned, controlled, and expedited. Not only does this generate more production planning overtime, it also tends to create the demand for more planners than are really needed.

- Material handling costs increase because more work needs to be moved.

JIT implies that lot sizes be cut dramatically. In fact, the ideal lot size for JIT is one piece; of course, that is an ideal rather than a reality. The important point is that manufacturing managers must insist that their employees always find more ways to cut lot sizes. But planners and supervisors subconsciously feel more comfortable when they have a lot of inventory, not less. This attitude needs to be overcome by educating workers because the presence of more work inventories is costly and leads to decreased delivery performance, not improvement; the more work on the floor, the longer it waits to be processed at work stations.

Reducing lot sizes can be accomplished by:

- Eliminating buffer inventories (discussed later in this chapter).

- Reverse loading (See Chapter Sixteen on short-interval scheduling).

- Implementing manufacturing cells (discussed later in this chapter).

Small lot sizes actually reduce lead time because the work moves through production faster. Inventory levels drop accordingly.

Case Study: A Zipper Manufacturer Cuts Lot Sizes 24 percent. A zipper manufacturer in the South analyzed and implemented many different ideas for reducing lot sizes. Included were:

• Eliminating safety stocks.
• Moving part lots through manufacturing rather than waiting for full lot completion. This tended to smooth the flow of work in the plant and reduce wait times. Eventually, the lot size was reduced to match the part-lot sizes.
• Cutting vendor lot sizes.

The company cut its lot sizes by 24 percent.

HOW TO IMPLEMENT A MANUFACTURING QUALITY SYSTEM

JIT manufacturing cannot work if there is a large amount of defective work on the production floor. When inventory levels between operations are low (the essence of JIT), then most of the inventory must be good or the machines will shut down while waiting for acceptable parts. When many parts are defective, more inventory must be pumped into the system to compensate for the defective work. And that increases the lead times, causing further problems. This simply defeats the purpose of JIT.

Manufacturing quality can be implemented by following the guidelines established by the quality principles explained earlier in this book, in Chapters Six, Seven, and Eight. Manufacturing quality is a prerequisite for near defect-free production, and near defect-free production is a necessary qualification for successful JIT.

Case Study: An Electrical Manufacturer Installs Manufacturing Quality Program and Reduces Defects 31 percent. Following the guidelines similar to the ones described in earlier chapters on quality, an electrical products company in the East installed a manufacturing quality program and reduced its defect level by 31 percent. This allowed the company to begin work on a JIT installation.

In all cases, it is imperative that defect levels be reduced to a low level before the JIT program is installed. That specific level is a matter of judgment and reflects a decision properly reached after consultation with the quality manager, materials manager, and production manager.

HOW TO IMPLEMENT A KANBAN SYSTEM

JIT is remarkably similar to short-interval scheduling (SIS) in its use cf the Kanban Card. The Kanban Card triggers the release of work to individual workstations just as the dispatching batch ticket does in SIS. In fact, the study of SIS (described in detail in Chapter Sixteen) can help indoctrinate the JIT user.

In JIT, the Kanban Card is generated by the production schedule for a given period of time, normally in five- or ten-day increments. A Kanban Card is used to authorize the use of a specific number of parts for a downstream operation, as well as to release a given quality of parts from a supplier (an upstream operation).

The parts as shown on the Kanban Cards are also reflected on a production schedule, which is the department's authorization to manufacture for the time period. For each workstation within the department, a daily schedule is made with its supporting Kanban Cards.

Every Kanban Card is physically attached to the container holding the parts at the workstation where they are produced, and it accompanies the container to its downstream destination, the next workstation. At that station, the worker removes the Kanban Card after that container's parts have been received and returns the card along with the empty container to the previous operation, via a dispatching or schedule clerk who marks completion of the container of parts on the production schedule.

At the previous operation, the worker attaches the Kanban Card to the parts container to show that the parts have been completed at that station and are now ready for release to the next operation. The Kanban Card is then affixed to the full container, and the parts are physically moved to the next workstation. The dispatching clerk marks the movement on the production schedule, which tracks the movement of all inventory within that department.

Authorization to manufacture a container of parts is triggered by three events:

1. Authorization is shown on the production schedule.
2. The parts are available.
3. The Kanban Card accompanies the parts.

To use the Kanban system effectively, parts must always be kept in standard containers and the 5- or 10-day schedule window must be frozen. It cannot be changed to reflect emergency orders or other changes. This permits the orderly flow of work through the system.

A typical Kanban Card is shown in Figure 15-2.

Case Study: Manufacturer's Trim Million With Kanban. An Ohio-based automotive supplier with $160 million annual sales trimmed $10 million from its finished goods inventory, consolidated two plants, and eliminated the need for a 400,000 square foot warehouse after it applied the Kanban Card system to its operations.

Another, larger company with six divisions encompassing 21 plants installed the Kanban Card system and reduced its inventory carrying costs $7 million.

One of this company's plants makes starter motors and then feeds them to 10 automotive assembly plants across the USA, with shipments every two hours. The Kanban Card allows the plant to carry an average of seven hours of raw material inventory, nine hours of work-in-process, and eight hours of finished goods through-

XYZ MACHINE WORKS	
KANBAN CARD	
PART NUMBER: *Z 43A-5*	CONTAINER NUMBER: *DP - 47*
PART NAME: *ROTOR ARMS*	NO. OF PIECES IN THIS CONTAINER:
ORIGINATING WORK CENTER: *CNC MILLING*	DESTINATION WORK CENTER: *WELDING*
ORIGINATING STOCK LOCATION: *CNC MILLING LOCATION BR*	DESTINATION STOCK LOCATION: *FABRICATION LOCATION BS*
SCHEDULE PERIOD: *7/10 - 7/20*	

Figure 15-2   Kanban Card

out the entire plant. Those numbers were arrived at after experimentation showed them to be the minimum that could be carried in the different inventories without disrupting operations.

HOW TO MOVE TOWARD THE USE OF MANUFACTURING CELLS

True JIT requires the use of cellular layouts in manufacturing, as opposed to traditional functional layouts. A functional layout is one in which all of the same kind of machines are grouped together. For example, in a machine shop, all automatic screw machines are placed together in one area; in the next operation, all milling machines are located together; in a subsequent operation, all drills are placed together; and so on throughout the entire plant. This is the kind of layout that has been popular in most U.S. and European manufacturing plants since rapid industrialization took place in the nineteenth century.

But with the advent of JIT, managers have come to realize that the lowest possible inventory levels are associated with manufacturing cells. In a manufacturing cell, successive operations are physically located adjacent to one another. In the machine shop example, if a single automatic screw machine processed a part and then passed it on to a milling machine immediately adjacent to it, and then the milling machine processed that same part and passed it on to a drilling machine immediately next to it, that process would be considered a manufacturing cell.

The obvious advantage of a cell is that it eliminates *any* inventory between operations. In a functional manufacturing layout, an entire lot of parts is manufactured in milling, then all of the parts are sent to the drilling department. Those parts constitute the work-in-process inventory. But in a cell, the part is moved from machine to machine as soon as it is made, and the individual workstations are balanced to process the same number of parts every hour.

A not-so-obvious advantage is that in a cell, the same operator may run all of the different machines. In the example given, one operator could run the screw machine, the mill, and the drill. But even if different operators are used, they will all gain familiarity with the groups of parts they process, because they are all working side by side.

They will also have instant communication. When a downstream operation has a quality problem, the worker from that operation can walk five yards away and discuss the problem with the upstream operator whose machine caused the problem. Their very proximity helps defeat problems. Instant communication!

A manufacturing cell eliminates much of the material handling and temporary storage requirements always present in a traditional functional manufacturing plant, particularly one that has no JIT system. One great advantage is the reduced need for expensive plant space, because the temporary storage areas are no longer needed.

In actual practice, it is difficult and expensive to tear up an entire functional manufacturing layout and replace it entirely with cells. The obvious problem is the cost of relocating equipment. Also, in the cell arrangement, if one machine in the entire sequence of machines breaks down, then the entire line goes down. Another factor is that customer parts requirements are constantly changing, and those changes may necessitate frequent relocation of different pieces of equipment to accommodate the schedule, which is not a practical way to do business.

It is better to identify a series of parts representing a small portion of the plant's capacity and start with that as an experiment. Then, perfect the manufacturing cell before gradually extending the concept to further operations. Careful analysis and thought are required to reach the optimum balance of functional and cell types of manufacturing.

Case Study: A Machinery Company Uses Cells for Special Jobs and Reduces Customized Product Costs by One-Third.   A textile machinery company in New England faced the problem of mixing its standard winding machinery production with customized machinery orders in the same production stream. The company had a functional layout and, inevitably, the customized production took a back seat to getting out standard production orders. Since custom machinery brought a high profit margin to the company, the manufacturing manager had to find some way to deliver the machinery to customers on time and at a reduced cost.

The company cleared a corner of the plant and installed a manufacturing cell in which individual pieces of equipment used to process custom work (along with the special tooling needed in its manufacture) were placed in a line, with all pieces of equipment in close proximity to each other. Operators were trained to handle several different pieces of machinery. The fact that all of the operators worked closely together helped improve quality, and the cell concept reduced inventories, lead times, overtime, and labor costs. The company actually reduced the *entire* cost of the custom operation by one-third.

HOW TO ELIMINATE BUFFER INVENTORIES

Many Japanese companies have approached this problem differently than American companies. In the United States, most companies going through the exercise of removing their safety stocks do it gradually, piece by piece, after installing a JIT component program (such as the Kanban Card). Many Japanese companies remove their safety stocks all at once, or they cut the buffer stocks in half before the JIT program commences or right at the beginning of the JIT installation. They do this to stimulate the elimination of sources of delay among operations, to reduce quality and process problems, and to get their people thinking hard about process improvements. In essence, they bite the bullet. The other 50 percent is removed later and the process repeated. The downside of this method is that an overwhelming number of problems will cause problem-solving specialists to spread their efforts too thin and downtime will grow accordingly.

There is a certain logic behind what may first appear to be a precipitous Japanese move. Safety, or buffer, stocks make employees lazy and comfortable. They know that if errors are made, the safety stocks will protect them. In theory, that makes a lot of sense. In actual practice, the size of buffer inventories tends to grow and grow while managers rely on them more and more and think of process improvements less and less. That is the reality.

Case Study: A Military Products Company Reduces Safety Stock 81 percent. In most manufacturing operations, probably the most effective method for reducing buffer inventories is to eliminate all safety stock—except that which provides emergency stocks for machine breakdowns. A company making large aluminum deep-drawn products for military vehicles and similar applications found that it was carrying an average of 56,000 pieces of work-in-process inventory. The operations for this company can be seen in Figure 15-3 in the vertical column on the left.

The plant made about 1000 of these deep-drawn hubs per hour, or 8000 per day. Because its operations were fairly well balanced, with the appropriate number of machines to handle a constant flow at each step of the production process, it produced 8000 pieces per day for all operations.

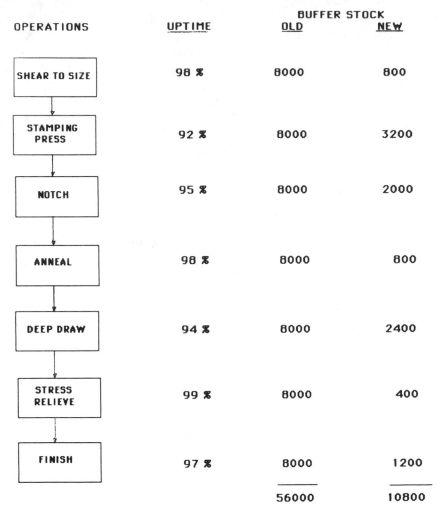

OPERATIONS	UPTIME	BUFFER STOCK OLD	BUFFER STOCK NEW
SHEAR TO SIZE	98 %	8000	800
STAMPING PRESS	92 %	8000	3200
NOTCH	95 %	8000	2000
ANNEAL	98 %	8000	800
DEEP DRAW	94 %	8000	2400
STRESS RELIEVE	99 %	8000	400
FINISH	97 %	8000	1200
		56000	10800

Figure 15-3   Buffer Inventory Reduction

It also carried about one day's stock for each operation as a buffer. As shown at the bottom of the third column, "Old Buffer Stock," the total buffer stock for the entire plant was 56,000 pieces. The second column, "Uptime," reflects the actual percent of the time the machines were in operation as indicated by the maintenance records for those machines.

The last column, "New Buffer Stock," shows the quantity of inventory needed to cover machine downtime only *for one week*. This is calculated by taking the downtime percent and multiplying it by 40,000 pieces (the average daily production per operation times five working days per week). The formula is:

$$Downtime = (100\% - Uptime)$$

Average weekly production/operation =
$$8000 \text{ pieces per day} \times 5 \text{ days/week} = 40{,}000 \text{ Pieces}$$

$$New Buffer Stock = Downtime Percent \times 40{,}000 \text{ Pieces}$$

EXAMPLE:

$$\text{For "Notch," Downtime} = (100\% - 95\%) = 5\%$$

$$5\% \times 40{,}000 \text{ Pieces} = 2000 \text{ Pieces}$$

Finally, the bottom of the last column on the right shows the total of all the new buffer stock needed: 10,800 Pieces.

The reduction in buffer stock is:

$$Column\ 3 - Column\ 4/Column\ 3 \times 100\%$$

In this case, $56{,}000 - 10{,}8000 = 45{,}200/56{,}000 \times 100 = 80.7\%$.

HOW TO EXTEND THE JIT PROGRAM TO VENDORS

Over the last several years, it has become increasingly evident that companies must consider their suppliers' operations when implementing new programs such as JIT. For example, if a company implements JIT but doesn't include its vendors, then the program simply won't be as successful; it may even fail.

Increasingly, companies have come to view their vendors as full and important partners of any new undertaking. JIT is particularly relevant here, because vendors must deliver quantities of parts and materials just in time. They must share the practices started by their customers.

Some companies have gone so far as to locate their vendors close to their operations to cut down on the transportation time and cost of shipping materials between plants and to allow vendors to ship small quantities many times per day as opposed to one or two shipments per week.

The primary advantage here is that vendors are able to form a more close-knit and cohesive team with their customers and can supply better products, at a cheaper price, ship it on time, and in JIT quantities. The disadvantage is that when the customer wishes to change vendors, that decision becomes exceedingly more difficult. In any case, vendors closer to their customers will do a better job in a JIT program.

Case Study: An Automotive Supplier Joins in JIT Effort. An automotive supplier making parts for radiators located its new plant adjacent to its main supplier and embarked jointly on a successful JIT program. Both companies realized large inventory savings and lead time reductions, and their continued cooperation led to a significant improvement in product quality.

16_____

Short-Interval Scheduling: A Complete Planning and Control System for Increasing Worker Productivity

One of the major problems confronting manufacturing managers today is how to increase worker productivity. With a shortage of skilled or competent workers and the resultant increase in labor costs, there is constant pressure to increase production with fewer employees. Many companies who find themselves in this situation turn to short-interval scheduling (SIS).[1]

What is SIS? How does it produce operation economics? Simply stated, short-interval scheduling is a method for assigning a planned quality of work to be completed by a specific time and with a means to determine that the quantity of work is completed within the specified time limit.

The interval of time assigned to complete a job is usually one hour. The time interval can vary according to a situation. The basic thought behind this system is that time is one of management's most precious assets. If you can positively control

---

1 Adapted from the author's book *Short-Interval Scheduling* (New York: McGraw-Hill, 1968).

sixty minutes in most hours for most employees, you can improve efficiency and profitably.

SIS imbues each supervisor with the critical importance of utilizing effectively all of his available resources. It highlights substandard operations, thereby placing the supervisor in a critical area at a critical time—where the supervisor must be in order to improve operating methods.

Probably the most enticing advantage of SIS is that it instills in both workers and supervisors an immediate sense of urgency to get the job done. The effect is psychological and occurs because SIS establishes obtainable goals on a *short-range basis*. The frequent appraisals of performance ensure that employees will produce at standard levels, or close to it, throughout the day. When daily output totals are the only guide to performance, a supervisor does not learn that an employee has not been turning in full performance until the day is over, *and then it is too late to take corrective action*. In business operations time lost can never be regained.

HOW TO ESTABLISH WORK STANDARDS

To establish work standards for the short-interval scheduling program, we must define the units of measure that are to be scheduled, and then find out how long each unit of measure takes to perform. This is called the job-time relationship. As we develop this study and investigate this relationship we will see that it is aimed at alerting the supervisor to recognize *off-schedule* conditions in the briefest practical time. We will find the answers to the following questions:

* What *does* the employee do?
* How *much* does he or she do?
* How *often* does he or she do it?
* How *long* does it take?

Rarely, in any operation, is a supervisor fully cognizant of what is involved, and how long it takes to do a job. This may sound like a shocking condemnation of people in supervisory positions, but it isn't. For example, in a routine stamping operation, parts are stamped, annealed and inspected. If we had a supervisor in such an operation, would he be able to enumerate and define the quantities of each type of stampings at each station? Could he or she give a reliable estimate of how long it should take to process the stampings? Could he or she accurately predict how often the stampings would come across a given press? Chances are that the supervisor could not give us the desired information. To be really effective, these standards must be known. Why isn't the average supervisor aware of them? Simply because he or she has not been trained to cope with production problems in terms of a schedule.

SIS is a new way of looking at job-time relationships. It proposes that all elements of given operation be known to the supervisors, and places a unique tool in their hands to control the flow of work. The unique tool, of course, is SIS. The knowledge is provided by the work standards.

How to Define the Unit of Measure for Work Standards

Defining the proper unit of work, to which the time element is applied, may appear on the surface to be an elementary task. With skill and experience it usually is. Defining the proper work unit must never be underestimated. SIS specialists undertake considerable study and analysis to arrive at the proper unit of measure. Some cases are relatively easy. Others are complex. The proper unit of measure is the foundation of the work standard. You must exercise care that the unit of measure is a uniform factor.

In most industrial operations a great deal of attention is focused on standards. Consequently, the activities that are measured by standard engineering procedures (time study, MTM, standard data work factor, etc.) have a well-established unit of measure. However, it is of little value to the foreperson who has neither the time nor the desire to interpret a standard, so expressed, into something that can be worked with. This kind of arrangement exists in too many situations, but to be an effective tool, work standards must be converted to pieces per hour for the supervisor's use.

To help understand the basis of preparation for the units of measure, the following table is a simplified version of the typical standard data sheets of a fabricating plant. Observe the unit of measure. Relate this to the listed activity in the table to see how it was derived.

ACTIVITY	UNIT OF MEASURE	TIME ALLOWANCE	PIECES PER HOUR
Stock press	Care	3.30	—
Change die	Die change	25.00	—
Set-upstop and square bends	Set up	6.70	––
Set-up double bends	Set up	13.40	—
Read bundle card	Card	.50	—
Press brakes			
1 Bend	Piece	.40	150
2 Bends	Piece	.43	139
3 Bends	Piece	.56	107
4 Bends	Piece	.60	100
5 Bends	Piece	.70	86

Notice that there is no attempt to establish a precise, scientific unit of measure. Breakdown of the work into elemental components is not of any consequence, nor is it desired. Scheduling, not work measurement, is the key factor.

How to Establish a Unit of Measure for Maintenance Work

Units of measure are easy to define in a production activity because of the availability of data and the repetitive feature of the work. How do we arrive at consistent units for maintenance work, when the job is largely nonroutine? Not too much attention has been directed to maintenance work, at least not in the way production operations have been measured. Defining nonroutine jobs becomes more difficult. However, if recognition is given to the elements that comprise maintenance work, we will discover that the task is not as formidable as it may seem.

Each job is composed of units that are readily identified and measured when each unit is segregated. For example, an electrician installs a lighting system. The installation is the total job. Measurable elements would be running conduit, hanging fixtures, installing switches, reading architectural prints, etc. From each of these elements a unit of measure can be derived.

There are three basic types of maintenance work: preventative maintenance, routine maintenance, and emergency maintenance. Of the three, only the first is predictable, repetitive, and most similar to a routine production operation. An oiler's work, for example, is generally within the realm of preventative maintenance. The elements of the job are easily definable. An oiler fills oil cans, greases and oils bearing, and cleans machinery. Routine and emergency maintenance, on the other hand, are for the most part nonrepetitive. Even here, if we analyze the components of each task, as in the example of the electrician, the unit of measure can be established.

Establishing Units of Measure in Engineering Work

Engineering functions are seldom measured. As with maintenance, there is a certain reluctance to tackle the nonroutine or technical activity. Such fears are groundless. The engineering function, like the clerical or production operation, can be defined provided that we first break down the job into its component parts. It must be mentioned, however, that this technique is applicable to the more basic type of engineering activity rather than research and development application.

In the engineering department of a door manufacturing plant, detail engineers interpreted and transposed information from architectural drawings basing the standards on the *sources documents*; the following units of measure were established.

ACTIVITY	UNIT OF MEASURE	TIME ALLOWANCE	PIECES PER HOUR
Door Frames			
Drawings			
Form 225-frame elevation	Drawing	15 Min.	4
Form 416-buck section	Drawing	20 Min.	3
Schedules			
Form 703-Apt. house	Line	1 Min.	60
Form 707-detail	Line	2 Min.	30
Schedule corrections	Entry	4 Min.	15
Floor Plan corrections	Page	10 Min.	6

This plant tried to use the broadest possible unit of measure. Several observations revealed that for a door frame drawing the amount of time required was very consistent. The drawing was selected as the unit. It would have been more exact to use a smaller unit of measure, say a line or entry. But we are not chasing exactness, particularly at the expense of the supervisor who must apply these standards.

The element of supervisory time must be considered. The schedules, it was found, required widely varying amounts of time. The next smallest unit was the line, which proved to be consistent. This became the unit of measure for the schedules.

Key Principles for Selecting Units of Measure

There are a few basic principles that can aid in the selections of units of measure.

- The unit selected should be the broadest possible unit available.
- It must be that type of unit that can be expressed as a quantity per hour.
- If *any* type of paper work is involved, such as in clerical and engineering applications, the unit of measure should be located in the source document.
- It must be easily measured to save the supervisor's time before assigning work.

GROUND RULES FOR DETERMINING REASONABLE EXPECTANCY FOR MANUFACTURING JOB TIMES

SIS is not based on precise, scientific work standards. There is no need for this. In fact, to further the understanding of the concept, work standards in SIS applications are termed "reasonable expectancies."

A reasonable expectancy is defined as the quantity of work that can be produced by an average employee under normal working conditions in a given period of time. The period of time is usually one hour.

The reasonable expectancy is defined in terms of the unit of measure. For example, in the stamping department, we have determined that stamping is the best unit of measure. The reasonable expectancy would be expressed as the number of stampings that can be processed by a worker in one hour.

Whenever reasonable expectancies are being determined, certain criteria must be established. The ground rules are:

- *Test the job under consideration under normal working conditions.* No attempt should be made to isolate the worker or impose ideal working conditions. If the measurement is to be representative, the reasonable expectancy must be established under actual working conditions.
- *Make sure the individual(s) being studied is working at a reasonable and consistent pace.*
- *As in all work standards, make enough studies to assure accuracy of the data.* As a general rule, four separate studies will be sufficient.
- *Use historical data with caution.* It might contain lost time or foreign elements in the operation.
- *Use "pure time" as the basis for the reasonable expectancy.* "Pure time" can be defined

as that time necessary to perform a given job, exclusive of all unusual forms of lost time.

The reasonable expectancy is different from the exact standards commonly used in industrial operations. The standards presently in use have built-in allowances for delays; whereas reasonable expectancies do not. When a "batch" of reasonable expectancies are assigned to a worker, we are telling him or her to perform a reasonable amount of work for the given time period. No attempt if made to speed up activity. Neither is the worker allowed the luxury of built-in wasted time. A fair day's work is expected. The reasonable expectancy has the effect of stressing the role of supervisor scheduling the work rather than the work measurement itself. SIS emphasizes scheduling as the key factor in obtaining smoother work flow and operation efficiencies.

How to Prepare an Activity Report

In almost any given operation, the major portion of a workload consists of a few basic tasks. For example, an inspector's basic job is to inspect product; this will occupy at least half of his or her time, while the remaining tasks are devoted to communicating problems to workers, calibrating gauges and other related activities. It is the job of the *activity report* to specify these tasks, to record how often they are performed and when they occur. The activity report will determine the total workload and is the basis for constructing reasonable expectancies. (See Figure 16-1.)

To start the report, all job duties of the employee are listed on the left side of the sheet. This list should be carefully reviewed with the individual concerned and also with his or her supervisor, in order to cover all the activities performed. It is best to have the activities described in as simple terminology as is possible.

To establish the time period when the employee performs each task and how often the task is done, divide the middle of the sheet into time periods. For the purpose of this analysis two to four periods are adequate. When the described activity has been performed, the employee puts a hash mark in the proper column. At the conclusion of the workday, the activity report is collected by the supervisor and a fresh report form is issued the following day.

This tally should be completed each day by the employee for a period of one month. Sufficient data will then have been gathered to indicate all responsibilities and the frequencies of occurrence.

Measuring Manufacturing Job Time

During this period the reasonable expectancies of all the tasks are set. Because you are interested in normally paced activity, rather than exact time measurements, do not use a stopwatch. The best way to observe the amount of time usually needed to complete a job is to use a wristwatch or pocket watch to help arrive at approximate time levels. Be sure the five guidelines for establishing reasonable expectancies are

Name: JACK PIERCE							WORKLOAD CALCULATIONS	
Job: INSPECTOR		ACTIVITY REPORT				Date: WEEK OF JUNE 7 (5 DAYS)		
Description Of Activity	Unit of Measure	Volume				Totals	Reasonable Expectancies MINUTES	Total Workload MINUTES
		7 AM to 9 AM	9 AM to 11AM	11:30 AM to 1:30 PM	1:30 PM to 3:30 PM			
ROVING INSPECTION GRINDERS	PIECE	20	25	20	15	80	1.00	80
ROVING INSPECTION HONING MACHINES	PIECE	25	25	20	20	90	1.00	90
ROVING INSPECTION TUMBLERS	PIECE	25	25	20	20	90	1.00	90
GATE INSPECTION FINISHING DEPT.	BASKET	3	3	4	2	12	15.00	180
GAUGE CALIBRATION	GAUGE	20	0	0	0	20	5.00	100
POSTING TO SPC CHARTS	CHART	20	20	20	20	80	1.50	120
WRITING INSPECTION REPORTS	PAGE	10	12	8	12	42	4.00	168
FEEDBACK TO OPERATORS	DISCUSSION	22	5	12	6	45	5.00	225
OPTICAL COMPARATOR INSPECTION	PIECE	10	12	6	9	37	3.50	130
SHAFT BALANCE INSPECTION	SHAFT	12	5	15	0	32	7.00	224
TOTALS:								1407

Figure 16-1 Activity Report

in use. What is important is that the time considered be "pure time" and does not include periods of time when the employee is waiting for work, or suffers unusual interruptions that would not be considered routine.

Once you are fortified with approximate reasonable expectancies, "batch" the work and assign it to the employee. Observe the employee while he does the work and check the accuracy of the reasonable expectancies. By doing this several times you can verify the reasonable expectancies established and change those expectancies that are incorrect.

How to Determine the Workload

Once the data have been sharpened and judged to be reliable, the data are applied to each day's activities, as determined by the activity report, to arrive at the amount of time required to handle the volume of work. The data will provide the necessary information to assign work to each employee and workstation.

Using the same activity report described above, fill out the two columns on the right marked *Reasonable Expectancies* and *Total Workload*. Next to each activity, denote the reasonable expectancies in number of pieces per unit of measure. After each activity enter the volume of work recorded on the activity report.

For example, using the Activity Report shown in Figure 16-1, notice the reasonable expectancy that has been written in the second column from the right. Immediately to the right of that column is the total workload for each task as described in the first column on the left.

The first activity, "Roving Inspection Grinders" occurred 90 times for inspector Jack Pierce during the week of June 7. The reasonable expectancy for each piece inspected at the grinders was found to equal one minute.

The workload is determined by multiplying the total amount that activity occurred by the reasonable expectancy. Here, 90 pieces inspected × 1 minute = 90 minutes total workload time for "Roving Inspection Grinders" for the entire five-day week.

Similarly, calculate each of the total workload times for every activity. Then add together the "Total Workload" column and, in this case, calculate a total weekly workload of 1407 minutes (see bottom right-hand column).

Since there are 2400 minutes in each work week (60 minutes/hour × 40 hours/week) the workload for Jack Pierce during the week of June 7 was:

$$1407 \text{ minutes}/2400 \text{ minutes} \times 100 = 58.6\%$$

It now becomes apparent that an excess of time is either lost or wasted. For an eight-hour day, it is not surprising to see that work accomplishment is only 40 percent to 60 percent of total capability. We have now arrived at the basis for future reduction in personnel. When the short-interval schedule is installed and in operation, these reductions can be made.

Developing the Job Data Sheet

For every individual and for every work station there will be a multitude of established reasonable expectancies. To correlate this information, you should prepare *job data sheets*. This will consist of the activity, described briefly, the unit of measure and the reasonable expectancies, expressed in pieces per hour. Figure 16-2 is an example of such a job data sheet.

Each job data sheet lists the daily activities first, with the other duties following in descending order of frequency. Notice that in Figure 16-2 the last two jobs have been assigned a straight time allowance. Because they occur infrequently the job itself becomes the unit of measure, and the time required to perform the job becomes the reasonable expectancy. It would be impractical, for example, to express "fill blueprint machine with ammonia" as six times per hour, when the job occurs only once a week.

How to Handle Unscheduled Work

A certain amount of work cannot be scheduled feasibly and assigned reasonable expectancies. This amount of work will vary according to the situation. Each task will have to be judged by its own standards. The reason the nonroutine work cannot be scheduled is because standards cannot be established and used practically. If (a) the work is occasional and small or (b) there are a large number of very small "batches" which must be kept together or (c) the work does not lend itself to scheduling, then it is better to handle this work outside of the system.

Many work-standard specialists claim that any work can be measured and standards of performance established. This is probably true. But there are some instances where the cost of establishing and applying standards exceed the anticipated gains. This kind of work can be handled more appropriately by estimating and adding it to the production plan outside of the schedule.

HOW TO ESTABLISH EQUIVALENT UNITS OF MEASURE TO COMPARE OPERATIONS

When measuring productivity some conversion factors must be introduced to establish a frame of reference against which all operations can be measured. This is the purpose of the *equivalent unit of measure.*

An equivalent unit is an applied factor that reduced different standards of performance to one common element. These factors are always based on time; usually a fraction of an hour. The equivalent unit must be one that can readily be multiplied or divided in terms of varying standards. The simplest equivalent unit conversion factor is 60 units to the hour. Let us assume that we have four different operations to measure, each with a different standard. Through our studies and analysis, we have established the reasonable expectancies.

DEPARTMENT: BLUEPRINT ROOM		REASONABLE EXPECTANCY
DESCRIPTION OF ACTIVITY	UNIT OF MEASURE	HOURLY
Make Blueprints	Copy	140
Make Thermofax Copies	Copy	120
Make Photostats	Copy	110
Layout Job for Paste-Up	Layout Sheet	12
Write Labels	Label	60
Tag and Stamp Plans	Plan	75
File Folders	Folder	125
Enter Orders and Stamp	Order	75
Trip to Maintenance for Ammonia	Trip	30 Min.
Fill Blueprint Machine with Ammonia	Job	10 Min.

Figure 16-2 Job Data Sheet

OPERATION	PIECES PER HOUR
#1	3,000
#2	360
#3	150
#4	480

We need a common element for these standards. By expressing each operation in equivalent units, we can reduce each operation to the same base.

OPERATION	PIECES PER HOUR	EQUIVALENT UNITS
#1	3,000	60
#2	360	60
#3	150	60
#4	480	60

Imagine that all four of these operations are measured for an hour. If all the workers attained the exact scheduled pieces per hour, they would have earned 240 equivalent units, or 100 percent schedule productivity. Suppose they varied in their actual output. The picture may then look something like this:

OPERATION	PIECES PER HOUR	EQUIVALENT UNITS	ACTUAL EQUIVALENT UNITS	PRODUCTIVITY
#1	3,000	60	30	50%
#2	360	60	50	83%
#3	150	60	70	116%
#4	480	60	60	100%

Operation #1 produced 1,500 pieces for the hour. Since 60 equivalent units were scheduled per hour, this operation earned only one-half of 30 equivalent units. Operation #3, on the other hand, produced 174 pieces. This represents 16 percent more than scheduled and therefore earned 116 percent. Total operation productivity was 87.5 percent (210/240) = 87.5 percent).

How to Use a Conversion Chart to Simplify the Job

We have now established an index to measure any conglomerate activity. We can determine either individual or departmental schedule productivity. We also see that some amount of arithmetic is necessary to make the calculations. These calculations can be simplified with the use of a conversion chart.

As we have established 60 equivalent units to the hour, the problem of mathematical conversion is simple. The use of the conversion chart enables you to quickly plot your daily schedule control sheet. Figure 16-3 illustrates a typical conversion chart. This chart was established using five-minute time intervals, which have been found to be sufficiently accurate for both control and labor reporting. Any finer breakdown is unnecessary and takes too much of the supervisor's time.

pieces per hour	EQUIVALENT UNITS FOR EACH FIVE-MINUTE TIME PERIOD											
	5	10	15	20	25	30	35	40	45	50	55	60
5		1	1	1	2	2	2	3	3	3	4	5
10		2	2	3	4	5	6	6	7	8	9	10
15	1	3	3	5	6	7	8	9	11	12	13	15
20	1	4	5	6	8	10	11	13	15	17	18	20
25	1	5	6	8	10	12	14	15	15	21	23	25
30	2	5	7	10	12	15	17	20	22	25	29	30
35	2	6	8	11	14	17	20	23	26	29	32	35
40	3	7	10	13	16	20	23	26	30	33	36	40
45	3	8	11	15	19	22	23	26	30	38	42	45
50	4	9	12	16	20	25	29	33	37	41	46	50
55	4	10	13	18	23	27	32	36	41	46	50	55
60	5	10	15	20	25	30	35	40	45	50	55	60
65	5	11	16	21	27	32	38	43	49	54	59	65
70	6	12	16	23	29	35	41	47	52	58	64	70
75	6	13	18	25	31	37	44	47	52	62	69	75
80	7	14	20	25	33	40	47	54	60	66	73	80
85	7	15	21	28	35	42	50	57	64	71	78	85
90	7	15	22	30	35	45	53	60	67	75	82	90
95	7	16	23	31	39	47	55	63	71	79	87	95
100	8	17	25	33	41	50	58	67	75	83	91	100
105	8	18	26	35	44	52	61	70	79	88	96	105
110	9	19	26	37	45	55	64	74	82	91	100	110
115	9	20	28	38	48	57	67	77	86	96	105	115
120	10	20	30	40	50	60	70	80	90	100	110	120
125	10	21	31	41	52	62	73	83	94	105	116	125
130	10	22	32	43	54	65	76	87	97	108	119	130
135	11	23	33	45	56	67	79	90	101	113	125	135
140	11	24	35	45	58	70	82	94	105	117	130	140
145	12	25	36	48	60	72	86	94	109	121	134	145
150	12	25	37	50	62	75	89	100	112	125	138	150

Figure 16-3 Equivalent Unit Conversion Chart

DEVELOPING EFFECTIVE PRODUCTION CONTROL TOOLS FOR SHORT-INTERVAL SCHEDULING

Production planning and control is the function that decrees what work will be done, how the work will be done, where the work will be done and when the work will be done.

In actual practice, the planning function and the control function are separate. *Planning* has the responsibility of utilizing plant operating facilities to produce a low-cost, high quality product. *Control* has as its objective the task of keeping work flowing through on schedule and instituting corrective action when the plan goes off course.

If the plan is faulty or if control is ineffective, processing costs increase and delivery dates lose their validity. The company loses business and profits drop.

Because so many variables can affect the flow of work through a plant, the planning and control people are usually on the "hot seat." They constantly feel a need for a "cushion," and they usually build it in. In most companies, one of two situations exist. Planning loads are deliberately made light because the planning group realizes that too many things can go wrong. Consequently, plant utilization is low compared to plant capacity. Delays and lost time become the accepted way of life and a potentially dangerous modus operandi is established. Other planning groups load to the absolute maximum even though, time and time again, the production organization demonstrates its inability to come through. Replanning and frequent changes in the schedule are the order of the day. This situation is just as damaging as the first. In both cases, accomplishments are far below the potential of the facilities and the people.

Probably the most tragic aspect of either circumstance is that this poor way of doing a job is rapidly communicated to the first-line supervisor and assimilated. It is the easy way out, after all, the supervisor is only emulating his managers. When this unfortunate circumstance occurs, control and operating efficiency go out the window. The supervisor will hold on to more people that he actually needs and will use them as a cushion to protect himself from a fluctuating, spasmodic work flow.

The successful SIS program has its roots in production planning and control. It is here that the production forecast and plan are formulated. And it is upon these instruments that the schedule control is based. It naturally follows that if a major error is made in the forecast it will be transmitted through the production plan and could wind up by reversing the very purpose of the schedule control which controls the work. The SIS program, by necessity, must begin with the design of the forecast and production plan. Once these documents have been perfected the short-interval schedule can be installed.

How to Implement Short-Interval Scheduling

Let us make an important distinction before we discuss the forecast. As just mentioned, planning loads the manufacturing departments and control follows up in regard to progress on the schedule. Both functions are defined, in the customary tradition, as the responsibility of production planning and control. SIS changes this relationship. The responsibility for schedule accomplishment is separated from the responsibility for schedule preparation—just as it is now.

The important distinction is that the sole responsibility for the meeting of the manufacturing schedule belong to the manufacturing organization, specifically the supervisor and his managers.

To support this relationship, a secondary and supporting principle is made. The foreperson must be given a definite schedule for which he or she is held accountable and this schedule should be for a short period of time. Ideally, the schedule should indicate the total labor hours output required by labor classification and machine center so the supervisor can properly allocate the workload.

Schedules are released in short incremental perhaps for a day, three days or a week, depending on the complexity of the operation. The supervisor receives only that workload scheduled for the short run, Future work is retained in production planning and is only released to the foreperson when he or she finishes the current work schedule. Receiving only the work that is required on a definite schedule from planning eliminates the need for the supervisor to operate from a "hot" list.

Work assignment with SIS clearly stipulates that one source (the employee) can be assigned work by another source (the supervisor). The same principle must be extended to the planning department. It assigns the workload to the foreperson who, in turn, assigns work to the employee.

To carry out this principle, it is necessary to clearly assign the responsibility for meeting schedule dates to the supervisor. Production planning will support the procedure by issuing sequenced operation schedules on a periodic basis.

Forecast for Short-Interval Scheduling

Short-interval scheduling begins with the dating of orders after the manufacturing information is prepared. Presumably, these orders are within the overall capacity of the plant (or business) and the company has accepted the responsibility to meet the delivery dates. This may result in workload above or below capacity for a short period of time. An annual forecast is made to provide management with a guide as to the amount of production required by month for the coming year.

Initially, the annual forecast is prepared one year in advance and updated on a monthly basis. Depending on the type and complexity of the business, many different methods are used. Some are very simple and easy to prepare while others are quite sophisticated and involve computers. Either way, they must all be reviewed and adjusted periodically for fluctuations in demand.

A large garment warehouse, using SIS, predicts volume on a monthly basis for a one-year period. Its forecast, predicted on anticipated sales, is broken down for the warehouse in each of the six basic sections. A section forecast looks like this:

Warehouse   Section: SORTING   Date Made: 11/18/X8

JAN.	FEB.	MARCH	APRIL	MAY	JUNE	JULY	AUG.	SEPT.	OCT.	NOV.	DEC.
100	175	180	210	235	250	200	180	200	160	170	170
80	150	180									
80	86	110									

To keep the forecast current, it is updated every month. The total actual volume of the preceding three months is divided by the total planned volume for the same period.

The figure obtained represents the percentage of actual orders based on forecasted volume. For example:

	JANUARY	**FEBRUARY**	**MARCH**	
Actual volume	80,000	150,000	180,000	= 410,000
Planned volume	100,000	175,000	180,000	= 455,000
Percent of forecast mfg.	80%	86%	100%	

$$\text{Therefore:} \quad \frac{\text{Actual Volume}}{\text{Planned Volume}} = \frac{410,000}{455,000} = 90\%$$

Beginning with April, all forecasted volume is then adjusted to the new calculated rate of 90 percent of volume. For example, April's planned volume is now 189,000 (the old forecasted figure of 210,000 × 90 percent) and May's planned volume is now 211,500 (the old forecasted rate of 235,000 × 90 percent) and so on. All new monthly figures are then tempered by recent sales trends in the company.

The important point about the forecast is that one be made. No matter how difficult it is to determine the forecast and regardless of the multitude of variables associated with the product or service, it is a necessary step in formulating the overall plan.

Using the Production Plan as a Method of Control

The forecast must be translated into a workable production plan for all of the operating departments. A master plan based on the forecast is prepared, dovetailing all production activities. All orders are dated in line with the scheduling policy and operations are dated with a start and completion time.

In determining rules for individual department plans, the length of productive time for the operations is a governing factor. Productive time, in turn, is based on established reasonable expectancies and adjusted to department performance. The need for individual operation dating increases as the cycle time per operation increases.

Tips for preparing a good production plan. Many companies work with a minimum of planning in the production planning stage. To contrast the information of a poor plan versus an informative, reliable and workable plan, compare Figure 16-4 with Figure 16-5. The plan shown in Figure 16-4 displays only a minimum of

STAMPING DEPARTMENT PRODUCTION AND EXPEDITING SCHEDULE WEEK OF: 4/25 – 4/30						
Lot Number	2370	2453	3567	4523	2388	18760
Customer	Davis Co.	Jon. Al.	Guis Co.	Guis Co.	East Bend	East Bend
Gage and Size	032 × 12"	150 × 25"	016 × 10"	016 × 15"	080 × 17"	040 × 23"
Die Number	1a12	1a25	2b10	2n15	1r17	1r23
Cost Center	1650— 4	1650— 18	1650— 4	1650— 4	1650— 7	1650— 5
Order Quantity— Pieces	300,000	100,000	160,000	160,000	75,000	225,000
Order Quantity— Lbs.	175,00	470,000	47,000	60,000	195,000	110,000

Figure 16-4   Simple Production Plan

ALLIED ALUMINUM - STAMPING SCHED.
WEEK ENDING: 4/30

					PRESSES												ANNEAL			TOTAL DEPT.
					1	2	3	4	5	6	7	8	9	10	1100 Total	1	2	220 Total	1320
MACHINE HOURS AVAILABLE →					110	110	110	110	110	110	110	110	110	110		110	110		
LOT NUMBER	GAUGE X SIZE	DIE NO.	QUANTITY	PRESS PCS./HR.											Total	1	2	Total	
2370	032 x 12	1AL12	300,000	3000	100										100		40	40	140
2244	150 x 25	1AH25	100,000	1000		100									100				100
2325	016 x 10	1AL10	180,000	3000			60								60		20	20	80
2313	016 x 12	1AL125	210,000	3000				70							70		24	24	94
2270	016 x 15	1AL15	160,000	2500					64						64	18		18	82
2265	020 x 17	1AL20	10,000	200						50					50				50
2324	040 x 15	1AH15	100,000	1000							100				100				100
2311	050 x 20	1AH20	60,000	2000								30			30	8		8	38
2312	ICE TRAYS	1FQ12	200,000	4000									50		50	20		20	70
2313	ICE TRAYS	1FQ12	200,000	4000									50		50	20		20	70
2296	050 x 32	1AL32	75,000	1000										75	75	12		12	87
2250	125 x 13	1AH13	160,000	2000								80			80		20	20	100
2359	052 x 17	1AL17	90,000	2000						45					45	12		12	57
2302	090 x 16	1AH16	100,000	3000										33	33				33
TOTAL SCHEDULED LABOR-HOURS →					100	100	60	70	64	95	100	110	100	108	907	90	104	194	1101

LABOR-HOURS NEEDED TO MEET SCHEDULE

TOTAL SCHEDULED LABOR-HOURS	1101
ADD: STOCKERS - FIXED CREWING	120
UNSCHEDULED WORK ALLOWANCE	100
TOTAL LABOR-HOURS NEEDED	1321

LABOR-HOURS AVAILABLE FOR SCHEDULE

NUMBER OF EMPLOYEES ON ROLL MULTIPLIED
BY HOURS PER WEEK = 40x40 =   1600

LABOR-HRS. AVAILABLE	1600
LESS: ABSENTEE ALLOWANCE	48
TOTAL LABOR-HOURS AVAILABLE	1552
TOTAL LABOR-HOURS NEEDED	1321
OVER-UNDER	231

PLANNED SURPLUS OF 5.8 WORKERS (231/40)

Figure 16-5 Detailed Production Plan

information and is in sharp contrast with the plan shown in Figure 16-5. Comparing the two, it is easy to see that Figure 16-5 follows these vital guidelines:

- Depicts scheduled machine hours and labor-hours clearly.
- Make sure individual and departmental machine loads are obtainable at a glance.
- Measures scheduled machine hours and labor-hours against capacity.
- Lists production standards, in easy to understand form, for the supervisor's use.
- Enables management to prepare daily work schedules.
- Indicates overloaded conditions and provides sufficient flexibility for adjusted load to capacity.
- Provide an indication of excess, or short, manpower staffing.
- Shows all unscheduled work that is to be processed by the department.

How to Assign Work

Once a production plan has been implemented, it is necessary to break the plan down into daily increments for assignment of work and, subsequently, some procedure must be devised to assign the work to individual operator and work stations. This is the principle of dispatching work in the lexicon of short-interval scheduling, it is termed "sign-out."

Sign-out in SIS indicates the assignment of work to employees in quantities that have been converted to a total time requirement for each assignment. Batching is the physical accumulation of work to be signed-out in equal increments of time, usually one hour. The batch ticket displayed in Figure 16-6 is such a document used to dispatch and assign work.

Following the principle sign-out in its entirety, each batch of work would have a batch ticket attached when distributed. The key to the success of SIS is that it lets its users tell an employee when a job batch should be completed in advance of his or her starting on the job. The batch ticket tells the employee when the batch of work should be finished and gives the employee the opportunity to communicate with the supervisor about any condition that may be preventing him or her from attaining this goal. Most traditional forms of work measurement lack this direct communication between employee and supervisor at the job level where it counts. In addition, they suffer from what might be termed the "post-tally sin." That is, an employee does not know how well he or she has succeeded in the attainment of production goals for a delayed period of time, ranging from one day to one month, and in some cases, never. Even then, when an employee is appraised, it is done only in a very general way with little or no knowledge of how specific assignments were performed. The real loss of potential under the "post-tally" approach is not, oddly enough, in lack of knowledge of how well an employee is doing but rather in not knowing in time when, at any given time, an employee is available to take on additional work. This factor alone is a prime reason why the SIS approach can

JOB: #8768-A	BATCH TICKET	BATCH NUMBER #1450-136
NAME: M.L. GREEN	ITEM: #3732 ORDER LINE ITEM	SCHEDULED BY: R. MYER
DESCRIPTION: SEE MANUAL PG. 96	REF. JOB DATA LIST ME-17	SCHEDULED TIME: 1.00 HOURS
START TIME	STOP TIME	ELAPSED TIME
8⁰⁰/AM	9¹⁵/AM	1.25 HOURS
REMARKS 15 MIN. LOST — WAITING FOR SUPPLIES		

Figure 16-6   Job Lot Ticket

improve production above that which may now be realized under the "post-tally" forms of traditional work measurement.

How the Schedule Control Keeps Supervisors on Top of the Production Plan

A weekly production plan has been developed and a method for dispatching work has been provided. But how does the supervisor control the work itself and dovetail results with the production plan? Another tool must be placed in the supervisor's hands in an effort to utilize resources for complete control of individual work stations at short intervals of time. This tool is the ore of the SIS program and is called the "schedule control."

The control document and how it works. The function of the schedule control is to keep the supervisor on the alert regarding the production plan, and to aid in checking progress of the plan on a regular cycle. Use of this control document allows the supervisor to plan ahead in order to remain on schedule, even when schedule misses occur. Figure 16-7 is a modified schedule control that was adopted by a company in need of a control device to handle a relatively small and easy operation. The left side of the form lists the names of the operators. The time periods entered across the top of the form divided into four, two-hour intervals of the normal working day, plus an addition of two, one-hour periods to allow for the planning

EMPLOYEE	PLAN / ACT	7:00 AM to 9:00 AM	9:00 AM to 11:00 AM	11:00 AM to 1:30 PM	1:30 PM to 3:30 PM	3:30 PM to 4:30 PM	4:30 PM to 5:30 PM
STAMPING DEPARTMENT SCHEDULE CONTROL						DATE: 4/25	SHIFT: 2
BROWN	P	1500	1500	1500	1500		
	A	1280	1500	1500	1600		
JONES	P	1000	1000	3000	3000		
	A	1000	1000	2500	3600		
GREEN	P	2000	2000	1500	2000		
	A	2000	2000	1800	2000		
SWANSON	P	500	500	500	500		
	A	600	575	540	590		
PETERS	P	4000	4000	750	750		
	A	3200	3850	750	760		
MORRIS	P	700	700	800	800		
	A	700	700	800	800		
BAKER	P	1200	1200	1000	1000		
	A	1250	1170	980	1400		
	P						
	A						
	P						
	A						
	P						
	A						
BI-HOURLY TOTAL	P	10900	10900	9050	9550		
	A	10030	10795	8870	10750		
CUMULATIVE TOTAL	P	10900	21800	30850	40400		
	A	10030	20825	29695	40445		

Figure 16-7   Sample Schedule Control Form—Planned Versus Actual Production

of overtime. Each time period listed provides space to enter both planned and actual production. In this particular case, two-hour rather than one-hour intervals were considered sufficient to exercise control.

Using the scheduled batch tickets, the supervisor observed the number of pieces per hour required, doubled this figure (for the two-hour interval), and recorded this amount in the space "P" provided for each operator listed on the form. The supervisor then extended the double figures into as many time periods as needed, depending on the quantity of pieces to be produced as specified on the batch tickets. A sufficient quantity of batch tickets were calculated in advance, for each operation to fill the entire day, thereby enabling the supervisor to plan all material movements and have machines set up in time for production.

Every two hours the supervisor checked each operator listed on the schedule control. At each operation the supervisor saw what actual production was and entered this in the space "A" for that operator. Having completed the survey, the supervisor added the planned figures, based on the schedule for the two-hour period, and entered them in the "Bi-hourly Total" column. This "P" and "A" reflects one, two-hour period. The "Cumulative Total" space is for the entry of totalled "planned" and "actual" figures for all the work periods recorded. Planned figures, for each operator, are totalled and entered in the "A" column.

The supervisor now had a tool to help him measure, every two hours, each operation and performance of the entire department. If anything would occur to prevent the supervisor from attaining production goals, he or she was in a position to recognize it when it was happening and take timely corrective action.

If the supervisor should fall behind in production, he or she could plan to make up deficiencies by planning overtime or adding additional operators to recoup the loss. Should the schedule be surpassed, the supervisor could then plan additional work. What is important is that the supervisor is now in a position to recognize off-schedule conditions, and therefore is able to take corrective action before it is too late to act. Again, time once lost is time never regained.

Applying the Equivalent Unit to the Schedule Control

The schedule control just illustrated does not use equivalent units. Its basic use is to pinpoint troublesome conditions that prevent the schedule from being attained. It cannot be used to calculate productivity. If this form is modified for the use of equivalent units, productivity can be measured. If we compare the schedule control in Figure 16-7 with the schedule control in Figure 16-8 we see that the latter uses equivalent units, thereby showing individual and departmental productivity. A tighter control can now be attained.

FINDING THE OPTIMUM SHORT INTERVAL FOR JOB TIME

The importance of finding the best short-interval of time for a given operation cannot be minimized. There is no hard-and-fast rule stipulating the time for assignment and follow-up of work. The length of the best short-interval will vary from one type of work to another.

Even with the same department, these intervals may be completely different. A common sense approach to the complexity and measurability of each operation

STAMPING DEPARTMENT SCHEDULE CONTROL									DATE: 4/25 SHIFT: 2	
EMPLOYEE	P L N A C T	7:00 AM to 9:00 AM	9:00 AM to 11:00 AM	11:00 AM to 1:30 PM	1:30 PM to 3:30 PM	3:30 PM to 4:30 PM	4:30 PM to 5:30 PM	TOTAL EQUIVA- LENT UNITS	PRODUC- TIVITY %
BROWN	P	120	105	120	105			450	96
	A	110	105	105	110			430	
JONES	P	120	105	120	105			450	100
	A	120	105	120	105			450	
GREEN	P	120	105	120	105			450	103
	A	120	105	130	110			465	
SWANSON	P	120	105	120	105			450	101
	A	115	100	125	115			455	
PETERS	P	120	105	120	105			450	92
	A	115	100	115	105			415	
MORRIS	P	120	105	120	105			450	99
	A	120	90	125	110			445	
BAKER	P	120	105	120	105			450	96
	A	100	105	120	105			430	
	P								
	A								
	P								
	A								
	P								
	A								
EQUIVALENT UNITS BI-HOURLY	P	840	735	840	735				
	A	785	700	840	765				
EQUIVALENT UNITS CUMULATIVE	P	840	1575	2415	3150			SHIFT PRODUCTIVITY 3150/3090 = 98%	
	A	785	1485	2325	3090				

Figure 16-8 Sample Schedule Control Form—Equivalent Unit Measurement

must be adapted. For example, in the overhaul of a large rolling mill that may take several weeks, it would be wise to establish intervals over two hours. Yet, in a clerical operation, the one-hour cycle is predominant and in the fast moving mail order business time cycles of twenty minutes are common.

There are several factors that must be studied to establish and maintain the optimum short-interval. The interval must be practical and effective. As in the case of a rolling mill, a one-hour check would be excessive due to the nature of the job. It would not yield satisfactory control. A condition of excess control would prevail. The supervisor would be spending too much time on the control and would be sacrificing his ability to supervise the technical aspects of the job. Each job must be examined from the standpoint of the length of time that the supervisor must spend on the activity.

As a general rule, the more repetitive the operation, the shorter the interval can be. Most production activities of the repetitive and intermittent type lend themselves to hourly intervals. However, stationary assembly operations, multiple crew operations or just complex and involved operations may go two to four hours, before the check is applied. Maintenance jobs, such as repairing machinery, is a case in point.

On rare occasions, a day or two may constitute the most practical interval. At this point, however, we are beginning to lose the attributes of the short-interval for control. A product engineer engaged in research work, for example, is not engaged in that type of work that lends itself to control intervals of one day, and, in many cases, may go as long as two or three days. In cases of this nature, it may be wise to reconsider the advisability of applying SIS. Again, the judgment of the interpreter must be applied. He or she must decide whether his control system will achieve what is wanted, within the budgeted cost.

Guidelines for Setting Short Intervals

The governing factors for establishing optimum short-intervals of control are:

- Make the interval brief enough to enable you to take corrective action in time to keep the schedule current.
- Make sure it doesn't take an excessive amount of time to keep the schedule current. Remember, you must balance your time between the technical and administrative portions of your job.
- Keep the interval short enough to motivate the employee to achieve the goal.

There is the example of the drive to Buffalo along the Thruway. When there was no hourly goal and markers were not spaced along the Thruway, achieving the goal became a very difficult task. When both goals and markers were present it suddenly was apparent if the schedule was not being met, and additional efforts in subsequent time periods allowed the goal to be accomplished.

TRACKING MISSED SCHEDULES TO ELIMINATE PRODUCTION DELAYS

Beginning with the forecast and production plan and extending through the supervisor and the line operation, we have installed a method of control to permit a smooth flow of work and to keep costs in line. At this stage of installation of SIS, management is made aware on a short-interval basis of any significant deviations from standard. If production is low or staffing out of line with existing orders it is now quickly recognized in time for management to take the necessary steps.

Recognizing the problem, however, does not solve it. The schedule control has only highlighted the substandard area. With this control the supervisors are able to investigate the causes of failure to attain the schedule and, in many cases, take corrective action. An additional control that will aid them and direct their immediate attention to solving the problem is called the "schedule miss report."

How to Set Up a Schedule Miss Report

The schedule miss report is an arm or extension of the schedule control. In any given time period, if the schedule isn't made, supervisors are required to make out a schedule miss report. There are several good reasons for using this additional control form. First, the supervisors are forced to recognize the impact of below par operations. The more schedule misses there are the more they are required to complete schedule miss reports stating reasons for poor performance in their sections. This directs not only their attention, but their supervisor's attention to the problems at hand.

Second, the supervisors' thinking is directed toward fining the reason for delays. On the report, they must list the corrective action taken to eliminate the causes of each and every delay. The nature of the system is such that their managers will closely scrutinize these critical reports in an effort to find patterns of delays and do something themselves. Any recurrent delay provokes supervision and focuses all of its resources on the problem. Additionally, problem employees are highlighted and can be handled through intelligent use of the schedule miss report. The schedule miss report is soon interpreted as a stigma and supervisors becomes quite anxious to improve their situation. Their managers direct their attention to helping the supervisors find the answers to the problems. This pressure is subsequently felt by the individual employee and he or she, in turn, becomes subject to the same motivation.

What to Look for When Tracking Missed Schedules

To give full value for expended effort a schedule miss report should answer certain questions:

- What work center and operations are involved?
- How many equivalent units were missed? If the schedule is missed by 5 percent or less, it is customary not to call this a schedule miss report unless the schedule in constantly missed by this amount.)
- What was the reason for the miss?
- What corrective action was taken?

Figure 16-9 is a schedule miss report used by a garment warehouse and is typical of the forms in use.

WAREHOUSE SCHEDULE MISS REPORT						Section: *DISTRIBUTING* Date: *10-12-X9*	
Employee	Job	Equival. Units			Time Per.	Reason For Miss	Corrective Action Taken
		S C H E D	A C T U L	M I S S D			
DOBBS	DISTRIB-UTOR	60	50	10	7-8	NO BACKLOG OF WORK	STOCKER'S MOVES TO BE RESCHEDULED.
FASON	"	60	30	30	9-10	RAN OUT OF RACKS	ELEVATOR BROKE DOWN. WILL ESTABLISH ALTERNATE SUPPLY.
WALE	MARKER	60	50	10	9-10	MARKER BROKEN	ADDITIONAL STANDBY MARKER ORDERED.
BROWN	"	60	45	15	10-11	NONE GIVEN	EMPLOYEE NOT DOING JOB. GIVEN WARNING

Figure 16-9   Schedule Miss Report

HOW SHORT-INTERVAL SCHEDULING GETS VITAL INFORMATION TO TOP MANAGEMENT

The basic reasoning behind every report issued to top management is:

- Does this report give management the information necessary to make prompt, reliable, and effective decisions?
- Is the report clear and concise?
- Is the report designed to highlight the significant information?
- Can the executive reading the report scan it and quickly digest the information that is vital to him?

SIS provides top and middle management with reports that are geared to "action" information. Through the use of management-by-exception techniques, only vital information that management needs to know is reported.

Management-by-exception can be defined as that which does not meet standard expectations or that which significantly deviates from the norm. For example, the garment warehouse, previously mentioned, was scheduled to process 3,000 garments per day. Using the exception technique of reporting, the warehouse manager would receive only the information reporting when production fell below or exceeded 3,000 pieces. This is the extreme case of exception reporting. In practice, a report should be given to the managers daily. If production fell below requirements, the deficit would be highlighted so that management's immediate attention would be drawn to the figure. The deficit may be printed in red ink or it may be circled, to name two methods.

Each report to management should be designed to save the time of the executive reading the report and to capture his or her attention. In SIS reports the vital information of productivity, cost, and other pertinent information are recorded in this fashion.

Companies must make a profit. They must ensure their success in order to survive. If an individual needs medical attention he or she calls a doctor. If a company is not healthy, then it too must get help. This is the function of SIS. It assists the company on the way to recovery. Even more important to the company, it helps the company "before" ills arise, thereby allowing it to remain healthy. During the course of the program, the company develops effective methods of doing business. The profit position is restored, and, although some individuals may be laid off temporarily to help effect the cure, the company can look beyond this to the day when it will attract new business and rehire those individuals.

Short-interval scheduling is not the answer to a company's prayers. There will never be that moment in time when a manager can push the "button" and everything goes exactly as planned. SIS is a system that, when used intelligently and with proper application, will produce economies and allow a company to remain in business profitably.

17

How to Use Labor Reports to Increase Productivity

The best devised work standards program is totally ineffective without the proper method of communicating performance results on the production floor to manufacturing managers and supervisors. Labor reporting is the method in common use today to handle just that problem. With the advent of the computer, the cumbersome job of accumulating job data, calculating performance results, and publishing these data has become very simple and straightforward.

Manufacturing companies experience an increase in productivity of up to 50 percent when labor reporting is installed (although the most usual range is from 15 percent to 35 percent). Nevertheless, in situations where little or no control has been exercised over the work force, 50 percent savings have occurred.

HOW TO IMPLEMENT A LABOR REPORTING SYSTEM IN SIX STEPS

Figure 17-1 describes the steps needed to implement a labor reporting system in a manufacturing operation.

Step 1: Set work standards for plant operations.

Step 2: Post work standards to job routing. A routing describes the sequence of operations. For example, in a fabrication shop making drum rolls, the routing with incorporated standards would look like Figure 17-2. All operations are performed in the sequence shown on the routing.

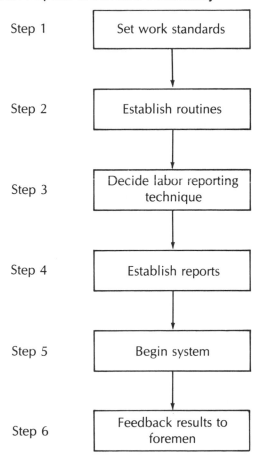

Step 1 — Set work standards

Step 2 — Establish routines

Step 3 — Decide labor reporting technique

Step 4 — Establish reports

Step 5 — Begin system

Step 6 — Feedback results to foremen

Figure 17-1 Steps in Labor Reporting System

50″ DRUM ROUTING		
OPERATION CODE	OPERATION DESCRIPTION	STANDARD LABOR-HOURS
001	Stock Plate	.50
002	Flame Cut 12″ × 50″ Plate	1.25
003	Roll to 50″ Drum	1.70
004	Weld in Heads	2.10
005	Turn Drum ¼″	2.65
006	Inspect	.25

Figure 17-2 Sample Job Routing

DYNAPAC MFG INC
SHOP ORDER DIRECT PRODUCTIVE WORK—FINISHED OPERATIONS

JOB NUMBER 5000-1015
PROGRAM NO. LABR20

COST CTR.	PART NUMBER	DESCRIPTION	SHOP ORDER	OPER NO.	PIECES COMP.	ACTUAL HRS	STANDARD HRS	PER-FORMANCE	CLOCK NO.	EMPLOYEE	COMMENTS
4131	821150	HEAD-PIPE	MO18320	0100	8	6.00	6.88	114.60	1041	KANE, DANIEL	
						6.00	6.88	114.60			
4131	821150	HEAD-PIPE	MO18320	0100	8	8.90	8.56	96.10	876	TALMADGE, HENRY	
						8.90	8.56	96.10			
COST CENTER TOTAL **						14.90	15.44	103.60			

Figure 17-3 Sample Daily Performance Report

234

Step 3: Explore the technique of labor reporting. Very simply, you should decide on the method of reporting operator's time on each job to the computer. This is usually done through time cards designed to have job time recorded on them. An alternative is a computerized shop floor system, where operators punch job data directly into CRT terminals and computer printouts are made daily.

Step 4: Determine reporting formats. See the discussion below.

Step 5: Begin the system. This is the payoff point.

Step 6: Feed reports back to forepeople. Forepeople in turn use the reports to control their operations and increase productivity.

USING THE DAILY PERFORMANCE REPORT TO TRACK WORKER PRODUCTIVITY

Dynapac, Inc., of New Jersey, a manufacturer of vibratory compaction equipment, uses a labor reporting system to control the productivity of its hourly production workers. Figure 17-3 illustrates a page from its daily labor report (it is called "Shop Order Direct Productive Work—Finished Operations"). This report is similar to the labor control technique described in Chapter Four except that it is computerized and shown here in contrast to the manual system. The entries on this report are self-explanatory other than the cost center number and shop order number which are numbers indigenous to Dynapac. The report reveals the performance of individual works as well as machine (cost center) performance.

USING THE LOST TIME REPORT

Figure 17-4 shows lost time for Dynapac every week by account description. Training, rework, tooling problems, and others have cumulative lost time hours posted to their individual accounts. This report is issued weekly and is called "Indirect Work By Account Number."

HOW TO SAVE MONEY USING LABOR REPORTS

Case Study: Dynapac Saves $104,000. Dynapac, recaptured approximately 200 labor-hours per week by identifying and eliminating the reasons for downtime. This resulted in an annual savings of:

$$200 \text{ labor-hours} \times 52 \text{ weeks} \times \$10 \text{ per hour} = \$104,000$$

Case Study: 20 Percent Drop in Downtime. A steel piping fabricator in the east cut its downtime annually by 20 percent with a resultant savings of $95,000 by identifying and eliminating machine downtime reasons.

Case Study: A Pharmaceutical Company Saves $260,000. One year after using labor reporting, this company claimed savings of $260,000 by identifying lost time by operator, machine, shift, and product. The ensuing analysis clearly indicated major tooling and material problems that were subsequently eliminated.

JOB NUMBER 5000-2035
PROGRAM NO. LABR40

DYNAPAC MFG INC
INDIRECT WORK BY ACCOUNT NUMBER
WEEK ENDING 11/22/X1

ACCOUNT NUMBER	DESCRIPTION	COST CENTER	ACTUAL HOURS	
1101	TRAINING	4114	2.20	
			2.20	** ACCOUNT TOTAL
1102	REWORK	4112	13.50	
		4114	74.20	
		4230	47.90	
		4234	33.60	
		5300	45.10	
			214.30	** ACCOUNT TOTAL
1104	JANITORIAL	4112	9.70	
		4113	22.30	
		4114	27.80	
			59.80	** ACCOUNT TOTAL
1105	MATERIAL HANDLING	4234	46.90	
			46.90	** ACCOUNT TOTAL
1109	MISC-OTHER	4113	17.50	
		4114	3.10	
			20.60	** ACCOUNT TOTAL
1110	SET UP	4113	4.80	
		4114	3.00	
			7.80	** ACCOUNT TOTAL
1114	TOOLING	4112	12.00	
		4114	4.90	
			16.90	** ACCOUNT TOTAL
1115	$$$ INVALID ACCOUNT NO.	4114	8.80	
			8.80	** ACCOUNT TOTAL

Figure 17-4 Sample Lost Time Report

236

JOB NUMBER 5000-2035
PROGRAM NO. LABR40

DYNAPAC MFG INC
INDIRECT WORK BY ACCOUNT NUMBER
WEEK ENDING 11/22/X1

ACCOUNT NUMBER	DESCRIPTION	COST CENTER	ACTUAL HOURS	
1121	WAITING TIME	4103	3.30	
		4114	2.00	
		4120	7.20	
		4234	7.30	
			19.80	** ACCOUNT TOTAL
1418	LABOR PL20-90952	5310	21.60	
			21.60	** ACCOUNT TOTAL
1419	LABOR PL20-90953	5310	20.80	
			20.80	** ACCOUNT TOTAL
1420	LABOR PL20-90954	5310	5.20	
			5.20	** ACCOUNT TOTAL
			444.70	*** FINAL TOTAL

Figure 17-4 Sample Lost Time Report

237

18

Manufacturing Engineering Techniques That Keep Quality High and Production Costs Low

HOW TO IMPROVE THE EFFECTIVENESS OF MANUFACTURING ENGINEERING

Manufacturing Engineering bridges the gap between the product engineering and production functions. Its job is to take the design offered by product engineering and make it a reality. Manufacturing engineering plans the production process which includes:

- Selecting the machinery and equipment
- Determining the operating method
- Selecting the tooling
- Establishing the work standards
- Working with QA to select sampling plans and inspection methods
- Providing process instructions for operators
- Planning facility and work station ergonomics layouts
- Costing operations
- Maintaining plant and equipment in working order

In addition to performing the tasks stated above, the manufacturing engineers must work effectively with design engineers, production managers, planners, and a host of other support line people. This means establishing systems that assure the effective working relationships needed to get the job done. With product engineering, for example, it means participating in design reviews early in the new product development cycle so that manufacturing engineers can adequately plan and implement their own procedures and tasks *before* production of the product starts, not during or afterwards.

QUESTIONNAIRE FOR EVALUATING YOUR MANUFACTURING ENGINEERING DEPARTMENT

Manufacturing engineering has a multitude of tasks to accomplish before it can be termed a successful venture. The major aspects of its performance can be examined by using the questionnaire that follows.

The manufacturing engineering questionnaire was developed by Management Sciences International, Inc., a quality improvement consulting firm, from its experiences in a variety of industries over a period of approximately 10 years. The consulting company attempted to isolate and identify those elements it considered most critical to the success of a viable manufacturing engineering effort.

The questionnaire has been used in such diverse industries as construction machinery, medical devices, plastics companies, furniture manufacturers, knitting mills, shelving manufacturers, and aluminum plants. Its use is applicable to almost any manufacturing facility, regardless of the products manufactured.

Organizing and Managing the Manufacturing Engineering Function

Q. Does manufacturing engineering report directly to the top manufacturing person (director of manufacturing for the company or plant)?

A. Manufacturing engineering should always report to the person responsible for the entire manufacturing function to assure its fair representation in the manufacturing process. If manufacturing engineering reports to the production manager, for example, it will take a back seat to getting the goods out the back door, and that could spell disaster.

Q. Does manufacturing engineering have a charter that outlines its primary responsibilities?

A. Manufacturing engineering should have a clearly defined charter that spells out the functions described in this questionnaire. The purpose of a mission statement is to assure the dedication of manufacturing engineers to those major tasks necessary for manufacturing products in the most economical manner possible.

The following major manufacturing engineering functions should be described in the charter.

- Work standards
- Tooling
- Methods
- Equipment selection
- Product costing
- Quality plans
- Plant/work station ergonomics layout
- Process instructions
- Plant maintenance/engineering

The nine functions shown here are the primary responsibility of the manufacturing engineering department, although there are some obvious overlaps (working with purchasing on equipment selection and QA on quality plans, for example). A typical manufacturing engineering organization to handle these jobs is shown in Chapter Two.

Q. Are the manufacturing engineers professionally trained and capable of carrying out their mission?

A. This is a subjective but important question. Professional manufacturing engineers will be able to execute the jobs listed above effectively. The evaluation of their capability and preparedness is the responsibility of the manufacturing engineering manager and his or her boss, the VP of Manufacturing.

Process Engineering

Q. Are product designs complete so that manufacturing engineering can take those designs and implement its own procedures?

A. If the design is incomplete and has no specifications for, say, the type of plastic that will be used for a particular product, then manufacturing engineers will be unable to do their job of defining the production processes needed to make the product.

To go into production and meet all product goals (i.e., budget, delivery, quality, and quantity goals), it is mandatory that all design specifications be complete so that manufacturing engineers can make the new product a successful undertaking in production.

Q. Are design reviews conducted, not only to assure high quality, but also to allow manufacturing engineering to shape product engineering opinions regarding the design to enhance manufacturing reproducibility?

A. Designing a product that meets customer needs is only half the battle. The other half is making sure that the product runs well in manufacturing so costs can be held down. In design review sessions, manufacturing engineers help shape the design by showing product designers the implications of a design that is difficult to make in production.

Q. Do manufacturing engineers consider how the product will be manufactured?
A. The following elements of manufacturing the product must be taken into consideration:

- Machines and equipment that will be the most cost efficient and produce the highest quality possible for the new product.
- The optimum plant layout and work station ergonomics.
- Inspection and sampling plans that will assure high quality of production.
- The most efficient material handling equipment and work flow.
- Process instructions that are easy for operators to use.
- Full and complete operator training.
- Availability of drawings, process sheets and bills of materials.
- Proper maintenance of machinery and equipment.
- Costed production operations.
- A complete list and description of supplies to be used to support production.
- Work standards and incentive systems that do a good job of measuring operating efficiencies and that motivate performance.

Q. Do the work standards described above provide for adequate allowances such as start-up or break time?
A. All work standards must accurately reflect standard operating conditions. If the union contract, for example, specifies a five minute start-up, the work standard must account for that allowance.

Q. Is the work flow balanced so that synchronized operations occur?
A. If, in a series of progressive operations, all operations except one take ten minutes and the variant operation takes twenty minutes, a genuine bottleneck prevents the smooth flow of production. All operations need to be balanced to assure uninterrupted work flow.

Production Cost Estimating

Q. Are all necessary inputs for costing present in the costing procedure?
A. Costing must take into consideration the following production elements:

- Bills of materials.
- Machinery and equipment to be used.
- Materials and parts to be produced.
- The value-added portion of labor and overhead and the material costs.
- Tooling to be used.

- Supplies that will be used and/or consumed, such as welding rod.
- Material handling and packaging methods.
- Work standards.
- Production run quantities.
- Setup times.
- Training costs.

Q. Are after-the-fact reports made on cost estimates to determine how accurate the projection was?

A. This critical ingredient of the production costing process is often overlooked. Since budgets are prepared based on cost estimates, trouble can arise when those estimates are off base. A feedback procedure from cost accounting to the production costing section of manufacturing engineering will help keep this important function on track.

Tooling

Q. Do the procedures for tooling include all necessary elements?
A. Tooling procedures must account for:

- A well-defined authorization and approval methodology for all tooling requests.
- Records that show tool cost, tool life, production problems with tooling, and vendor records of purchased tooling.
- Worn tool disposal.
- Methods for studying alternative tooling that is cheaper and does a better job.

Plant Engineering and Maintenance

Q. Is there a maintenance job order system?
A. If there isn't you can rest assured that maintenance is not only not providing the type of support production needs, but that it is also costing much more money that it should. A maintenance job order system, described in Chapter Twenty, if a mandatory first step in restoring order and system to the maintenance function.

Q. Are all maintenance jobs classified as routine, preventive, or emergency?
A. They should be. The best way to find out how much time maintenance spends on reacting to problems rather than performing routine and preventive work—a less rewarding effort—is to keep track of emergency time. In an uncontrolled situation, emergency work can comprise up to 80 percent of the workload. A more reasonable figure is somewhere around 10–20 percent depending on the age of the equipment and other related factors.

Q. Are work standards applied to maintenance work?
A. Here again, it is important to do so. The more that standards can be applied,

the better the chances of planning and regulating the activities of maintenance. And maintenance is a costly activity, consuming expensive parts by high-priced labor using costly tools.

Additionally, with adequate work standards, realistic schedules can be made regarding the number of people needed by craft for the time period. It is all too easy to hire extra electricians, pipefitters, and other craftsmen that simply are not needed.

Q. Are there reliable preventive maintenance schedules?

A. There must be, particularly today when machine tool cost upwards of $750,000. The magnitude of expense dictates two- or three-shift use for all of those tools. They are too expensive to sit around idle. And when they break down, operators will be idle. Preventive maintenance (PM) is increasingly a crucial ingredient in today's factory.

Q. Are ancillary systems such as sewage disposal, air compressors and boiler room equipment given the proper attention to assure the needed uptime?

A. If, for example, the recirculating system for an acid etch breaks down, then production comes to a halt, at least for the finishing end. If a substation breakdown occurs, then electricity for the plant stops. A fully developed plant engineering system assures the proper functioning of these critical subsystems.

Q. Are tools and consumable supplies accounted for and stored in safe locations?

A. A tool control procedure is necessary to prevent loss and improper usage. Most tools should be locked up every night and all of them should be identified and recorded in a tool log that tracks when the tool was purchased, who made it, its costs, any repairs during its life and when it was disposed of. All of this information—and control—is needed so the right decisions on the type and quantity of tools can be made.

The same degree of control should be exercises for supplies. Records need to be maintained for usage and problems so intelligent purchasing decisions can be made.

Q. In storerooms containing tools and supplies, are stock levels monitored to prevent stockouts?

A. If they're not, then stockouts will occur, and production costs will escalate when crews are idled for lack of the right tools and supplies—and intolerable condition.

Q. Are all withdrawals from the storeroom accompanied by a requisition?

A. The withdrawal of a tool or supply item should be under the same vigorous control as inventory.

Q. Are stores periodically reviewed to remove obsolete items?

A. Nothing is as frustrating as attempting to use a tool that doesn't work because the production part has changed but the old tool is still being inventories because somebody forgot to make the accompanying tool change.

Stores need to be reviewed every year (or more frequently in a high turnover operation) and obsolete items removed from inventory. The cost writedown is invariably resisted by cost accountants with the result of a large cache of unusable tool and supplies piling up in stores because nobody wants to challenge the numbers people. The job of manufacturing engineering is to make sure those kind of ridiculous mistakes aren't made.

19

How to Buy Equipment That Pays Back 20 Percent and More

One of the keys to success for an manufacturing company is the amount of capital it invests to grow and to improve its profitability. A wise and productive use of capital allows a company to stay ahead of ever-burgeoning labor and materials costs.

Capital costs must be planned to support the company's operating plans and marketing strategy. If a company plans to increase sales of its product by 50 percent, then capital plans must be made to support that action (assuming that additional capital resources are needed).

The relationship can be seen in the following diagram, which traces the marketing strategy of a railroad car manufacturer through its capital plan:

- MARKETING STRATEGY—Expand freight car business 25 percent
- OPERATING PLAN—Building plant in South
- CAPITAL EXPENDITURES—1st Year—$6.75 million; 2nd Year—$4.25 million]

GUIDELINES FOR ENSURING SMART CAPITAL EXPENDITURES

Every capital budget must be established using certain guidelines to assure that capital dollars are being expended wisely. A plastics machinery manufacturer uses these guidelines:

- *Return-on-investment should equal to exceed a stated percentage.* That percentage will vary depending on economic conditions and the cost of money. A desired return today of 15 percent is not uncommon. Twenty years ago the ROI may have been stated at 10 percent. In any case, ROI should exceed interest a company could earn by investing its money in short-term liquid money market instruments.

- *The capital budget should support company strategic goals* as well as the manufacturing operating plan.

- *To establish discipline in the capital expenditure process, forecasted capital costs should not exceed 95 percent of plant and equipment depreciation* (unless a new product line or major expansion of an existing product line is specified).

- *All expenditures for capital over $1,000 must be approved* by the plant manager; over $2,000 by the vice-president of manufacturing, and over $5,000 by the president. Capital is defined as a tangible asset investment that yields returns over periods of time exceeding one year.

- *Capital plans will be prepared for a three-year period* and will be updated annually.

- *All capital expenditures will be post-audited annually* by the financial department to assure that projected returns-on-investment are being attained.

Sample Capital Budget

The capital budget (in total) for an oil field supply manufacturer is shown in Figure 19-1. During the coming year the company plans to spend $1,850,000 on both machinery and equipment as well as a small plant expansion. Of this, $1,000,000 will be financed by the states's industrial revenue bonds, a loan apparatus established by the state to encourage capital investment within the state. The balance of $850,000 will be financed through dollars earned on sales.

Figure 19-2 is a detailed capital expansion plan of a construction equipment manufacturer. It lists individual expenditures by area for the company. Normally, both Figures 19-1 and 19-2 are made by a company to describe capital expenditures.

OIL FIELD SUPPLY COMPANY
CAPITAL BUDGET
19X1

Machinery and Equipment	$1,000,000
Plant Expansion	850,000
Subtotal	$1,850,000
Less: Industrial Revenue Bonds	1,000,000
Cash Expenditure Needed	$ 850,000

Figure 19-1 Sample Capital Budget

CALCULATING RATES OF RETURN ON CAPITAL INVESTMENTS

When rating capital investments for return on investment, there are many acceptable methods but all of them are based on two direct methods of calculation: (1) payback and (2) present value.

		INVESTMENT BUDGET SPECIFICATION				CWD
BUDGET						
Company: XYZ		Date: 8-5-X1				Local currency Amount in: ($1,000)
Item No.	Description	Budget Year 19X2				REASON PAYBACK
	BLDGS AND FACILITIES					
1.	Paint Bldg.—Planner	100.				C 3.1
2.	Personnel Bldg. Repairs	30.				M
3.	Blacktop—Yard Storage	75.				E
4.	Security Fencing	30.				C
5.	Snow Plow Truck	15.				R
6.	Safety Equipment	20.				S
7.	Landscaping/Grounds	10.				E
8.	Breakdown Fund	50.				—
9.	Heater/Fab Bay	5.				R
10.	Emerg. Lights/Office	2.				S
	FAB DEPARTMENT					
11.	(2) Irco Positioners	40.				C 3.5
12.	Memory for Programmer	10.				C
13.	A/C for Programmer	2.				M
14.	Spool Welder	15.				C 1.08
15.	Plate Storage Machine	35.				S
16.	Vacuum Lifts	10.				S
17.	Caddy Lifts-Drum	5.				S
18.	HTC-Backgage	10.				C
19.	Mig Welding Equipment	20.				R
20.	Lifting Magnets and Devices	10.				S
21.	Jigs and Fixtures	30.				—
22.	Parts Washer for Sheet Metal	15.				E
23.	Planner Tools/Jigs	50.				E
24.	Welding Robot	150.				C 3.0
25.	Tap Attachment—Trumpf	30.				C
26.	Press Brake and Tooling	90				C 2.0

Figure 19-2 Sample Capital Expansion Plan

Item No.	Description	Budget Year 19X2				REASON PAYBACK
	ASSEMBLY DEPARTMENT					
27.	Tire Changer	20.				C 1.2
28.	CC-4X Tooling	30.				—
29.	CA-12PD Tooling	30.				—
30.	Power Tools	10.				E
31.	Jigs and Fixtures	10.				—
32.	New Steam Cleaners (2)	10.				R
33.	Planner Prog. Assembly	50.				E
34.	DBL Roller Progressive	75.				E
	Q.A. DEPARTMENT					
35.	Gages and Test Equipment	20.				E
36.	Insp. Area Expansion	20.				E
	MISCELLANEOUS					
37.	Office Eq.—Pers. Dept.	5.				E
38.	Used Fork Lift—Maint.	5.				E
39.	Service Platform—Maint.	5.				E
40.	Mite-Lift Maintenance	5.				E
41.	Power Tools—Maint.	10.				E
42.	New Floor Sweeper	15.				R
43.	Fixture Dept.	50.				C
	TOTAL	1220				

Figure 19-2 Sample Capital Expansion Plan (continued)

Using the Payback Method

The payback method uses a simple calculation to reveal the number of years it will take to recover the initial investment. The payback method is easy to use but it is reliable only if the returns are evenly distributed over the years and if the investments to be compared are equal in amount and have the same life expectancy and little or not residual value.

Example: A capital investment of $100,000 that is expected to produce annual incremental returns of $20,000 with no residual values over a fifteen-year life if recovered in five years, as shown here using the payback method of calculation:

$$\frac{\$100,000 \text{ Investment}}{\$ 20,000 \text{Annual Payback}} = 5\text{-Year Payback}$$

The reciprocal of this investment equation reveals the percentage of payback:

$$\frac{\$20,000 \text{ Annual Payback}}{\$100,000 \text{ Investment}} = 20\% \text{ Return on Investment}$$

The payback method assures that the value of money tomorrow is the same as the value of money today. That assumption is incorrect, however, because of the difference in time. When confronted with a choice, anyone would prefer to have $100 today rather than one year from now. At 18 percent, an investment of $100 today will yield $118 in one year. Should an opportunity arise where a person could alternatively invest his $100 at 15 percent, he or she would reject it, simply because the present value of the money is greater at 18 percent than at 15 percent.

Using the Present Value Method

In similar fashion a rate of return can be calculated for a capital investment by discounting the estimated future returns at an interest rate that equates the present value of the returns with the investment. This rate of return is the present value of money (it can also be termed the discounted rate of return).

Example: In the previous example a $100,000 capital investment was calculated to yield returns of $20,000 per year with no residual value of the asset at the end of fifteen years, its useful life. The present value is determined as follows:

A. *Calculate the Payback*

$$\frac{\$100,000 \text{ Investment}}{\$\ 20,000 \text{ Annual Return}} = 5 \text{ Years}$$

B. *Determine the Present Value Factor*

Use the Payback Percentage Table shown in Figure 19-3 to find the factor that comes closest to the payback period. In the 18 percent column 5.092 is the closest number to 5 years on the horizontal line for 15 years. Since the asset has a useful life of 15 years the present value factor is taken from this line.

C. *Calculate the Present Value*

$20,000 Annual Return × 5.092 = $101,840 Present Value of Investment

In this example, the present value of the annual return is approximately equal to the present value of the investment. The investment will earn slightly above 18 percent. If an investment program criterion stated that 20 percent was the minimum return required, then this investment would be disqualified.

Notice that using the payback method yields a return of 25 percent. The payback method, however, does not take into account the difference in money value over different time periods, while present value does.

(N)	4%	5%	6%	8%	10%	12%	14%	15%	16%	18%	20%	22%	24%	25%	26%	28%	30%	35%	40%
1	0.962	0.952	0.943	0.926	0.909	0.893	0.877	0.870	0.862	0.847	0.833	0.820	0.806	0.800	0.794	0.781	0.769	0.741	0.714
2	1.886	1.859	1.833	1.783	1.736	1.690	1.647	1.626	1.605	1.566	1.528	1.492	1.457	1.440	1.424	1.392	1.361	1.289	1.224
3	2.775	2.723	2.673	2.577	2.487	2.402	2.322	2.283	2.246	2.174	2.106	2.042	1.981	1.952	1.923	1.868	1.816	1.696	1.589
4	3.630	3.546	3.465	3.312	3.170	3.037	2.914	2.855	2.798	2.690	2.589	2.494	2.404	2.362	2.320	2.241	2.166	1.997	1.849
5	4.452	4.330	4.212	3.993	3.791	3.605	3.433	3.352	3.274	3.127	2.991	2.864	2.745	2.689	2.635	2.532	2.436	2.220	2.035
6	5.242	5.076	4.917	4.623	4.355	4.111	3.889	3.784	3.685	3.498	3.326	3.167	3.020	2.951	2.885	2.759	2.643	2.385	2.168
7	6.002	5.786	5.582	5.206	4.868	4.564	4.288	4.160	4.039	3.812	3.605	3.416	3.242	3.161	3.083	2.937	2.802	2.508	2.263
8	6.733	6.463	6.210	5.747	5.335	4.968	4.639	4.487	4.344	4.078	3.837	3.619	3.421	3.329	3.241	3.076	2.925	2.598	2.331
9	7.435	7.108	6.802	6.247	5.759	5.328	4.946	4.772	4.607	4.303	4.031	3.786	3.566	3.463	3.366	3.184	3.019	2.665	2.379
10	8.111	7.722	7.360	6.710	6.145	5.650	5.216	5.019	4.833	4.494	4.192	3.923	3.682	3.571	3.465	3.269	3.092	2.715	2.414
11	8.760	8.306	7.887	7.139	6.495	5.988	5.453	5.234	5.029	4.656	4.327	4.035	3.776	3.656	3.544	3.355	3.147	2.752	2.438
12	9.385	8.863	8.384	7.536	6.814	6.194	5.660	5.421	5.197	4.793	4.439	4.127	3.851	3.725	3.606	3.387	3.190	2.779	2.456
13	9.986	9.394	8.853	7.904	7.103	6.424	5.842	5.583	5.342	4.910	4.533	4.203	3.912	3.780	3.656	3.427	3.223	2.799	2.468
14	10.563	9.899	9.295	8.244	7.367	6.628	6.002	5.724	5.468	5.008	4.611	4.265	3.962	3.824	3.695	3.459	3.249	2.814	2.477
15	11.118	10.380	9.712	8.559	7.606	6.811	6.142	5.847	5.575	5.092	4.675	4.315	4.001	3.859	3.726	3.483	3.268	2.825	2.484
16	11.652	10.838	10.106	8.851	7.824	6.974	6.265	5.954	5.669	5.162	4.730	4.357	4.033	3.887	3.751	3.503	3.283	2.834	2.489
17	12.166	11.274	10.477	9.122	8.022	7.120	6.373	6.047	5.749	5.222	4.775	4.391	4.059	3.910	3.771	3.518	3.295	2.840	2.492
18	12.659	11.690	10.828	9.372	8.201	7.250	6.467	6.128	5.818	5.273	4.812	4.419	4.080	3.928	3.786	3.529	3.304	2.844	2.494
19	13.134	12.085	11.158	9.604	8.365	7.366	6.550	6.198	5.877	5.316	4.844	4.442	4.097	3.942	3.799	3.539	3.311	2.848	2.496
20	13.590	12.462	11.470	9.818	8.514	7.469	6.623	6.259	5.929	5.353	4.870	4.460	4.110	3.954	3.808	3.546	3.316	2.850	2.497
21	14.029	12.821	11.764	10.017	8.649	7.562	6.687	6.312	5.973	5.384	4.891	4.476	4.121	3.963	3.816	3.551	3.320	2.852	2.498
22	14.451	13.163	12.042	10.201	8.772	7.645	6.743	6.359	6.011	5.410	4.909	4.488	4.130	3.970	3.822	3.556	3.323	2.853	2.498
23	14.857	13.489	12.303	10.371	8.883	7.718	6.792	6.399	6.044	5.432	4.925	4.499	4.137	3.976	3.827	3.559	3.325	2.854	2.499
24	15.247	13.799	12.550	10.529	8.985	7.784	6.835	6.434	6.073	5.451	4.937	4.507	4.143	3.981	3.831	3.562	3.327	2.855	2.499
25	15.622	14.094	12.783	10.675	9.077	7.843	6.873	6.464	6.097	5.467	4.948	4.514	4.147	3.985	3.834	3.564	3.329	2.856	2.499
26	15.983	14.375	13.003	10.810	9.161	7.896	6.906	6.491	6.118	5.480	4.956	4.520	4.151	3.988	3.837	3.566	3.330	2.856	2.500
27	16.330	14.643	13.211	10.935	9.237	7.943	6.935	6.514	6.136	5.492	4.964	4.524	4.154	3.990	3.839	3.567	3.331	2.856	2.500
28	16.663	14.898	13.406	11.051	9.307	7.984	6.961	6.534	6.152	5.502	4.970	4.528	4.157	3.992	3.840	3.568	3.331	2.857	2.500
29	16.984	15.141	13.591	11.158	9.370	8.022	6.983	6.551	6.166	5.510	4.975	4.531	4.159	3.994	3.841	3.569	3.332	2.857	2.500
30	17.292	15.373	13.765	11.258	9.427	8.055	7.003	6.566	6.177	5.517	4.979	4.534	4.160	3.995	3.842	3.569	3.332	2.857	2.500
35	18.665	16.374	14.498	11.655	9.644	8.176	7.070	6.617	6.215	5.539	4.992	4.541	4.164	3.998	3.845	3.571	3.333	2.857	2.500
40	19.793	17.159	15.046	11.925	9.779	8.244	7.105	6.642	6.234	5.548	4.997	4.544	4.166	3.999	3.846	3.571	3.333	2.857	2.500
45	20.720	17.774	15.456	12.108	9.863	8.283	7.123	6.654	6.242	5.552	4.999	4.545	4.166	3.999	3.846	3.571	3.333	2.857	2.500
50	21.482	18.256	15.762	12.234	9.915	8.304	7.133	6.661	6.246	5.554	4.999	4.545	4.167	4.000	3.846	3.571	3.333	2.857	2.500

Figure 19-3 Payback Percentage Table

20

How to Recapture One-Third of Wasted Maintenance Labor Hours

It has been established by many seasoned manufacturing professionals that an effective maintenance program has the potential to recapture a full one-third of wasted labor hours. So many labor-hours of production time are lost to:

- Production machine breakdowns
- Production machine repairs
- Production machine adjustments
- Service equipment failures:

fork trucks	boilers
cranes	buildings
monorails	lighting
air compressor	scrubbers
welding machines	electrical equipment
tools and fixtures	conveyors
piping	pressure vessels
air conditioners	pumps
heating equipment	(and so on)

It is obvious from this small and incomplete listing that the potential for failure is high and that the need for a trained maintenance work force coupled with workable maintenance procedures is necessary.

```
┌─────────────────────────────────────────────────────────────┐
│            FURNITURE MANUFACTURING COMPANY                   │
│               MAINTENANCE ORDER REQUEST                      │
├─────────────────────────────────────────────────────────────┤
│  ORIGINATOR _____      DATE WRITTEN _____    │
│  DEPARTMENT _____      MACHINE/LOCATION _____     │
├──────────────────────────┬──────────────────────────────────┤
│  WORK REQUEST:           │                                  │
│                          └                                  │
│                                                             │
│                                                             │
├─────────────────────────────────────────────────────────────┤
│  CHECK ONE     □ EMERGENCY     □ ROUTINE                     │
│  IF ROUTINE, SPECIFY COMPLETION DATE _____            │
│                              _____    │
│                              SIGNATURE OF ORIGINATOR         │
└─────────────────────────────────────────────────────────────┘
```

Figure 20-1   Maintenance Order Form

HOW TO USE THE MAINTENANCE ORDER FORM
TO KEEP MAINTENANCE WORK HOURS DOWN

A furniture manufacturer in the South uses a maintenance order form to control maintenance work and keep maintenance work hours as low as possible. The system is based on the following procedure:

1. *Make sure all requests for maintenance work by an production of support department have a work order.* Figure 20-1 is a sample maintenance work order. The originator sends the original request to the maintenance department and holds a copy for follow-up. The furniture company insists that all requests for maintenance help be made through the general foreman. This lets management monitor the need for assistance and keeps it aware of the problems in the functional areas.

2. *Note whether the emergency block has been checked on the form* (this task should be performed by the maintenance manager). If the block has been checked, forward the request quickly to the maintenance superintendent for immediate action. If the routine block is checked:

- Note the required date of completion
- Estimate and record the hours required to do the job on the work order.
- Place the work order in a tickler file of jobs to be done.

3. *Assign work orders to crafts daily* for completion based on the labor- hours estimated by maintenance.

The furniture company management estimates that before it began its maintenance work order system it was losing 500 direct labor-hours per week due to disorganization and confusion. Those 500 hours, in this case, represented a $4,000 weekly loss (over $200,000 annually) that was recaptured with the start-up of a maintenance work order system.

HOW TO SCHEDULE COMPLEX MAINTENANCE WORK AND REDUCE MAINTENANCE LABOR

Maintenance work cannot always be scheduled through the simple use of tickler file. Jobs of a more complex nature or jobs of simply longer duration require a Gantt chart technique.

Such a Gantt chart is shown in Figure 20-2. It represents the scheduling of pipefitters for a fourteen-week period in a hardware manufacturer's plant. The job numbers are in the left-hand column while the time scheduled to be expended is shown by the solid horizontal bars. The notch above the fifth week represents today's date, and the dotted horizontal lines show actual time taken. Job #44K, for example, was originally scheduled to take two week, but it actually took three weeks to complete.

Job #16LZ was completed on time, while Job #40R is currently one week behind schedule.

The hardware company estimates that intelligent application of scheduling techniques in the maintenance area, including the use of Gantt charts, has resulted in a 10 to 12 percent reduction of maintenance labor.

```
┌──────────────────────────────────────────────────────────────────────┐
│                    HARDWARE SUPPLY MANUFACTURER                        │
│                 MAINTENANCE SCHEDULE FOR LARGE JOBS                     │
├──────────────────────────────────────────────────────────────────────┤
│        CRAFT:   PIPEFITTERS                                             │
├──────────────────────────────────────────────────────────────────────┤
│  WK. NO. → 1   2   3   4   5   6   7   8   9   10   11   12   13   14   │
│  JOB # 44K  ============                                                │
│  JOB # 16LZ       =================-                                    │
│  JOB # 40R              =======-                                        │
│  JOB # 51LZ                           _____              │
│  JOB # 72RS                                         _____        │
└──────────────────────────────────────────────────────────────────────┘
```

Figure 20-2   Maintenance Schedule—Gantt Chart

HOW ONE COMPANY SAVED 30 PERCENT BY INSTALLING A MAINTENANCE WORK CLASSIFICATION SYSTEM

A textile machinery company in New England classifies all maintenance work in one of the following categories:

- *Emergency*—Work needed to immediately restore production such as a machine breakdown, loss of air supply, or electrical failure. This category of maintenance receives preference over the other described below.
- *Routine*—Work needed to *improve* the functional characteristics of a working piece of equipment. A screw machine, for example, currently producing at 60 percent efficiency can be scheduled for upgrading to increase its efficiency rating to 80 percent. This type of maintenance work can be scheduled to repair at the convenience of both production and maintenance people.
- *Preventive*—Service of machines and equipment before they need repairs. Preventive maintenance aims to increase equipment uptime through scheduled, periodic servicing including adjustments, lubrications, and overhauling.

The textile machinery company at one time had an uncontrolled maintenance function. Early analysis of the amount of time spent on each of the three categories of maintenance revealed:

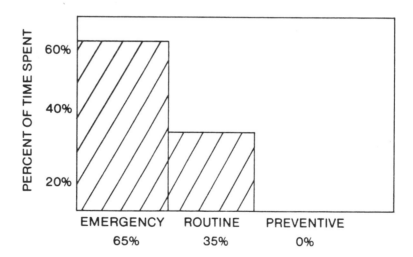

The company soon installed a maintenance work order system coupled with effective time estimating of work to be done by craft, Gantt chart scheduling of longer term maintenance work, and training for crafts members in these techniques. The results, within a period of two years, looked like this:

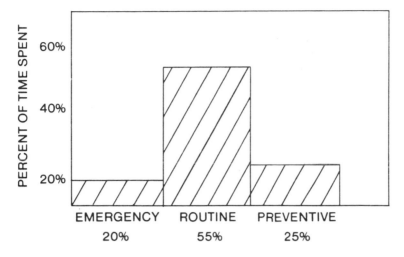

EMERGENCY   ROUTINE   PREVENTIVE
   20%   55%   25%

Their estimated savings in dollars by craft exceeded 30 percent for total maintenance dollars. Dollars expended were reduced by $275,000 per year.

MEASURING MAINTENANCE EFFECTIVENESS WITH THREE CONTROL CHARTS

It is not enough simply to install effective disciplines within the maintenance activity. Controls must be established to monitor progress. A mining equipment manufacturer in the Midwest uses the following controls to maintain the large savings in labor it achieved.

1. Maintenance Hours as a Percent of Production Hours

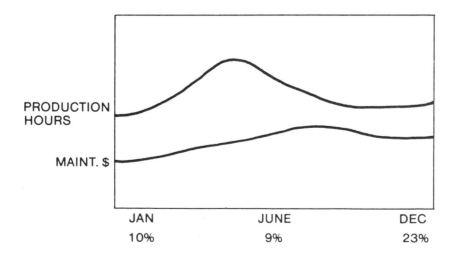

JAN   JUNE   DEC
10%   9%   23%

In this case, maintenance hours showed an unfavorable trend. Not enough dollars were shaved from the maintenance budget to keep in pace with the downturn in production hours beginning mid-year.

2. Total Maintenance Dollars as a Percent of Cost-of-Sales

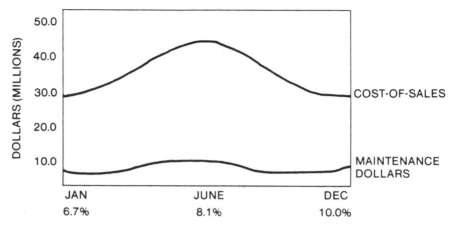

Here, too, the trend is up, although the total percentage average (about 8 percent) is considerably below the prior year's performance of 12 percent. Again, industry or regional averages are not really significant. What counts is *improvement.* So long as a company's maintenance department's control indicators are constantly improving, criticisms cannot be leveled.

3. Maintenance Supply Costs as a Percent of Total Maintenance Dollars

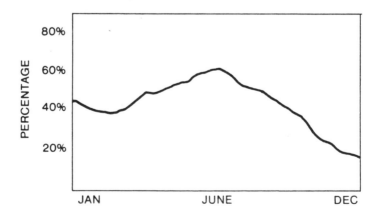

Here, a steady and noticeable trend is evident. Maintenance management exercised good control over the expenditure of maintenance supply costs.

21

How to Cut New Product Development Costs by 25 Percent

The introduction of new products in manufacturing is as essential to company survival today as any other factor discussed thus far, and its impact on manufacturing costs can be immense. Most American corporations *need* new products to survive; the forces of competition dictate that. The marketplace of today is forever changing; new consumer needs and emerging technologies are the two predominant factors coupling to force and ever-increasing number of new products on the market. Furthermore, internal development of new products is rapidly replacing external acquisition as the number one method of growth.

In such an environment, manufacturing executives should be prepared for constant change. The introduction of new products within manufacturing is traumatic experience. New machinery must be acquired, methods changed, work standards set, tooling built, people trained, quality requirements established, production processes modified, new materials purchased, inventories monitored, and so on.

All of these favors, and more, create demands in manufacturing that must be successfully achieved within budgeted goals.

Because of the increasing complexity of new products, the former method of having each functional area (marketing, engineering, and manufacturing) handle its own role in new product development is not longer a viable method. Too many interrelated factors exist. The successful company today is turning toward project teams (a form of matrix organization) to launch new products.

USING A TEAM APPROACH TO NEW PRODUCT DEVELOPMENT

Figure 21-1 depicts the project team approach to new product organization. A project manager for the new product (in this case referred to as Product "A") reports to the company president, along with the operating vice-presidents of marketing, engineering, and manufacturing. The product manager has a functional (dotted line) relationship with the managers of Product "A" in marketing, engineering, and manufacturing. These latter managers report directly to their vice-presidents but take functional direction from the project manager regarding the launching of Product "A" in the company.

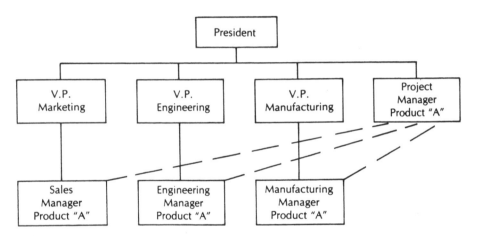

Figure 21-1   New Product Organization—Product Team Approach

USING THE CRITICAL PATH IN PROJECT PLANNING

New product introductions, particularly for technological or large projects, are normally quite complex. One method of scientifically planning all the activities in such a project is called "Critical Path." This technique provides a road map for the critical and most time-consuming activities in the new product introduction network. It aims at providing control through advance planning of each segment of the project including its timing and sequencing.

Figure 21-2 is the critical path diagram used by a machine tool manufacturer for introduction of a new, complex machine tool (referred to normally as CA-1PD). It lists all of the many segments critical to the success of the new product introduction (most of these are in manufacturing).

All events are listed in sequential order to establish the relationship of priorities. Pages 1 and 2 list all of these segments; page 3 shows all of the segments (or events) time-phased.

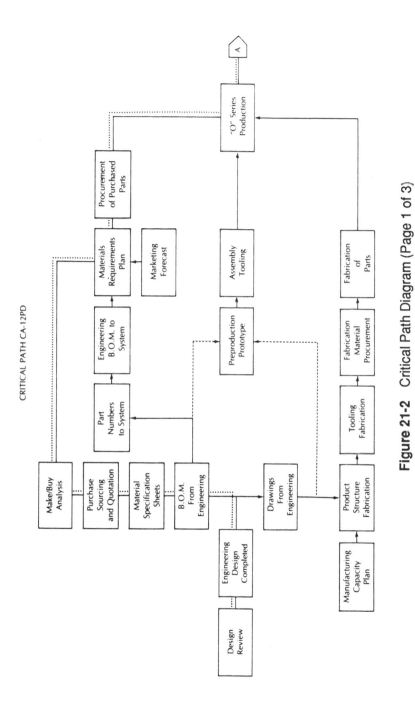

CRITICAL PATH CA-12PD

Figure 21-2 Critical Path Diagram (Page 1 of 3)

259

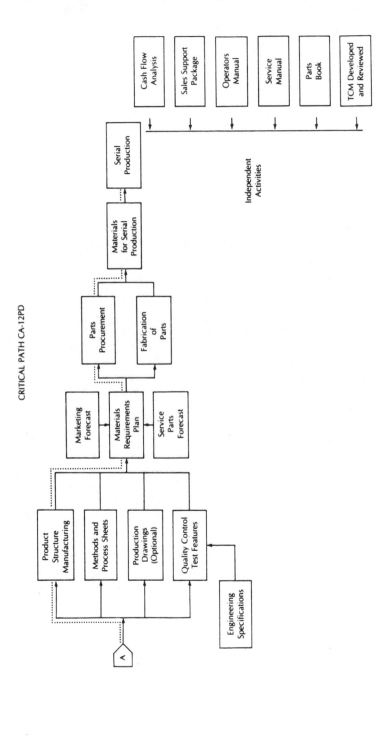

CRITICAL PATH CA-12PD

Figure 21-2 Critical Path Diagram (Page 2 of 3)

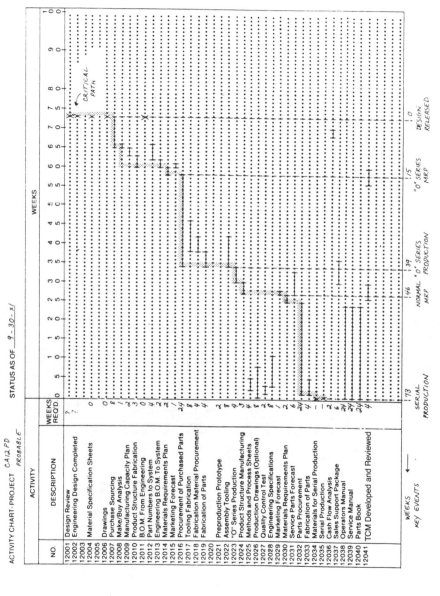

ACTIVITY CHART-PROJECT _CA12 PD_
PROBABLE   STATUS AS OF _9-30-x/_

Figure 21-2 Critical Path Diagram (Page 3 of 3)

261

On page 3, time periods in weeks are listed sequentially on the top from right to left. Events are shown in the left-hand column. The critical path can be seen by the shaded line. An examination of each of these events will explain the steps necessary to control the introduction of new products in manufacturing and will explain how the different manufacturing functions contribute.

EVENT	EXPLANATION	RESPONSIBLE DEPARTMENT IN MFG.
Design Review	Review of design by manufacturing to determine cost, production capacity, tooling quality characteristics, and purchasing requirements	Prod., QA, Materials, Mfg., Engr.
Engineering Design Completed	Self-explanatory	Project Mgr.
Material Specification Sheets	The specification of materials in the product; for example, what type of steel to buy	Materials, Mfg., Engr.
Drawings	Release of all product drawings from product engineering	Mfg., Engr., QA, Prod.
Purchase Sourcing	Where to buy parts and materials for new product	Materials
Make/Buy Analysis	Determination of whether it's cheaper to manufacture or purchase	Mfg., Engr., Materials
Manufacturing Capacity Plan	Determination of product quantity factory can produce	Mfg., Engr., Prod.
Product Structure Fabrication	The sequential listing of operations with accompanying methods, tooling, standards, and inspection instructions	Mfg., Engr., QA
B.O.M. from Engineer	The release of the Bills-of-Material so purchasing can order parts	Materials
Part Numbers to System	Assignment of part numbers to product components for ordering and scheduling production	Materials

EVENT	EXPLANATION	RESPONSIBLE DEPARTMENT IN MFG.
Engineer B.O.M. to System	The release of B.O.M. for planning purposes such as inventory planning	Materials
Materials Requirements Plan	The establishment of the new product within the MRP system	Materials
Marketing Forecast	Transportation of the market forecast into a production plan	Materials, Production
Procurement of Purchased Parts	Purchase of parts for "O" series production	Materials
Tooling Fabrication	Purchase or manufacture of tooling for new product in machining and fabrication areas	Manufacturing Engineer
Fabrication Material Procurement	Purchase of raw materials (as opposed to completed parts)	Materials
Fabrication of Parts	Fabrication of "O" series production parts for new product	Production
Preproduction Prototype	The assembly of one machine tool for fixed testing	Prod., Mfg., Engr.
Assembly Tooling	Purchase or manufacture of tooling for new product in assembly	Mfg. Engr.
"O" Series Production	Pilot manufacture of several new product machines to establish mfg. methods and standards	Prod., QA, Mfg. Engr., Materials
Product Structure Manufacturing	The final, refined sequence of operations originally set under "Product Structure Fabrication"	Mfg. Engr., QA

EVENT	EXPLANATION	RESPONSIBLE DEPARTMENT IN MFG.
Methods and Process Sheets	Setting of process methods and standards; reflected on process sheets (operator instructions)	Mfg. Engr.
Product Drawings (Optional)	Preparation of isometric drawings which show assembly sequence	Mfg. Engr.
QA Test	QA tests and instructions	QA
Engineering Specifications	Description of tolerances, locating holes, reference dimensions refined to meet manufacturing requirements	Mfg. Engr., QA Prod.
Marketing Forecast	Revisions to the original sales forecast	Materials, Prod.
Materials Requirements Plan	Revisions to the original MRP	Materials
Service Parts Forecast	Forecast of parts needed to service machines in customer's hands	Materials
Parts Procurement	Purchase of parts for production volume	Materials
Fabrication of Parts	Fabrication of production parts	Production
Materials for Serial Prod.	Arrival of inventory for sustained production	Materials
Serial Production	The start of production	Production
Cash Flow Analysis	Analysis of cash generated by sales of new product	None

EVENT	EXPLANATION	RESPONSIBLE DEPARTMENT IN MFG.
Sales Support Package	Advertising, training aids for customers, literature, etc.	None
Operator's Manual	How to operate the new machine tool	None
Service Manual	How to service the new machine tool	None
Parts Book	Spare parts availability and ordering information	None
Less Developed Reviewed	Standard costs developed for new product	Mfg. Engr., Materials

HOW THREE COMPANIES CUT THEIR NEW PRODUCT COSTS BY 25 PERCENT—AND MORE

The start-up of any new product in manufacturing is inevitably projected within certain budgetary limits. These self-imposed restraints comprise a goal—and goal to be either met or beaten.

The keys to coming in under budget are (1) thorough planning and (2) rigorous execution. Three case examples will show how three different companies reduced new product costs by 25 percent or more using the project management approach.

Case 1: Shrink New Product Develop Time

A manufacturer of construction cranes reduced the expected time of introducing a major new product almost in half, thereby paring new development costs approximately one-third. It did this by carefully sequencing the events in the new product development cycle, and analyzed them for potential time reductions. These are two typical steps taken:

1. It eliminated "O" series production. The company moved directly from prototype development into early production.
2. Rather than wait to order parts from vendors all at once (a large share of the new development lead time) it had R&D identify long lead time parts in advance, and ordered those parts early in the development cycle.

Case 2: Methodize Production Operations and Train Operators Early

A consumer products company took advantage of a long "O" series to methodize operations, perfect tooling, develop process instructions for operators, and train operators in the new methods. This extended training program allowed manufacturing to cut the expected learning curve in half during early production and reduced start-up costs by 25 percent.

Case 3: Focus on Perfecting New Product Design

In another case, a manufacturer of mechanized outdoor products found during the prototype run that the product had been poorly designed for manufacturing. Tolerances were unrealistic, wrong materials had been specified, and assembly fits were next to impossible to maintain consistently. This *early* identification of severe problems gave R&D the time to redesign the product on a crash basis without substantially delaying the new product introduction. Accounting estimated that development costs would have been doubled had the new product moved ahead under the original configuration.

22

Twelve Ways to Negotiate Successfully With the Union

Very few manufacturing managers have non-union plants (although the list is growing slowly but steadily). Living with the union, whichever one that may be, has been commonplace in American industry for the past forty to fifty years.

Every two or three years, manufacturing managers must sit down with their union and negotiate a contract. It is at this critical period when the entire tone of relations is established for the duration of the forthcoming management-union contract. During negotiations is also the time when management is most susceptible to "giving away the store."

Therefore, it is imperative that manufacturing managers, and other member of the negotiating team, learn those fundamentals necessary to protect the company's position vis-a-vis the union in basic negotiations.

There are twelve ways to do just that; twelve methods for focusing on success during union negotiations. Some of these points reflect upon organization and personal negotiating style, while others concern themselves with different parts of the management-union contract that are significant in terms of economic impact on the operating economy.

RECENT UNION AND LABOR TRENDS

Before reading the 12 methods, there are certain recent trends that any manufacturing manager should be fully aware of in union negotiations. These are trends that will probably hold for some time in the future—probably until about the year 2000.

The dominant trends is that union membership is down and appears as if it will continue downward for the foreseeable future. Even if there is a sever recession, any upward pressure for union membership will probably remain dormant simply because there will be fewer opportunities as more people become unemployed and companies scale back or eliminate their expansion plans.

During the 1980s, unions participated in many give-backs. In the 1990s, there will be increased pressure on companies to return those give-backs, but the force of union demands will be blunted by reduced company profitability in the face of economic slowdowns.

This, of course, puts the manufacturing manager in the driver's seat during negotiations. You will be able to apply enormous economic leverage to resist inflationary union demands for increases in wage rates and benefits.

Regarding employee benefits, the trend is to have employees share the explosive costs of such benefits as medical and hospitalization insurance. These items are becoming so prohibitively expensive that companies can no longer afford to handle them without some assistance from their employees. Expect this trend to continue well into the next decade.

One area where unions have been successful in applying pressure has been in acquiring extensive layoff benefits, at least among the country's largest companies, such as the automotive manufacturers. This will not extend to most manufacturing companies simply because they cannot afford it. It will remain a negotiable issue for many years to come, but unions will gain very little in layoff benefits from most companies; there will be stiff resistance.

Overall, although unions will attempt to seize sizable pay and benefits increases, their gains will fall far short of their demands. The 1990s should be an opportune time for manufacturing managers to minimize labor costs of all types.

Regardless, the following 12 negotiating tactics can be used in any business climate, good or bad. They constitute an approach that manufacturing managers can take to assure they walk away with gains from the negotiating table.

METHOD 1: USE AN OPERATING MANAGER AS YOUR NEGOTIATING TEAM CHAIRMAN

A plastics machinery manufacturer in New England found this out the hard way. Formerly, the vice-president of personnel headed the negotiating team. An independent analysis revealed that the company's settlements had been considerably higher than the industry average. Thereafter, the vice-president of manufacturing, along with the president, co-chaired the negotiating team.

The operating manager is the person who must live with the provisions established in the contract, not the personnel manager. The operating manager's success or failure at the bargaining table affects his or her department's costs, not the personnel manager's.

Because the operating managers have the most to win or lose, they should be in the driver's seat. The personnel managers, by contrast, want labor peace—they will sometimes go to extraordinary lengths to achieve that. It makes sense to place the authority and responsibility in the hands of the person whose operations are most affected by negotiations—the manufacturing manager.

METHOD 2: PLAN YOUR ATTACK

One idea has been stressed throughout this book—planning. In an manufacturing enterprise, planning balances the scales with vigorous execution of plans as the counterweight. Nowhere is this more important than in union negotiations. A company must thoroughly prepare its position in advance of negotiations in four distinct areas:

Anticipate Union Demands. Anywhere from six months to one year before negotiations, company representatives should get together, and through a series of meetings, anticipate what demands the union will present at the bargaining table. Management will need to separate those issues the union feels strongly about from those they will compromise on.

Gather Industry and Area Compensation Data. Statistics of hourly rates, incentive pay, overtime, and related data abound for company executives interested in discovering these data for both industry and local area comparisons. These statistics strengthen a company's hand when union representatives begin making demands exceeding normal industry and local area compensation.

*Plan What You'll Give the Union.*If you know in advance just how much you will (or can) give, you are in a better position to begin your negotiations low enough so the eventual settlement does not exceed the guidelines originally established. One of the worst mistakes a negotiation team can make is to be unaware of its limitations. Shrewd union negotiators are trained to spot that vulnerability quickly and to take maximum advantage of it.

Plan What You'll Get from the Union. It is simply not enough to approach the bargaining table with only concessions in mind. Remember that negotiations are give and take. They get something and you get something. If you establish give and take (trading) early in negotiations, the company is probably going to walk away from the table with more than it originally expected.

METHOD 3: AVOID VULNERABILITIES

One of the best poker hands in negotiations is held by the side that knows it is bargaining from a position of strength. When going to the table, company representatives must let the union know (subtly or indirectly, of course) that business is bad, orders are down, backlogs have dissipated, layoffs are imminent, etc.

The best time to negotiate a new contract is during a down period. A machinery manufacturer in the East does 65 percent of its business during the first sixth months of the year, and 35 percent during the last six months. It negotiates its contract in August when business is poor. That factor alone strengthens its hand at negotiations.

Another approach taken by companies whose business is good is to build ahead of schedule in preparation for a possible strike. This tactic can also place the company in a position of lessened vulnerability.

Company negotiators should determine the demographics of the union membership. Age, marital status, employees living with parents, employees whose spouse work, and other related factors all have a bearing on pressure felt by the union during contract talks. A membership which can live comfortably during an extended strike strengthens the union's position and helps neutralize company advantages. The company negotiator must probe that factor and determine its relevancy in negotiations.

METHOD 4: LET THEM FIGHT FOR WHAT YOU WANT THEM TO HAVE

An astute negotiator for an aluminum company in the South trains future company negotiators by telling them to let the union fight for everything the company is prepared to give them, although the company has already decided to make those concessions anyway.

The psychology behind that approach never fails. If the company presents its entire package up front at the start of negotiations, union negotiators will have won concessions without a fight. They will feel cheated and will then *begin to ask for more.* They need the process of negotiation to extract concessions so their sense of self-worth can be confirmed. An astute management negotiating team will recognize that principle and "string out" its concessions after long hours of tough negotiations.

METHOD 5: KEEP JOB CLASSIFICATIONS BROAD

A plant manufacturing automotive accessories in Tennessee ran into this problem. It had six different classifications. There were constant jurisdictional disputes among assemblers about who should be doing what, right down to the smallest details. Grievances were rife. Management and union wasted time arguing about unimportant details of job assignments. Assembly productivity declined because of all the infighting.

During negotiations the company proposed, and the union accepted, a reduction in the number of assembly job classifications from six to two. The union was as tired of bickering as management was. Almost immediately after negotiations the problems ceased and assembly productivity increased.

Broad job classifications prevent constant fighting about assignments among workers. Management's prerogatives about assigning work does not become an issue and workers enhance their job skills through a variety of job assignments.

METHOD 6: LIBERALIZE TEMPORARY JOB TRANSFERS

A temporary transfer occurs when an employee is moved from his or her regular job to another job in a different classification for a temporary period of time. Flexibility in temporary transfers allows management to minimize labor costs, and it is an issue that should be pursued by negotiators.

The same company described in Method 5 was successful in expanding the temporary transfer clause of its contract. Previously it had allowed management to temporarily assign a worker to another job for five days. During negotiations that period of time was expanded to fifteen days.

The value of temporary transfers is clear. A company is unable to materially forecast its labor needs by classification for any length of time. Sales increase or decrease, product mixes change, machine breakdowns occur, and so on. If a company was forced to post permanent job bids for these multitudinous changes it couldn't respond quickly enough. The job bid process is a lengthy one. From time of posting the job to appointment of a candidate (not to mention job bumping) the process can take up to two weeks. By that time the need for the temporary transfer may have expired, and the company will have lost an opportunity to respond to market demand.

METHOD 7: MINIMIZE UNION BUSINESS TIME

Union stewards and committeemen love nothing more than to be allowed to leave their regular jobs and roam the plant talking to other employees and hearing their complaints. After all, they are elected political representatives of their membership and they as such, must please their membership or lose the next election for union representatives.

Since increased union time on business ferments trouble for management, the company must minimize union time. One way to do that is to specify during negotiations that union time away from the job must be only in answer to a worker's grievance. To control this, managers should insist that shop stewards get permission from their forepeople before leaving their work stations, and that a log of union time be kept. The log will show time away from the job, employee contacted, and nature of the complaint. Failure to enact such a procedure is tantamount to managers permitting free union time and access. The time to nail this down is a contract negotiations.

METHOD 8: INSIST ON VACATIONS BY THE WEEK, NOT THE DAY

It becomes a logistics nightmare for managers if union employees are allowed to take their allowed vacation time in days rather than weeks. Nail this one down at the negotiating table.

METHOD 9: WORK OVERTIME BY DEPARTMENT SCHEDULE

Equalization of overtime has its limits. One of Ford Motor Company's assembly plants shut down in recent years. One of the many reasons for its demise was that overtime was equalized plant-wide rather than by department or job classification. When part of the plant was scheduled for ten-hour days almost every job on the assembly line changed at the end of eight hours. Not only was time lost to make the change, but also many workers were required to be assigned to jobs they knew nothing about. The result was mass confusion, high costs, and low car quality.

METHOD 10: KEEP WORK STANDARDS OUT OF THE CONTRACT

Admittedly, this is hard to do. Work standards is one area on which unions focus. Too many labor contracts hamstring management's ability to administer work standards. Union challenges, if legitimized by contract, can tie up an entire time study department and prevent the installation of work standards necessary to maintain high productivity. Make this a prime demand of management!

METHOD 11: SET STRINGENT REQUIREMENTS FOR HOLIDAY PAY

Insist, in the contract, that employees must work two days before and two days after the holiday to become eligible for holiday pay. The alternative is employees taking long weekends.

METHOD 12: SPECIFY DISCIPLINE ONLY GENERALLY IN THE CONTRACT

A clause such as "Management shall have the right to discipline employees for infractions of company rules" is all a company wants. Don't specify levels of discipline and punishment for infraction of rules; any such clause will open the door to negotiation of disciplinary action and will erode management's authority—and ability to maintain discipline.

23

How to Use the JOBSCORE™ Checklist to Hire the Right Managers for Your Company*

Hiring the right kind of managers is an absolute must if companies are to succeed and flourish in today's demanding marketplace. Everybody knows that. Less well known are specific techniques that heighten the ability of companies to hire the best candidates possible.

One easy-to-use technique is a checklist that enables manufacturing managers to *objectively* evaluate and compare job candidates. The checklist, called the JOB-SCORE,™cuts through the emotion and subjectively of the hiring process. It focuses management's attention on those major characteristics called "factors," that job candidates need to be successful on the job. It guides the selection process by determining how individual job candidates stack up against those important factors.

---

* JOBSCORE™ is a trademark of Management Sciences International, Inc. Reprinted from "Hiring the Best Managers," by Martin R. Smith (Monterey, Calif.: *Small Business Reports*, October 1989). Reprinted with permission.

HOW THE JOBSCORE™ CHECKLIST WORKS

Each factor on the JOBSCORE™ is assigned a numerical point value, weighted as to its importance. Job candidates receive points for each factor; the closer they come to meeting the intent of the factor the more points they receive. When the checklist is completed all points are totaled for each job candidate. The candidate with the most points is the one who, in all probability, will be the one most likely to succeed.

Please note that subjectivity can never be completely eliminated from the hiring process. Managers must still determine the factors that they consider critical and then estimate how closely job candidates measure up. All of this is subjective. What the JOBSCORE™ does is to reduced subjectivity to a minimum.

Case Study: How a Machinery Manufacturer used JOBSCORE™ to Pick the Best Candidate for the Job

Figure 23-1 is an example showing how JOBSCORE™ can be used in actual practice. In this case, a machinery manufacturing company selected nine factors to be used to evaluate job candidates for the position of quality assurance director. These factors are written in the column marked "Factor Evaluated."

"Must haves": The First Screen.   At the bottom of that column is a list of "Must Have" factors, including college degree and ten years experience. All candidates must first possess these "Must Have" characteristics to be considered in the running. It is the first screen.

Ratings.   The next column, "Rating" describes the degree by which candidates came closest to fulfilling the intent of the factors being evaluated. For example, the first factor evaluated, "Major Type of QA Experience" has three possible ratings, depending on the answer most closely matching the candidate's experience: plant, corporate, or staff. In this case the highest rating was assigned to plant since management of the machinery company wanted to stress the importance of hands-on experience.

Weight.   The following column, "Weight" is an indication of the relative importance that management has placed on the different factors. A 10 represents the most important while a 1 represents the least important.

Note that the possible numerical values for rating and weight are listed on the lower left-hand portion of the form.

In this example three candidates are being evaluated: Jones, Toya and Shaw. Their individual scores for each factor evaluated are the product of the weight times the rating as determined by managers assessing each candidate. In the first factor, for example, Jones had mostly corporate experience so Jones' his score was the weight of 8 multiplied by 4, the numerical value of the rating for corporate

JOBSCORE™	JOB: DIRECTOR, QUALITY ASSURANCE			DATE:　7-12		
FACTOR EVALUATED		RATING	WEIGHT	**TOTAL POINTS**		
				Jones	Toya	Shaw
Major Type of QA Experience In:	Plant	5	8	32	40	16
	Corporate	4				
	Staff	2				
Types of QA Programs Installed	Prevention	5	10	50	50	10
	Inspection	1				
Accomplishments of Former Positions	Bottom-Line	5	10	50	50	10
	Peripheral	1				
Success of Programs Installed	High	5	10	50	50	0
	Low	0				
Orientation	Total Business	5	7	35	14	14
	Technical	2				
Jobs Held Other Than QA	Line	5	6	12	30	30
	Staff	2				
Communication Skills	High	5	8	40	40	24
	Average	3				
	Low	0				
Understanding of Market & Customers	High	5	7	21	35	21
	Average	3				
	Low	0				
Salary Level Relative To Years Worked	High	5	5	25	25	15
	Average	3				
	Low	0				
Must Have: College Degree						
10 Years Experience Currently QA Manager or Director						
Some Machinery Experience						
TOTAL POINTS:				315	334	140

RATING	WEIGHT
5　Most Value	10　Most Important
4　Above Average Value	To
3　Average Value	1　Least Important
2　Below Average Value	
1　Minimum Value	
0　No Value	

Figure 23-1 Sample JOBSCORE™ Used by a Machinery Manufacturing Company

experience. Toya, who had a lot of plant experience scored a 40, the product of a weight of 8 times 5, the rating level for plant experience.

At the conclusion of the evaluation, points were totaled for all three candidates. Shaw was completely out of the running while Toya led Jones in a horse race of 334 to 315 points. This type of result—two candidates fairly close together—is not uncommon. The company selected Toya over Jones mainly because of Toya's plant experience and bottom-line orientation, a characteristic that was apparent during the course of the evaluation.

THREE KEY ADVANTAGES OF THE JOBSCORE™ CHECKLIST IN EVALUATING JOB CANDIDATES

The selection of the factors, the assignment of numerical ratings, and the weight of each factor—these are the crucial decision that make the JOBSCORE™ a very useful technique. They must be determined carefully.

There are three very good reasons for using this technique.

It forces management to clearly define the most vital job factors for enhancing the success of the new hire. Any attempt to use cookbook job descriptions can easily result in a failure of a succession of candidates. That is all too common.

It provides a rational and orderly method for evaluating the capability of several job candidates. This reduces the influence of peripheral characteristics that cloud the meaningful attributes needed for success on the job.

It meets EEO guidelines for candidate evaluation and can serve as a basis for a company's defense in case of a lawsuit for discrimination in hiring.

The JOBSCORE™ is a tool, not a magic wand. Its use must be tempered with the realization that it is only a technique that can be used in the selection process, and not the final and absolute determinant. It is, however, a very effective tool if used properly. You can use the blank JOBSCORE™ worksheet shown in Figure 23-2 to assist you in you company's management selection process.

JOBSCORE™	JOB:			DATE:		
FACTOR EVALUATED		RATING	WEIGHT	TOTAL POINTS		
	TOTAL POINTS:					
RATING 5 Most Value 4 Above Average Value 3 Average Value 2 Below Average Value 1 Minimum Value 0 No Value	**WEIGHT** 10 Most Important To 1 Least Important					

Figure 23-2   Blank JOBSCORE™ Form

24

Twenty-One Ways to Reduce Safety Costs In the Plant

Safety is one of the higher—but unrecognized—costs of manufacturing today. Lost labor time, medical expenses, insurance premiums, legal fees, and a host of other increasingly expensive costs are contributing toward the predominance of safety in the think of manufacturing managers. Spiraling regulations, such as those of the Occupational Safety and Health Administration (OSHA) and the Environmental Protection Agency (EPA), are focusing a great deal of attention on safety in the plant.

Astute managers are paying close attention to this trend, not only to minimize accidents and their attendant costs, but also to improve employee relationships throughout the organization. A well-planned and executed safety program brings managers and workers together in a common undertaking, which promotes cooperation.

METHOD 1: ESTABLISH A PLANT SAFETY PROGRAM

The following pages contain an actual safety program used by a major capital goods company to keep safety costs down and safety consciousness high.

SUBJECT: CAPITAL GOODS MANUFACTURER, SAFETY PROGRAM

PURPOSE: All effective safety programs must contain the following elements: management leadership, assigned authority and responsibility, established safety training and follow-up, safe and healthful working conditions, a safety record system, adequate medical and first aid capabilities, and personal acceptance by all employees. To implement each of these elements as an integral part of our company operations, to comply with the Federal Occupational Safety and Health Act and to minimize the number of accidents and the effects of injuries on the work capacity of all of our people and on the profitable operation of our business, our safety policy is hereby reaffirmed.

POLICY: It is our responsibility as a company to provide a safe job assignment and a safe place to work for each of our employees. To this end, every member of management has equal responsibility for achieving production efficiency in the safest known manner. In addition, each employee has the responsibility of performing his job and assisting others in performing their jobs in the safest possible way. All observed safety hazards or unsafe practices should be reported to supervision.

It is the policy of our company to give safety equal priority with production in carrying out our management's responsibility for providing a safe place of work, safe equipment and materials, and the establishment and insistence upon safe methods and practices.

Safety is an operating function, and we intend to exert every effort necessary to enhance the safe and healthful operation of every aspect of our company.

PROCEDURE: The formal Safety Program in support of our Policy Statement shall include but not be limited to the following actions:

A. Management Leadership
   1. Safety Committees shall be established and function on a regular basis as outlined below:
      a) Executive Safety Committee Membership
        1. President
        2. Vice-President, Manufacturing
        3. Personnel Manager
        4. Insurance Agent

        Activities—for regularly scheduled monthly meet-

ings, an agenda will be prepared to include along
with other items of importance—

    a) Minutes of meetings and recommendations of
plant safety committees.

    b) Plant injury, cost, and goal achievement
reports.

B.   Union/Management Safety Committee
1.   Safety Chairman.*
2.   Maintenance Manager.
3.   Representative hourly employees as appointed by the
Union Plant Chairman who should rotate every six
months on a staggered basis.
4.   All other employees shall receive appropriate safety
training as part of their job training for the work to
which they are assigned, shall adhere to good safety
practices at all times, report all hazardous conditions of
which they are aware, and be prepared for appropriate
discipline for violations of proper work practices.

C. Safety Training
1.   Job safety analysis
    a) Job safety analysis is a procedure used to review
job methods and identify safety hazards of each
step of that method.
        1. A written analysis is made itemizing each step
required to perform the job.
        2. The safety hazards are listed for each step of
the job.
        3. Ways are developed to eliminate or avoid the
hazards to prevent potential accidents.
    b) Implementation
        1. All managers and supervisors shall participate.
        2. A training program shall be established to
teach the elements of the program.
        3. Analysis of each hourly job will be completed
by the supervisors, approved by their manager.
        4. One copy shall be posted at the job location
and used to train new, reassigned, or temporarily assigned employees.

---

* An operating executive, normally.

2. New employees indoctrination and on-the-job training
   a) A training program shall be established to teach the elements of the program to all managers and supervisors.
   b) Supervisors shall formally train every new of resigned employee—
      1. How to do the job.
      2. Distribute job safety analysis and review with employee.
3. OSHA violation recognition and correction
   a) All supervisors shall be trained in requirements of OSHA standards and the most commonly cited violations.
   b) Each supervisor shall be aware of and maintain a current list of OSHA violations in his or her area.
      1. Formal inspection of own area should be made weekly with violations recorded.
      2. Additions and deletions should be made routinely as new violations develop of corrections are completed.
      3. All violations should be corrected where possible with other people and resources, others are to be submitted in writing to the Plant Engineer Supervisor.

D. Maintenance of Sale Working Environment
   1. Every effort shall be made to correct unsafe acts of employees and unsafe conditions rising in the plant which could result in accidents.
      a) The Union/Management Safety Committee shall make monthly plant inspections and report all discrepancies.
      b) Department managers shall be regularly assigned on a rotational basis to inspect area other than their own and report on housekeeping, safe practices and OSHA compliance.
      c) Supervisors shall inspect their own area weekly.
      d) Employees who fail to comply with safe practices and procedures, create unsafe conditions, or violate OSHA standards shall be subject to the normal disciplinary procedure.
   2. A running list of all unsafe conditions or poor housekeeping practices shall be compiled from the various

inspection reports, maintained current and reviewed by the Executive Safety Committee.

E.   Safety Record System
1.   Plant monthly accident report
a)   Completed monthly for submission to Executive Safety Committee.
2.   Minutes of Safety Committee meetings
a)   Executive Safety Committee minutes distributed.
b)   Hourly Safety Committee minutes submitted to Executive Safety Committee.
3.   Plant Inspections
a)   The Union/Management Safety Committee shall make monthly safety and housekeeping inspections of the total plant and submit a report of their findings and recommendations to this Committee.
b)   All managers shall make a monthly inspection of their assigned area and submit a report of their findings and recommendations to the Manufacturing Manager.
c)   All supervisors shall make a weekly inspection of their own area and submit a report of their findings and recommendations to their managers.
4.   Safety Improvement
a)   Safety performance is most objectively measured by the following experience factors—
1.   Number of medical treatment cases.
2.   Number of injuries resulting in lost or restricted work.
3.   Number of actual lost or restricted workdays.
4.   Actual dollar expenditures for treatment of occupational injuries.

F.   Medical and First-Aid Facilities
1.   First-aid training for all supervisors and specific U.A.W. employees shall be routinely updated.
a)   The Personnel Department will maintain records of such dates,
b)   Newly appointed supervisors shall participate in the appropriate training at the earliest possible date.
2.   Modernization and refinement of plant first-aid facilities shall be given a high priority with other capital appropriation projects.

3. Standards for pre-employment and return to work physical examinations shall be developed.

G. Personal Acceptance by Employees
   1. Plant safety scoreboards shall be prominently displayed and maintained in an up-to-date status.
   2. Safety posters and plant newspaper articles shall be used to effectively promote the safety program.
   3. The assignment of hourly employees on a staggered rotational basis to the Union/Management Safety Committee shall be used to provide concentrated training and exposure for a wide selection of the hourly group to the problems, difficulties, and concerns of management with accident prevention.

The safety program just described is a good start in reducing plant safety costs. It, in essence, is the first way. Following are the other 20. These will give you some ideas which, in turn, should generate others.

METHOD 2: SELF-INSURE YOUR COMPANY AND SAVE BIG DOLLARS IN PREMIUMS

Insurance premiums, particularly for workers' compensation, are high and growing higher annually. Many states will permit companies to self-insure themselves, thereby saving thousands of dollars in insurance premiums. Obviously, a company should have an excellent safety program and record to save money this way.

METHOD 3: GET FREE ADVICE ON SAFETY ISSUES AND SAVE MONEY

Insurance agencies and manufacturing companies of any size employ safety experts to advise customers on safety matters—and this service is always free. This is an excellent way to save money and establish an effective safety program.

METHOD 4: HIRE A NURSE TO SCREEN EMPLOYEES

A nurse will screen injured (or allegedly injured) workers, provide first aid, and keep lost-time accidents (a key indicator insurance companies use to raise your premiums) low. An experienced nurse will know when to turn back the shirker and when to excuse genuinely injured employees from work. *Nobody else is qualified to make that judgment other than a doctor.*

METHOD 5: HAVE WORKERS PARTICIPATE IN THE SAFETY PROGRAM

Without their active participation in the program, workers will not have the same degree of interest in reducing accidents. A well-conceived safety program will take full advantage of the full participation of every level of the organization.

METHOD 6: USE POSTERS AND AWARD TO MAKE
EMPLOYEES SAFETY-CONSCIOUS

One way to encourage attention to safety is through posters, newspaper articles, meetings, campaigns, awards, and similar publicity generating actions.

METHOD 7: GET THE UNION ON YOUR SIDE

Having union representatives participate in the safety program is tantamount to their full support. Once they are on the side of management they are likely to encourage worker participation.

METHOD 8: USE CONTROL REPORTS TO
MONITOR PROGRESS

Use of charts and statistics which report on safety progress is needed at the lowest organizational unit (usually the foreperson) to control accidents. A food processing company used the number of accidents (regardless of severity) to report on safety for each foreperson:

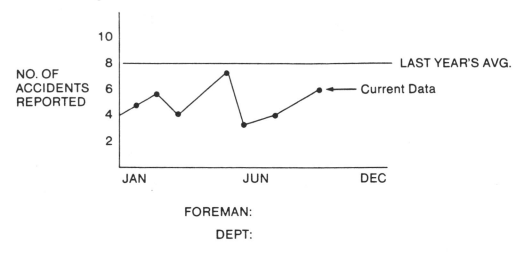

FOREMAN:

DEPT:

METHOD 9: USE ACCIDENT REPORTS TO
IDENTIFY AND CORRECT SAFETY PROBLEMS

Every accident should have a full and comprehensive investigation conducted *and* recorded on an accident investigation form, such as the one used by a hardware manufacturer (see Figure 24-1). This procedure will assure proper identification of problem areas coupled with rigorous corrective action.

METHOD 10: PUBLISH SAFETY RULES AND
DISCIPLINE OFFENDERS

Since adherence to safety rules in a matter of disciplinary action, it is necessary to post safety rules. Disciplinary action is sometimes necessary to correct poor employee safety practices.

METHOD 11: PROVIDE SAFETY TRAINING FOR ALL NEW EMPLOYEESS

An employee trained right the first time is likely to maintain the behavior pattern through repetition an recognition.

METHOD 12: MAKE SAFETY THE RESPONSIBILITY OF THE LINE MANAGER

Too many safety programs are run by Personnel. This virtually assures a lack of commitment by operating managers. Make the line manager just as responsible for safety as for production, cost, and quality.

REPORT DATE _____	PLANT ACCIDENT REPORT	SUPERINTENDENT _____
ACCIDENT DATE _____	ACCIDENT TIME _____	AM PM LOCATION _____

WITNESSES _____

INJURED EMPLOYEE(S) _____

DESCRIBE INJURY: LOST TIME: _____

FIRST-AID TREATMENT RECEIVED:

CORRECTIVE ACTION:

ESTIMATED COMPLETION DATE: _____

_____   _____
DATE   MANAGER'S SIGNATURE

Figure 24-1 Sample Plant Accident Report

METHOD 13: USE SELF-INSPECTION CHECKLISTS

Prepublished checklists used vigorously by line managers will point the way to corrective action. This list should be custom-made for each plant by a qualified safety professional.

METHOD 14: USE AN "INTERNAL EXPERT" ON SAFETY REGULATIONS

The proliferation of federal, state, and local safety laws demands the use of somebody in-house familiar with OSHA, EPA, and other regulations. Appoint somebody in the organization to that responsibility, and assure that he or she stays current with changes in the law. It will assure that the safety program remains up-to-date.

METHOD 15: INVESTIGATE ACCIDENT-PRONE EMPLOYEES

Every organization has a few if these unfortunate workers who attract accidents like flowers attract bees. Work with these people to correct their performance. Counseling sessions generally work quite well (but have them done by a medical professional).

METHOD 16: PROVIDE FIRST-AID TRAINING FOR EMERGENCIES

An awareness of some *key* people of both first aid and CPR techniques will pay off in emergencies. Local Red Cross chapters conduct these courses routinely.

METHOD 17: CONDUCT HOUSEKEEPING TOURS TO PREVENT ACCIDENTS

Good housekeeping is a must to prevent accidents. Cluttered work stations are a tip-off to potential safety problems. Housekeeping inspection tours help generate good housekeeping in the plant.

METHOD 18: HAVE THE PLANT MANAGER CHAIR THE SAFETY COMMITTEE

It is simply not enough to delegate that job to a line manager in manufacturing. The attention of the top person is mandatory to focus attention on safety.

METHOD 19: KNOW HOW TO USE FIRE EXTINGUISHERS

Employees should be aware of where fire extinguishers are available as well as which kind is used for wood fires, electrical fires, etc. A training program will familiarize employees with the different types of fire extinguishers and their uses.

METHOD 20: USE LEAD-FREE PAINT

Painted products using a lead-based paint involve the company with all kinds of regulatory attention and mandated controls including employee physicals and blood work, maximum exposure time, respirators, and the like. These requirements are *very* costly.

METHOD 21: USE SAFETY GLASSES ON EVERY JOB

Make the use of them mandatory. It is a lot cheaper to buy safety glasses than to pay for a lost eye, and much easier on one's sense of moral obligation.

Index